THE VITAL ROOTS OF
EUROPEAN ENLIGHTENMENT

THE VITAL ROOTS OF EUROPEAN ENLIGHTENMENT

Ibn Tufayl's Influence on Modern Western Thought

SAMAR ATTAR

LEXINGTON BOOKS

A division of
ROWMAN & LITTLEFIELD PUBLISHERS, INC.
Lanham • Boulder • New York • Toronto • Plymouth, UK

LEXINGTON BOOKS

A division of Rowman & Littlefield Publishers, Inc.
A wholly owned subsidary of The Rowman & Littlefield Publishing Group, Inc.
4501 Forbes Boulevard, Suite 200
Lanham, MD 20706

Estover Road
Plymouth PL6 7PY
United Kingdom

British Library Cataloguing in Publication Information Available

Library of Congress Cataloging-in-Publication Data

The vital roots of European enlightenment : Ibn Tufayl's influence on modern
Western thought / Samar Attar.
    p. cm.
  Includes bibliographical references and index.
1. Ibn Tufayl, Muhammad ibn 'Abd al-Malik, d. 1185—Influence. 2. Ibn Tufayl,
Muhammad ibn 'Abd al-Malik, d. 1185. Risalat Hayy ibn Yaqzan. 3. Philosophy,
Islamic—History. I. Ibn Tufayl, Muhammad ibn 'Abd al-Malik, d. 1185. Risalat
Hayy ibn Yaqzan. II. Title. III. Title: Ibn Tufayl's influence on modern Western
thought.
  B753.I54A92 2007
  181'.9—dc22
2007023013

ISBN: 978-0-7391-1989-1 (cloth : alk. paper)
ISBN: 978-0-7391-1990-7 (pbk. : alk. paper)
ISBN: 978-0-7391-6233-0 (electronic)

Printed in the United States of America

♾™ The paper used in this publication meets the minimum requirements of
American National Standard for Information Sciences—Permanence of Paper for
Printed Library Materials, ANSI/NISO Z39.48–1992.

For my German daughter, Lina Fischer,
in the hope that she will be a bridge between East and West.

TABLE OF CONTENTS

ACKNOWLEDGMENTS

I would like to thank Dr. Michael Kessler of Germany who encouraged me to collect these essays in a book form. However, my greatest debt is to Widener Library at Harvard University and to the university itself for having facilitated my research for many years and provided me with unique opportunities. For any errors or oversights I am solely responsible. I have worked on this project under severe personal hardship.

I shall always be grateful to Professor Lieve Spaas who published my first article on Hayy's influence on Robinson Crusoe and remained a very good friend to this day. I would also like to thank Professor Rafael Pinilla who encouraged me to continue working on Ibn Tufayl, and invited me to give a lecture on the Andalusian philosopher at his university in Cordoba, Spain in the spring of 2000.

Finally, I would like to thank the following publishers for granting me their permission to reprint my articles: Macmillan, St. Martin's Press, Cordoba University, and Stauffenburg Verlag. The articles are listed below:

"Serving God or Mammon? Echoes from Hayy Ibn Yaqzan and Sinbad the Sailor in Robinson Crusoe." In *Robinson Crusoe: Myths and Metamorphoses*. Ed. Lieve Spaas and Brian Stimpson. London, New York: Macmillan, St. Martin's Press, 1996, pp. 78–97.

"The Man of Reason: Hayy Ibn Yaqzan and His Impact on Modern European Thought." *Qurtuba* 2 (Cordoba), 1997, pp. 19–47.

"Beyond Family, History, Religion and Language: The Construction of a Cosmopolitan Identity in a Twelfth-Century Arabic Philosophical Novel." In *Adventures of Identity: European Multicultural Experiences and Perspectives*. Eds. John Docker and Gerhard Fischer. Tübingen: Stauffenburg Verlag, 2001, pp. 75–89.

PREFACE

In September 2003 when I was getting ready to leave for Boston, Dr. Michael Kessler of Germany sent me an e-mail message in which he asked me if I had a manuscript for him to be published at the time of the Frankfurt Book Fair in 2004. The fair, he explained, would be dedicated to East-West relation. I had written numerous papers on the topic. But there was no complete manuscript. I had half written projects. Kessler's request made me think of the necessity of producing a book on Ibn Tufayl who had a profound influence on modern European thought. The only possible way out was to collect some of my already published articles on this Arab-Andalusian philosopher known as Abubacer in the West, and to add a few new chapters to the collection.

My fascination with Ibn Tufayl goes back to childhood. My family owned a huge library in Damascus, Syria. As a child of eleven years old I was able to read many Arabic and foreign books. Authors such as Imru' al-Qays, Zuhair Ibn Abi Sulma, Ibn Tufayl, al-Ma'arri, Shakespeare, Goethe, Rousseau, Dostoevsky, Tolostoy, Chekove were all there. But I did not write about Ibn Tufayl till I was a middle-aged woman and living outside of the Middle East. The first opportunity I had was when I participated in a conference organized by Lieve Spaas and Brian Stimpson in London 2–5 September 1993 on "Robinson Crusoe: Myths and Metamorphoses." It was only then that I began to work seriously on Ibn Tufayl. I had known all along that Crusoe was inspired by Ibn Tufayl's book, *Hayy ibn Yaqzan*. No one who knows both texts very well could deny the similarities. My paper at the conference stirred a lengthy discussion. I was quite pleased and wished I could pursue my research on the Arab philosopher. Eventually the paper was shortened and published in a collection edited by both conveners of the conference.

The second opportunity came when I met Professor Rafael Pinilla of Cordoba University in Cairo in 1995. He asked me to write a new article on Ibn Tufayl for his journal, *Qurtuba*. In my new article "The Man of Reason: Hayy Ibn Yaqzan and His Impact on Modern European Thought" I have investigated the influence of Ibn Tufayl's book on the age of Enlightenment.

Between 30 July and 2 August 1998, the Goethe Institute in Sydney, Australia had organized an international conference on "Adventures of Identity: Constructing the Multicultural Subject." I wrote another paper on Hayy for the conference. The paper suggests that birth, family, blood ties, name, language, history and religion are neither necessary ingredients for the construction of identity, nor are they necessary for man's attainment of happiness. What constitutes personal identity for Ibn Tufayl is the proper usage of reason and inner light by human beings. "Beyond Family, History, Religion and language: The Construction of a Cosmopolitan Identity in a Twelfth-Century Arabic Philosophical Novel" was eventually published in a collection of essays in Tübingen, Germany in 2001.

Since the year 2000 I have been lecturing on *Hayy Ibn Yaqzan* at various universities and giving papers on this unique book in international conferences. On March 23, 2003 I was one of the contributors to BBC Radio 3 Sunday Feature on "Child On An Island: *Hayy Ibn Yaqzan* By Ibn Tufayl." The Presenter was Martin Wainwright and the Producer was Merilyn Harris. In 2006 I presented a paper on *Hayy Ibn Yaqzan* at the American Comparative Literature Association Annual Conference held at Princeton University, 23–26 March. My paper was entitled "Arab Roots of the European Sovereign Individual of Modernity."

During a short visit to Paris during the Christmas holidays of 2003 Ibn Tufayl's apparition followed me everywhere. In this city his pupils had once lived: Albertus Magnus (ca, 1200–1280), Thomas Aquinas (1224–1274), Voltaire (1694–1778), Rousseau (1712–1778), Diderot (1713–1784) and other Encyclopaedists, to mention only a few names. But whether they acknowledged him as their master or not is a different story. For the Parisians the spirit of these great men is overwhelming. There are statues and tombs everywhere. After all, the age of Enlightenment brought not only science to France and the rest of Europe, but also ideas, such as toleration, equality and freedom. The mentor who ignited the imagination of these great men is now relegated to the dust of history. Hardly anyone has heard of his name. But if he is to be resurrected from his grave in the guise of his protagonist, Hayy Ibn Yaqzan, and told about the violence that issued from the French Revolution, he would be very dismayed.

At the time of my visit to Paris one of the political issues that was hotly debated was the planned law to ban religious symbols from French public schools. President Jacques Chirac continued to stress the idea that France was a secular country, and that displaying religious symbols in state-funded schools violate the essence of the French constitution. On my way back to Boston on January 3, 2004, I read an interesting item of news which was reported in the *International Herald Tribune* on Sikhs asking the Indian prime minister to help keep turbans at school and to urge Paris to exempt them from the planned law. One wonders what ever happened to the concept of toleration in France? Hayy Ibn Yaqzan was neither a Moslem nor a Christian, nor a Jew although he was created by a Moslem philosopher. When he was placed among other people who entertained different ideas and seemed to worship different gods, he never criticized them, or tried to force them to adopt his way of thinking. What he did was to try to engage their reason. But once they refused to do so he left them alone. He knew very well that forcing others to adopt his ideas would lead to violence. Toleration is a very important key to peace.

The Vital Roots of European Enlightenment is a collection of essays some of which I have already published. But I have added new chapters and managed to examine the new literature written on the Andalusian philosopher. My purpose is twofold. First is to resurrect the memory of a forgotten man who left his traces on modern European thought, but was hardly acknowledged. Second is to entertain a wish that his ideas about equality, freedom and toleration may take root again not only in the West, but in particular among his own people and in the Islamic civilization that produced him in the past.

Samar Attar
Cambridge, MA
May, 2004

A CHRONOLOGY OF IBN TUFAYL AND SOME EUROPEAN THINKERS INFLUENCED BY HIM UNTIL 1859

1100 or 1110 Ibn Tufayl/Abubacer born in Wadi Ash, the modern Guadix, 40 miles northeast of Granada, Spain.

1126 Ibn Rushd/Averroes born in Cordova, Spain.

1163–1184 Ibn Tufayl serves as an adviser and physician at the court of Sultan Abu Ya'qub Yusuf of Morocco and Spain. Although he is trained in medicine he is very knowledgeable in philosophy, mathematics, astronomy, physics, other natural sciences and poetry. His scientific works are lost.

1160 or 1170 Ibn Tufayl writes an allegorical novel, *Hayy Ibn Yaqzan.* Hayy is a spontaneously generated boy on a desert island.

1169 or 1182 Ibn Tufayl invites Ibn Rushd/Averroes to the court of Sultan Abu Ya'qub Yusuf of Morocco and Spain and encourages him to write a commentary on Aristotle and other books which are eventually studied in European universities until the 17th century.

1185 Ibn Tufayl/Abubacer dies in Morocco.

1198 Ibn Rushd/Averroes dies in Morocco.

1241 Albertus Magnus, Dominican scholastic, bishop, and German patron of natural scientists arrives in Paris just as Averroes' commentaries on Aristotle are becoming available. After a few years his Italian disciple, Thomas Aquinas, who studies under him in Cologne follows him to Paris.

1245 Thomas Aquinas leaves Naples for Paris to begin his theological studies. Imitating Moslem philosophers, Aquinas attempts to synthesize philosophy and religion.

1256 Albertus Magnus writes against Averroes.

1271 Thomas Aquinas argues against the Averroists.

1281–1284 Siger of Brabant, member of the Parisian Faculty of Arts, who criticizes Albert Magnus and Thomas Aquinas and accepts the consequences of the Averroist philosophy, is persecuted by the Inquisition and dies in prison at Orvieto.

1349 Translation of *Hayy ibn yaqzan* into Hebrew by Moses of Narbonne.

Second half of the 15th century Translation of *Hayy ibn Yaqzan* into Latin by Pico della Mirandola, one of the most significant figures of the Renaissance. Pico died in 1494 at the age of thirty-one. His translation of *Hayy* was based on the Hebrew version. The son of a wealthy Italian prince, Pico studies at Bologna for two years, then wanders through the major universities of Italy and France for seven years. One year before his death he is exonerated of suspicions of heresy.

1516 Thomas More, *Utopia*.

1651 The first part of the Jesuit Baltazar Gracian's *El Criticon* is published in Spanish. Hayy's counterpart Andrenio is created. The nineteenth century German philosopher Schopenhauer describes the novel as one of the most important books ever written.

1651 Thomas Hobbe's *Leviathan* is published. The Anglican theologian Henry Hammond describes it as "a farrago of Christian Atheism."

1667 John Milton publishes his poetical work, *Paradise Lost*.

1671 Another Latin edition of *Hayy* rendered from the Arabic by Edward Pococke, son of the well-known orientalist professor at Oxford.

1672 Dutch version of *Hayy* appears in Amsterdam. Based on Pococke's Latin text. Name of translator is withheld.

c 1674 Charles Morton, an Oxford graduate, a mathematician and a master of many languages including Arabic opens his academy for dissenters in Newington Green. Defoe is a student from 1674 to 1679. At first a Royalist, Morton becomes a Puritan.

1674 English translation of *Hayy* by George Keith, a Scotsman and a prominent Quaker.

1676 The English Quaker William Edmundson, then in New Port, Rhode Island, is the first to attack slavery in English America.

1678 Robert Barclay, a Scot and a known Quaker theologian refers to *Hayy* in his book, *Apology*.

1681 *El Criticon* appears in London in English as *The Critick, one of the Best Wits of Spain*.

1683 The second Ottoman assault on Vienna fails. It marks the last offensive by an Islamic power against Western Europe.

1686 English translation of *Hayy* by George Ashwell, the Catholic vicar of Banbury, well known for his naturalist philosophy.

1687 Isaac Newton's *Philosophiae naturalis principia mathematica* is published.

1689 John Locke's *A Letter Concerning Toleration* is published anonymously in Latin.

1696 *El Criticon* appears in Paris in French as *L'homme détrompé, ou le Criticon*

1697 Charles Morton, Defoe's tutor in England, is appointed Vice-President of Harvard College in North America.

1697 Gottfried Wilhelm Leibniz writes a letter to Abbe Nicaise in which he refers to the excellent book *Hayy Ibn Yaqzan*, or the *philosophus auto-didactus*, translated into Latin by Dr. Pococke

1700 Pococke's Latin translation of *Hayy* reprinted.

1701 Another Dutch version of *Hayy* appears in Amsterdam. The old translation is revised by Adrian Reland. Engravings and indices of names and technical terms are added. Initials of the name of the translator are mentioned: S. D. B. Is Spinoza the translator, or perhaps one of his friends, Johan Bouwmeester?

1703–1713 Jean-Antoine Galland translates *Thousand and One Nights* into French.

1708 English translation of *Hayy* by Simon Ockley, a professor of Arabic at Cambridge.

1711 Ockley's translation of *Hayy* reprinted in London.

1715 The Grub Street English version of Galland's translation of *Thousand and One Nights* reaches its third edition. Among its first English readers are Swift, Addison and Pope.

1719 In a letter addressed to Lord Bathurst Alexander Pope refers to Hayy as the self-taught philosopher along with Alexander Selkirk, a Scottish sailor who lives alone on a desert island between February 1704 and January 1709.

1719 Publication of Defoe's *Robinson Crusoe*.

1721 Second edition of the Dutch translation of *Hayy* is reprinted in Utrecht.

1726 German translation of *Hayy* by Georg Pritius in Frankfurt.

1726 Swift publishes *Gulliver's Travels*

1726–1729 Voltaire lives in exile in England. He studies English, befriends Swift, Pope and others. English freedom of worship and thought appeals to him. The Quakers who admire *Hayy Ibn Yaqzan* are also admired by him. Bacon, Locke and Newton who have been influenced by *Hayy* to different degrees become his heroes.

1731 Ockley's English translation of *Hayy* is reprinted.

1733 Voltaire publishes the *Lettres Philosophiques*, or *Letters Concerning the English Nation*. The book appears first in English. More trouble awaits its author in France. The book is burnt and a warrant is issued for the author's arrest.

1742 Voltaire publishes his tragedy *Mahomet* in which he attacks all religions as the source of deceit.

1747 Voltaire publishes *Zadig*.

1754 Moses Mendelssohn, the German-Jewish thinker and admirer of the Arab-Jewish philosopher Ibn Maymun, or Maimonides, contemporary of Ibn Tufayl, meets Lessing in 1754. Their friendship is an important symbol of the Enlightenment.

1759 Voltaire publishes *Candide*

1759 Samuel Johnson (1709–1784) publishes *Rasselas*.

1762 Rousseau's *Émile* is published. The discovery of the child and the centrality of experience in his life.

1763 Kant publishes *The Only Possible Ground of Proof for a Demonstration of God's Existence*

1779 Lessing's *Nathan The Wise* is published in Germany. Tolerance is the key theme in the play.

1779 The Quakers decide to omit the positive reference to *Hayy Ibn Yaqzan* in the subsequent editions of Robert Barclay's *Apology*.

1781 Kant publishes the first edition of the *Critique of Pure Reason*.

1782 German translation of *Hayy* by Johann Gottfried Eichhorn in Berlin.

1784 Kant publishes his essay "An Answer to the Question: What is Enlightenment" in the December 1784 issue of the *Berlinische Monatsschrift*.

1787 Kant publishes the second edition of the *Critique of Pure Reason*

1788 Kant publishes *The Critique of Practical Reason*.

1793 Kant publishes *Religion within the Boundaries of Mere Reason*.

1859 Darwin publishes his book *On the Origin of Species by Means of Natural Selection, or the Preservation of Favoured Races in the Struggle for Life*.

I have read in the records of the Arabians, reverend Fathers, that Abdala the Saracen, when questioned as to what on this stage of the world, as it were, could be seen most worthy of wonder, replied: There is nothing to be seen more wonderful than man.

—Giovanni Pico Della Mirandola, *Oration of the Dignity of Man* (1486). Trans. Elizabeth L. Forbes

What a piece of work is a man!
how noble in reason! how infinite in faculty!
in form and moving how express and admirable!
how like an angel!
in apprehension how like a god!

—Shakespeare, *Hamlet*, Act II, 2

To be self-sufficient, hence not to need society, yet without being unsociable, i.e., fleeing it, is something that comes close to the sublime, just like any superiority over needs. In contrast, to flee from human beings out of *misanthropy*, because one is hostile to them, or out of *anthropophobia* (fear of people), because one fears them as enemies, is in part hateful and in part contemptible Nevertheless there is a kind of misanthropy (very improperly so called), the predisposition to which is often found in the mind of many well-thinking people as they get older. . . . evidence of this is to be found in the tendency to withdraw from society, the fantastic wish for an isolated country seat, or even (in young people) the dream of happiness in being able to pass their life on an island unknown to the rest of the world. . . , which the novelists or poets who write Robinsonades know so well how to exploit."

—Immanuel Kant, "Analytic of the Sublime" in *Critique of the Power of Judgment*, ed. Paul Guyer, trans. Paul Guyer and Eric Matthews. Cambridge: Cambridge University Press, 2000. 5: 276, p. 157

1

INTRODUCTION:
BURIED IN THE DUST OF HISTORY

A Forgotten Arab Mentor of Modern European Thinkers

The scientific activity is particularly interesting from the historical point of view because it is not simply creative but *cumulative*.
Our artists are not greater than artists of the past, our scientists
are not better than those of the past, but our scientists are un-
doubtedly more knowing. Michael Angelo stands upon the
shoulders of Phidias, but that does not make him any taller. On
the other hand, Newton stands upon the shoulders of Galileo
and because of that he can see further. . . .[1]

—George Sarton to Henry James

"It has on occasion been observed" Lawrence Conrad writes "that with
the possible exception of the *Thousand and One Nights*, no work from
the literary heritage of classical Islam has been published or translated so fre-
quently as Ibn Tufayl's *Hayy ibn Yaqzan* . . . . The scholarly literature is even
more extensive . . . . "[2] In another passage Lawrence observes that:

> In 1671 Edward Pococke published his *editio princeps* of the text of an
> Arabic manuscript his father had purchased[?] a journey to the Near
> East. The work was Ibn Tufayl's *Hayy ibn Yaqzan*, and Pococke had been
> attracted to it because . . . he regarded it as a book "in which it is
> demonstrated by what means human reason can ascend from contem-
> plation of the Inferior to knowledge of the Superior." Such themes were
> destined to evoke a favorable response in England during the Enlight-
> enment, and other scholars and literary figures were as taken by the book
> as Pococke had been. Whether Daniel Defoe modelled his *Robinson*

1

Crusoe on Ibn Tufayl's work is uncertain, but John Locke and others probably knew it and were influenced by it. The book was translated into numerous European languages, first from the Latin rendering that had accompanied Pococke's Arabic text, and later from the Arabic itself; by 1900 the work could be read in Dutch, English, French, German, Hebrew, Latin, and Spanish.[3]

Yet in spite of all these numerous translations and scholarly works of which Lawrence speaks about there is hardly anything that situates Ibn Tufayl squarely in the midst of modern European thought. Western theorists continue to ignore his profound influence on modern Europe. Ibn Tufayl, one of the genuine mentors of European philosophers and writers was buried in the dust of history. His book, *Hayy ibn Yaqzan*, had survived for more than nine hundred years, but only in the ghetto of Orientalist studies. Those who had borrowed freely from *Hayy*, had either kept silent about their debt for different reasons, or simply did not know that they were quoting this Arabic book. Illustrious names in Western thought are always paraded in books as the pillars of Western civilization, quite distinct from those 'Others' in the East. Their ideas about God, nature, man, society and history are exclusively the product of Western societies. They may be indebted to each other, but certainly not to non-Western aliens, particularly Arabs and Moslems.

One only has to look at any Western book on intellectual history to learn that "The modern origins of the history of ideas can be traced to the Enlightenment of the eighteenth century, to 'philosophic' historians such as Voltaire who tied progress to the growth of 'reason,' or the triumph of the human mind over superstition."[4] When modernity is discussed there is usually a reference to the Renaissance and Reformation, but then both periods are described as ones that tend to "look to the past for inspiration and guidance" says Franklin Baumer, for instance. "This was not true of the Moderns of the seventeenth century who looked more to the future and present. Sir Francis Bacon . . . a product of the Renaissance and Reformation, but also of the scientific revolution, was both prototype and epitome of this new sort of modernity."[5] The shift from the contemplative mode to the utilitarian one marks this revolution. Practical science becomes very important. As a result, the authority of great men, including Aristotle and Ptolemy, begins to be questioned, and eventually crumble. Book after book describes the scientific revolution and names great Western astronomers, or physicists, or mathematicians, such as Roger Bacon (1220–1292), Galileo Galilei (1564–1642), Sir Isaac Newton (1642–1727) and Leibniz

(1646–1716) among others, but fails to trace the origin and development of this drastic evolution of the new conception of knowledge in the world as a whole. This is mainly due to this very exclusive way of looking at Western societies as constituting separate and coherent entities very different from any other. The large divide created by historians between West and East seems to be responsible for many errors and misunderstanding in the transmission of knowledge in general.[6]

In his "Preface" to the *Encyclopedia of Enlightenment* published in 2003, Alan Charles Kors discusses the Enlightenment as "a set of tendencies and developments of European culture from the 1670s to the early nineteenth century (including in the American outposts of that culture."[7] He argues that "Enlightened culture . . . was matched by a set of dramatic phenomena . . . all of which had strikingly different histories according to time, place, circumstance, and group. These included . . . an increasingly critical attitude toward inherited authority in a large variety of human spheres, a sense that, armed with new methods and new powers, the human mind could reexamine claims upon it in a growing set of the domains of human life, including religion."[8] Furthermore, Kors highlights the ethical dimension of utility and the emergence of toleration as one of the most significant concerns of that time. Once again one wonders how did these "dramatic phenomena" spring up in a whole continent, which was not only oblivious to such concepts as empiricism, doubt, toleration, but also very hostile to them. The impression one gets from this repeated argument by Western scholars is that revolutions take place locally without the influence of the outside world, and that foreign ideas hardly travel beyond borders. But if the influence of others is conceded there is often the tendency to trace the original ideas to the Greek and Latin masters and the Renaissance.

To my mind, people have always lived in a global village throughout history. Ideas might not have traveled quickly, or on a large scale, as they do nowadays. But nevertheless they did manage to infiltrate other places. There were always travelers, merchants, missionaries, diplomats, students, and warriors to carry these ideas along to distant shores. People in general tend to be influenced by others who are more advanced than themselves. But this is not to deny the influence of people who are less developed on the ones who are more prosperous. New ideas are either eagerly accepted, or ferociously fought. Likewise, their sources are either named, or hidden. It is not always easy to fight against one's own prejudices, particularly when the new ideas emanate from one's enemy, or from people who are considered primitive, or barbarians. The compartmentalization of history, philosophy, science, and other branches of knowledge is a manifestation of this fear that keeps humanity apart. It denies basic ideas, such as interaction between people and possible influence of one on the other. The end result is that we have "Western history," "Western philosophy," "Western science," and "Western mind" as opposed to everything Eastern, as if there is one unified Western or Eastern mind! There is a wall that seems to perpetually stand between East and West. Even the most liberal intellectuals wallow in these terms. Of course, I am not calling for the study of universal history, or philosophy, or science, in lieu of regional studies. But I am very concerned about binary and rigid formulas, which do not take into consideration that people influence each other regardless of their race, religion, gender and culture, and that history is continuously in flux.[9]

In his portrayal of Hayy Ibn Yaqzan as an infant who grew up all alone on a deserted island, yet managed through his own reason and experiments to become an enlightened man without the help of parents, teachers, religious mentors, and society at large, Ibn Tufayl had presented to medieval Europe, which was on its way to discovering science, the prototype of a possible new human being. Not only did Hayy discover how to kindle fire, or to build a hut, or to domesticate animals, or to invent tools, but he also learnt how to become a physician, a biologist, an astronomer, a physicist, a psychologist and a philosopher.[10] No one helped him reach his goal except his reason and scientific experimentation.

When Francis Bacon (1561–1626) suggested that the mind be purged, presented as a scrubbed tablet, washed clean of fantasy and bookishness, in order to start anew, he was most probably thinking of the young man depicted by an Arab Moslem philosopher from Spain centuries ago. Bacon's modernity is traced back to his complaint to James I of England about the state of learning at the beginning of the seventeenth century. According to Bacon, both the Scholastic system and the humanist ideal that replaced it were responsible for the ills of the nation. His new logic called for a reconciliation between the empiricists and the rationalists and illustrated how induction would eventually lead to a knowledge of forms.[11] It is ironic, but not surprising however, that Bacon who most probably was aware of *Hayy Ibn Yaqzan*, had dismissed the Arabs' learning. In his *New Organon* (1620) he observed "neither Arabians nor the Schoolmen need to be mentioned, who in the intermediate times rather crushed the sciences with a multitude of treatises, than increased their weight."[12]

The late George Sarton, a humanist of the first order, assures us that "the search for the truth is not restricted to any single group or class or nation of men. If one takes the whole of the past into account, not simply one period, and all the chains . . . one finds that men of all kinds have shared in the work. No one can predict where and when the missing links of any chain will be discovered. . . ."[13] In his writing, Sarton always uses the metaphor of the giant and the dwarf, which is attributed to Bernard of Chartres and Newton in order to assert our indebtedness to each other and to stress the unity of science and mankind.[14] In a lecture entitled "East and West" Sarton regrets that, "We are used to think of our civilization as western, we continually oppose our western ways to the eastern ways, and we have sometimes the impression that the opposition is irreducible. 'Oh, East is East and West is West, and never the twain shall meet.'"[15] But to his mind, there is no logic in a statement such as this, for "The unity of mankind includes East and West. They are like two moods of the same man; they represent two fundamental and complementary phases of human experience."[16]

In his monumental book, *Introduction to the History of Science*, Sarton discussed early Jewish, Christian and Muslim scholars and their achievements, which gradually helped to create European civilization. Writing briefly on great philosophers, such as Ibn Sina, or Avicenna (d.1037), Ibn Bajja, or Avempace (1106–1138, 1139), Ibn Rushd, or Averroes (1126–1198) and many other illustrious names, he mentioned Ibn Tufayl, or Abubacer (1100, 1110– 1185, 1186) and praised his original philosophical romance, *Hayy Ibn Yaqzan*, without discussing its ideas in depth. According to Sarton, Hayy "is the history of a sort of metaphysical Robinson Crusoe proving the identity of revealed religion and philosophy, this philosophy being the extreme Muslim neo-Platonism. And as very few people are able to understand philosophy, it justifies the doctrine of the twofold truth. The introduction contains an account of the development of Muslim philosophy. The story itself includes a sketch of a natural classification of the sciences, a discussion of spontaneous generation, and miscellaneous scientific information."[17]

But one cannot blame Sarton to have made nothing more than that of *Hayy Ibn Yaqzan*. After all Sarton confesses in his Preface that his knowledge of Arabic language and culture is imperfect. The blame, I think, lies squarely with Arab and Muslim scholars and scientists who have neglected to study their medieval heritage in depth, not only to understand what their ancestors have achieved in all branches of knowledge, but also to show the continuous link between East and West. Unfortunately, most of the Arab and Muslim scholars nowadays tend to parrot what is written by Western scholars, either because they study in western universities and lack competence in reading medieval scientific Arabic, or because they study in eastern universities and lack an in-depth knowledge of European languages and

western science in general. Furthermore, there are many old Arabic manuscripts scattered in different libraries around the world awaiting serious
scholars to edit them, comment on them and publish them.[18] Many other
manuscripts are lost. We know that Ibn Tufayl, for instance, had written at
least two books on medicine, that he had a very advanced and useful theories in astronomy unlike those of Ptolemy and al-Bitruji, his own pupil
(d. 1185–1186), and that he had also written poetry. The short and sketchy
scientific references in Hayy's story were only meant as quick references to
more elaborate theories treated by Ibn Tufayl in his lost books and treatises.
One can never be sure if Ibn Tufayl, or other Muslim scientists, had in fact
advanced some new ideas which might have helped Copernicus, Kepler and
Galilei, for the complete story of Arabic science has not been told. Yet even
Sarton assures us—and one wonders on what basis—that the theory of Ibn
Tufayl's pupil, Al-Bitruji, the Latin Alpetragius, was erroneous and that "No
Muslim astronomer improved al-Bitruji's arguments."[19] But he speculates
that although Al-Bitruji's theory was erroneous, "it is the subject of considerable discussion and may be considered as one of the steps that led in-
directly to the astronomical revolution of 1543."[20]

In his book, *The Copernican Revolution*, T. S. Kuhn argues, "To astronomy . . . [Muslim scholars] contributed both new observations and new
techniques for the computation of planetary position. Yet the Moslems
were seldom-radical innovators in scientific theory. . . . Therefore . . .
Islamic civilization is important primarily because it preserved and prolifer-
ated the records of ancient Greek science for later European scholars.
Christendom received ancient learning from the Arabs."[21] Some historians
of science tend to present a similar argument up to this date. But one would
hope that this hypothesis which has by now assumed the shape of a scientific fact will be proven wrong in the near future, if and when Arab and
Muslim scientists begin working seriously on their dusty manuscripts
around the world.

Unfortunately, there are only a handful of books and articles in Arabic written on *Hayy Ibn Yaqzan*. None, to my knowledge, is done by a
physicist, an astronomer, a mathematician, or a natural scientist. Most of the
studies are exclusively written by philosophers, or historians. Yet even in
this regard they hardly scratch the surface and fail to situate this important
book in the main stream of world philosophy, or intellectual history.[22]
Books and articles written by Arabs and non-Arabs on *Hayy Ibn Yaqzan* in
English fare much better, but they are still entangled with orientalist discourse and seem to be unable to present this book as part of our world heritage.[23] There are signs however, which indicate that more critics are be-

ginning to be seriously interested in Ibn Tufayl in relation to other European thinkers. In 1994, G. A. Russell edited an interesting book entitled, *The Arabick Interest of the Natural Philosophers in Seventeenth-Century England* and wrote an article in which she investigated the possibility of Ibn Tufayl's influence on Locke. In her introduction she observes that:

> The immediate question that arises is whether the appearance of this unique narrative [*Hayy ibn Yaqzan*] and Locke's drafting of the first versions of the *Essay* were purely coincidental or whether there is a connection. The reason for raising such a query is that the publication of the *Philosophus autodidactus* at Oxford comes at a turning point in Locke's intellectual career. Scholars are largely agreed that it was in 1671 that Locke, for the first time in his writing, focused on the question of the nature of mind and its emergence out of experience without innate ideas. This empirical approach formed the nucleus of Locke's theory of knowledge and of what subsequently came to be known as the British Associationist School of Philosophy. Prior to this period, Locke's concerns were social, political, and practical and revealed no specific interest in the kind of epistemological issues which characterise his *Essay*.[24]

In a painstaking effort, Russell investigates Locke's friendship with Pocockes, father and son, at Christ Church, Oxford, when the Arabic text was being translated by Edward Pococke into Latin. The father, Dr. Pococke, who was the first Laudian Professor of Arabic at Oxford in 1636 had supervised the translation of his son and made sure that not only his friends in England knew about it, but also prominent European intellectuals. Russell also maps the dramatic shift in Locke's thinking vis-à-vis the human intellect as a result of the publication of *Hayy Ibn Yaqzan* in England. She traces Ibn Tufayl's basic ideas, which have ignited the interest not only of Locke but also of other seventeenth-century thinkers. Concepts, such as the nature of God, the law of nature, natural religion, and the role of religion in society are enumerated as key issues hotly debated at the time. In the second part of her essay, Russell talks briefly about "the Lockean notion of the mind as a *tabula rasa* where ideas are acquired by means of sensory experience and reasoning as opposed to the Cartesian notion of their innateness."[25] But she concentrates her efforts on proving, perhaps mainly to her skeptical western readers, how Locke might have been aware of Ibn Tufayl's book and consequently, perhaps influenced by it. She is puzzled by the fact that Locke made no reference to it, nor did anyone find it in his library. In her effort to explain Locke's silence about the matter, she feels obliged to attribute this to his "precarious existence and his cautious and highly suspicious attitude to others."[26] Of course, one understands Russell's dilemma and worries that unless a clear statement from the author is found in which he acknowledges his debt to Ibn Tufayl, her whole case will be easily dismissed by other Western scholars. This is not a peculiar example. If we are to examine any book, or article that deals directly or indirectly with the influence of Arabic, or Islamic ideas on the West we encounter a similar attitude, mainly because the authors of these books and articles understand the depth of hostility and irrationality of other scholars who insist on using binary terms, such as Western and Eastern and attempt to deflate any theory of influence by employing racial categories.

It is equally important, however, not to go to the other extreme and see influences everywhere, but to follow a reasonable and rational path by examining original texts suspected of being the source of other texts, by comparing, or contrasting their contents with or without having a solid proof of the alleged influence. The point, which I would like to stress, is that all of us are capable of producing great ideas regardless of our race, social class, religion, or gender. But life is like a Ferris wheel. One time we are placed on top of the world. The other time we are placed at the bottom.[27] Nevertheless, all of us can still contribute to civilization. History is never static, but always in flux. We can never ignore this assumption.

In this light, we must be very careful when we talk about our own scientific revolutions and inventions, and never claim that we alone are the first and the last who have discovered something. Ibn Tufayl borrowed from others and was humble enough to acknowledge his debt to many scholars, even those with whom he disagreed. This is, perhaps, where he differs from those who think that they must adopt a "scornful attitude toward the intellectual achievements of the past."[28] If I am trying to revive his name after hundreds of years of neglect, my aim is certainly not to say that he was the first, or the only mentor of modern Europe. There were other illustrious names and not necessarily Arabs, or Moslems. It is a high time to shift this racial-religious emphasis in the study of science, intellectual history, philosophy and literature from being exclusively western to something more humane. Indeed Spinoza (1632–1677) was a rebel whose God had nothing to do with the conventional Judeo-Christian God, and that he was associated with skepticism in modern philosophy and science. But one should also remember that he was standing on the shoulders of giants, such as al-Ghazali (d.1111) and Ibn Tufayl.[29] Unfortunately, Spinoza, the great philosopher, who is reported to have translated *Hayy ibn Yaqzan*, or ordered someone else to translate it into Dutch, seems to steal the limelight in all encyclopedias of philosophy, books on modern European thought, and the scientific revolution. His mentors, however, are relegated to the dust of history mainly because they are not western.

Richard Dawkins, who holds the Charles Simonyi Chair in the Public Understanding of Science at the University of Oxford, was invited to Harvard University to give the Tanner Lectures on Human Values on November 19, 20, 21, 2003. He gave two lectures on the first two days, namely, "The Science of Religion" and "The Religion of Science." On the third day there was a seminar in which other professors of psychology and philosophy participated. Dismissing religion as a social virus, Dawkins argued that religion is harmful and divisive; it has not helped people to adapt, or to survive. As a scientist, he stressed the significance of reason and evidence and totally rejected tradition and authority. Einstein, he said, was a great admirer of Spinoza, and religion for the scientist could only mean his own marvel at the universe.

I was stunned to hear part of Ibn Tufayl's argument albeit presented in a contemporary and simplistic format and accompanied by slides in order to demonstrate how harmful religion is. But three images in particular have caught my attention. One that represented tribal people wearing Arab robes and taking their gods with them to battle. The other was a tower that led to paradise, and presumably a suicide bomber who kills himself and other innocent people is aspiring to ascend to heaven. The third was the Indian-British writer Salman Rushdi and in the background the angry Iranian "clerics" who censored his thought and urged Moslems all over the world to kill him for publishing his *Satanic Verses*. These three powerful images gave the audience not only the hateful and misleading face of Islam as a religion, but of those races that adhere to it. In confusing his argument about a small group of fanatics with their religion Dawkins' thesis may easily lead to the persecution and harassment of Arabs and Muslims in Western countries, something, I am sure, the British scientist does not wish, or accept. When I asked him during the question-answer period whether a scientist should be also interested in history and endeavor to put his presentation in a historical perspective—for neglecting history, which is never static, but always in flux, can lead to dangerous consequences and consolidate stereotypical images of other people—he curtly replied that he detested all Abrahamic faiths, that he was not picking on Arabs and Moslems, and that his slides showed others as well.[30] But to my mind these brief captions that Dawkins showed to us at Harvard at these troubled political times froze and slanted history. Ironically, he used part of Ibn Tufayl's argument about the significance of reason, experimentation and evidence and used it inadvertently perhaps to damn Islam as a religion.

Ibn Tufayl's protagonist, Hayy Ibn Yaqzan, had no religion. He was not a Muslim, a Christian, or a Jew. He was not white, or black. When he matured on his own without the help of parents, society, or religious mentors, he managed to discover some power in the universe, and he gave it a name from the science of mechanics; i.e., the Mover of the Universe, not as God, Allah, or Yehua.[31] When he became acquainted with other human beings, he did not convert to their religion, or use subservient means to convert them to his. He realized that conventional rituals, literary interpretations of scriptures and abandonment of reason and evidence in favor of blind faith could be very harmful. He endeavored to reason with other human beings, but never sensationalized their shortcomings, or spoke with contempt about their religion, for Hayy believed that each one of us is endowed with reason. There is no doubt that he felt immense pity for those who neglected to use their reason, and thought that they would eventually use it if they had the will to do so. Hayy did not condemn religion per se. He saw some benefits to those who needed it.[32] On the other hand, he realized that truth was something relative, and that people who did use their reason did not exactly reach his own conclusions.

Hayy's basic argument is not really so much about the harmony between philosophy and religion as Léon Gauthier claims. Rather it is about us humans, about our diversity and the necessity to accommodate each other and the possible peaceful ways, which we may be able to use in order to avoid violence and bloodshed.

It is helpful, but not essential, to know that Western philosophers and writers had once owned, or read this Arabic book, in order to ascertain its influence on their works. The most important thing is to examine Hayy's innovative and modern ideas, such as his theory of knowledge, scientific method, system of education, concept of equality, freedom and toleration, the individual progress to perfection and the use of reason as a basis of evidence in contrast to authority in all its forms. These modern ideas seemed to have spread like fire from Moslem Spain to medieval Europe where once experiment was associated with black magic. But it was not until the seventeenth and eighteenth century that they began to take roots in European thought. "The Enlightenment . . . as Ernst Troeltsch and many others were later to say, was the hinge on which the European nations turned from the Middle Ages to 'modern' times, marking the passage from a supernaturalistic-mythical-authoitative to a naturalistic-scientific-individualistic type of thinking."[33] It is the spirit and the great ideals of this enlightened age that became the pride of Europe to this day.

On January 22, 2003 the American Secretary of Defense Donald Rumsfeld dismissed France and Germany as "old Europe." Responding to a reporter's question about European opposition to the use of force in Iraq, Rumsfeld said: "You're thinking of Europe as Germany and France. I don't. I think that's 'old Europe.' If you look at the entire NATO Europe today, the center of gravity is shifting to the East. And there are a lot of new members. And if you just take the list of all the members of NATO and all of those who have been invited in recently—what is it, twenty-six, something like that? [But] you're right. Germany has been a problem, and France has been a problem."[34]

The German-French reaction was swift. But the amazing thing is that the French and the Belgium, in particular, had invoked the Enlightenment. A French government spokesman, Jean-Francois Cope, noted pointedly that being old also meant being wise. He said: "An 'old' continent—a continent somewhat ancient in its historical, cultural, political, economic traditions—can sometimes be infused with a certain wisdom, and wisdom can sometimes make for good advice."[35] Belgium's Foreign Minister Louis Michel described Rumsfeld's insulting remark as a slap in the face. "Rumsfeld, who comes to teach a thing or two to 'old Europe,' the Europe of democratic values, humanist Europe, the Europe of the Age of Enlightenment, personally I find this hurts,"[36] the Foreign Minister said.

But one of the possible torches that showed Europe the path to enlightenment was this wild boy who matured and became wise at the age of fifty. His name was Hayy Ibn Yaqzan. He was created in the imagination of an Arab Moslem philosopher from Spain in the twelfth century. The negation of history, or the emphasis on the exclusiveness of one's own history, not only by the American Secretary of Defense, but also by the European officials shows this "scornful attitude" toward the Other, the denial of our indebtedness to each other and the selfish drive that dominates our lives.[37] Ibn Tufayl would never have dismissed the ancient philosophers. He would certainly disagree with them, or even criticize them, but he would always acknowledge his debt to them. On the other hand, he would never praise any specific race, or religion, or claim that they have exclusively achieved something that no one is able to achieve. For him we are all human beings, and are able to change the world if we use our reason.

NOTES

1. A letter by George Sarton to Henry James dated May 17, 1935. Sarton papers, Houghton Library, Harvard University. Quoted by Robert K. Merton in *The History of Science and the New Humanism: With Recollections and Reflections by Robert K. Merton* (New Brunswick, USA and Oxford, UK: Transaction Inc., 1988), xl.

2. See Conrad's "Research Resources on Ibn Tufayl and Hayy Ibn Yaqzan," in *The World of Ibn Tufayl: Interdisciplinary Perspectives on Hayy Ibn Yaqzan*, ed. Lawrence I. Conrad (Leiden; New York; Koln: E. J. Brill, 1996), 267.

3. See Conrad's "Introduction," to *The World of Ibn Tufayl*, 1.

4. See Franklin L. Baumer, *Modern European Thought: Continuity and Change in Ideas, 1600–1950* (New York; London: Macmillan & Collier Macmillan, 1977), 3.

5. Baumer, 27. Cf. what Herbert Butterfield says about the scientific revolution in his book, *The Origins of Modern Science 1300–1800*. Revised edition, (New York: The Free Press, 1965). The scientific revolution "outshines everything since the rise of Christianity and reduces the Renaissance and Reformation to the rank of mere episodes" 7. Jacob Bronowski and Bruce Mazlish quote Butterfield in their book, *The Western Intellectual Tradition: From Leonardo to Hegel*. (New York: Books for Libraries, A Division of Arno Press, Inc., 1979) and hail his views on the scientific revolution as those "of many contemporary historians. . . . " 107.

6. In *The Scientific Revolution: A Historiographical Inquiry* published by the University of Chicago in 1994, H. Floris Cohen tells us a very interesting story about how an "innocent" question posed by three Chinese graduate students at Cambridge University in 1937 has led their English biochemistry professor to take a crash course in Chinese and eventually publish several volumes on *Science and Civilization in China*. Of course, only Chinese scholars can assess the value of such a contribution. But the "innocent" (or not so innocent question) of the students is the one that interests me. Given the fact that Joseph Needham had written a large volume on the history of science in the 1930s the students inquired, "how it was that 'modern science originated only in Europe?'" 418.

Cf. Mohammad Ilyas, *Islamic Astronomy and Science Development: Glorious Past, Challenging Future* (Selangor Darul Ehsan, Malaysia: Pelanduk Publications, 1996). Ilyas asks a similar question, but more specific. How come that history of science books jump from the Greeks to the Renaissance as if the years 750–1100 never existed? Yet there were many prominent Arab and Moslem scientists during these years. 1–17.

7. See Alan Charles Kors, ed. *Encyclopedia of the Enlightenment*, vol. I (New York: Oxford University Press, 2003), xvii.

8. Kors, xvii.

9. On a lighter note, a very well-known Dutch-German orientalist was quite offended when I told him a few years ago that the delicious marzipan had perhaps originated in Damascus, my birth place, and that the German Crusaders had most likely taken it back with them to Germany in the Middle Ages. Before the marzipan we were talking about Dante and his possible debt to Islamic sources, most notably the Journey of Muhammad to Heaven and Hell and other literary works. I had taught *The Divine Comedy* in upstate New York many years ago when I was still a teaching assistant in the English Department. I did not speculate about Dante's debt to Islam at that time, but as a proof I brought to class specific texts to be read and compared with *The Inferno* in particular. The old German professor was anx-

ious to deflate my argument by all means. But when our conversation drifted to something very light like marzipan he was very furious. He must have thought that marzipan was a German symbol. No foreigner, particularly his own subjects, the Arabs and Muslims, could have taught his advanced country, which was not so advanced in the Middle Ages, how to make this confection of almond paste with sugar. Never mind that the loan word marzipan was Persian. But I must confess that the new German marzipan is far superior to any of its kind in the city of Damascus nowadays.

The reason I am telling this anecdote is that if an Orientalist, who has studied Arabic and Islamic culture and is expected to see the interaction between his subjects and other cultures, has this reserved and even hostile attitude about the most trivial thing, such as marzipan, how can we expect other Western scholars in other disciplines to be open-minded and receptive to theories of influence between East and West?

10. Note that Hayy had dissected his mother's body in order to find the cause of her death. Dissection of bodies seems to be a normal practice of a physician like Ibn Tufayl in twelfth-century Moslem Spain. Yet Robert Merton argues in his "Recollections & Reflections: George Sarton: Episodic Recollections by an Unruly Apprentice" that dissection is taboo in Arab-Islamic culture. Merton describes the defense of his dissertation as follows: "His [Sarton] first question struck me dumb: 'Mr. Merton, will you tell us, please, who discovered the greater circulation of the blood?'. . . . 'Of course, the greater circulation of the blood was discovered by William Harvey. Some claim that it was intimated in his lecture notes of 1616, although he didn't get around to publishing it until 1628. . . . But for historians of science, the recent excitement lies in the new confirmation . . . that the thirteenth-century Arab physician Ibn al-Nafis did indeed discover the lesser pulmonary circulation, long before its independent discovery first by Servetus and then by Columbo. It should be said, however, that he arrived at the lesser circulation, not through dissection, which was of course taboo in his culture, but on strictly theoretical grounds. . . .'" See *The History of Science and the New Humanism with Recollections. . . .*, xx–xxi. See also *Hayy Ibn Yaqzan*, ed. Jamil Saliba and Kamil 'Ayyad, 5th ed. (Damascus: Damascus University, 1962), 36–37, 39–40.

11. See James Collins, *A History of Modern European Philosophy* (Lanham; New York; London: University Press of America, 1986) Originally published by Milwaukee Bruce Publishing Company, 1954, 51–73. Cf. Franklin Baumer, *Modern European Thought*, 47–48.

12. Francis Bacon, *New Organon, Works*, trans. J. Spedding, R. Ellis, and D. Heath new ed. (New York: Hurd & Houghton, 1870–1872), 4: 77.

13. See Sarton's "The History of Science and the New Humanism" in *The History of Science with Recollections by Merton*, 31–32.

14. "Now as opposed to beauty, knowledge is cumulative and progressive. . . . It is in that sense that one must understand the saying ascribed to one of the most lovable scholars of the twelfth century, Bernard of Chartres, 'In comparison with the

ancients we are like dwarfs sitting on the shoulders of giants.'" See Sarton's "The History of Science and the New Humanism" in The *History of Science with Recollections*. 15–16 and footnote 1 on page 16.

15. Sarton, "East and West," in *The History of Science and the New Humanism*, 66.

16. Sarton, "East and West," in *The History of Science and the New Humanism*, 108.

17. See Sarton, *Introduction to the History of Science, Volume II From Rabbi Ben Ezra to Roger Bacon* (Baltimore: Carnegie Institution of Washington, The Williams & Wilkins Company, 1931), 354.

18. The historian of the seventeenth-century optics and of Arabic science, A. I. Sabra writes in *The Dictionary of the Middle Ages* that "the great majority" of those manuscripts that together constitute the surviving corpus of Islamic science, spreading today from libraries in Tehran and Cairo to Los Angeles, have never been examined by anybody. See "Science, Islamic" in volume 11, ed. Joseph R. Strayer (New York: Scribner, 1982–1989), 81.

19. See Sarton, *Introduction to the History of Science*, 295. Cf the arrogant assumption of T .J. De Boer in *The Philosophy in Islam* (1903), trans. Edward R. Jones (Richmond, Surrey: Curzon Press, 1994), 182. "He [Ibn Tufayl] was the *dilettante* of the philosophers of the West, and was more given to contemplative enjoyment than scientific work. Rarely did he set himself to write. We need not perhaps put absolute faith in his assertion that he could have fundamentally improved the Ptolemaie system. Many Arabs made a like assertion, without carrying it into effect."

20. *Introduction to the History of Science*, 298.

21. Kuhn, *The Copernican Revolution: Planetary Astronomy in the Development of Western Thought*. (Cambridge: Harvard University Press, 1957), 101. Cf. Thomas Crump. *A Brief History of Science As Seen Through the Development of Scientific Instruments*. London: Constable & Robinson Ltd., 2001, 35-36. Crump basically sums up the argument of most historians of science in his discussion of "Islam and the medieval legacy," but relies heavily on T. S. Kuhn.

22. See for instance Omar A Farrukh's *Ibn Tufayl (Abubacer) and his Philosophical Romance Hayy Ibn Yaqzan*. 2nd ed. (Beirut, 1959). Farrukh refers briefly and in passing to Ibn Tufayl's influence on Jewish philosophy in the Middle Ages, particularly Ibn Maymun, or Maimonides, Albertus Magnus, St. Thomas Aquinas, Spinoza, Defoe and others. See also the valuable, but very brief introduction of 'Abd al-Karim al-Yafi to *Hayy Ibn Yaqzan* (Damascus: Tlas Press, 1995). Al-Yafi has a very interesting thesis. He situates *Hayy ibn Yaqzan* in the genre of utopian literature, but unlike its genre it is more concerned with an individualistic utopia. According to him the word utopia is more likely to be derived from the Arabic *tuba* which denotes happiness and well-being than from the Greek word which refers to "no place." Al-Yafi groups *Hayy* with Plato's *Republic*, al-Farabi's *People of the Virtuous City* and Ibn Bajja's *Guide of the Solitary*. He also mentions that the first European writer to coin the term is Thomas More (1478–1535) in his Latin book translated into English as *Utopia* (1516). See 31–38.

A few Arabic studies on Hayy are concerned with Defoe's debt to Ibn Tufayl. See, for instance, Hasan Mahmud Abbas, *Hayy Ibn Yaqzan wa Robinson Crusoe: Dirasa muqarana* (*Hayy Ibn Yaqzan and Robinson Crusoe: A Comparative Study*) (Beirut: Al-Mu'assasa al-a'rabiyya lildirasat wa al-nashr, 1983).

23. See "Modern Studies on Ibn Tufayl and his Work" as part of Lawrence Conrad's "Research Resources on Ibn Tufayl and Hayy Ibn Yaqzan" in his edited book, *The World of Ibn Tufayl: Interdisciplinary Perspectives on Hayy ibn Yaqzan*, 285–93.

Examine for instance Sami S. Hawi's *Islamic Naturalism and Mysticism: A Philosophical Study of Ibn Tufayl's Hayy Bin Yaqzan* (Leiden: E. J. Brill, 1974). Hawi concentrates on Ibn Tufayl's philosophy and naturalistic outlook, epistemology and the plurality of the methods of knowing, the existence of God and His attributes, doctrine of pantheism and attainment of mystical experience. His aim is certainly not to situate *Hayy ibn Yaqzan* in world philosophy. Nevertheless, Hawi refers briefly to several western names here and there. In his conclusion, for instance, he argues, "Whether in his epistemology or in his pantheistic doctrine, he [Ibn Tufayl] was certainly awake to the same impulse which was behind Locke's epistemological determinations, Hume's agnosticism concerning causal relations, Spinoza's notion of universal subsistence, Husserl's phenomenological reduction, and the basis themes of Gestalt theory." 256.

24. See "The impact of the Philosophus autodidactus: Pocockes, John Locke and the Society of Friends" in *The 'Arabick' Interest of the Natural Philosophers in Seventeenth-Century England*. Leiden; New York; Koln, 1994, 224.

25. G. A. Russell, "The Impact of the Philosophus Autodidactus," 231.

26. Russell, "The Impact of the Philosophus Autodidactus," 252.

27. It was interesting for me to learn that George Hakewill, a chaplin to Prince Charles, afterwards Charles I, and the author of *An Apologie of the Power and Providence of God in the Government of the World*, 3rd ed., (London, 1635) had expressed the following views as quoted by Franklin Baumer in his *Modern European Thought*. Baumer wrote: "He [Hakewill] reminded his readers repeatedly of the "wheeling about of all things" in history. Like the turning wheel that eventually brings all its spokes back to the same point, just so did all the cultures of the world flourish, fade, and then perhaps flourish again. Actually, Hakewill preached in his own words, "a kind of circular progress." That is, civilization moved from one area or nation to another in different ages, so that while some members suffered, "yet the whole [was] in no way thereby endamaged at any time." The Greeks succeeded the Persians, Egyptians, and Chaldeans as leaders in the arts and sciences, and were in time succeeded by the Romans and Arabs, and now by the northern Europeans, who were able to improve upon all of them." 119–20.

28. In his chapter "Ancients and Moderns" Franklin Baumer argues, "It is not perhaps sufficiently understood that the scientific revolution was, among other things, a judgment on history. . . . But above all, it demanded a critical and *even scornful attitude* toward the intellectual achievements of the past, of antiquity as well as of medieval scholasticism. Aristotle, Galen, and the rest, for so long unquestioned

'idols' in their respective fields of knowledge, had to be overturned before the new science could bear fruit." *Modern European Thought*, 129. I have highlighted the phrase "even scornful attitude." For Ibn Tufayl who attempted to refute many scholars, including Aristotle and Ptolemy, a remark like this will be shocking. Scholars are not idols to be worshipped, then toppled and scorned, rather human beings who make mistakes. Baumer's observation, perhaps could also throw some light on Bacon's dismissal remark about the achievements of Arab learning and western scholastics.

29. In his introduction to *Hayy Ibn Yaqzan*, Ibn Tufayl evaluates the contributions of other philosophers and acknowledges his debt to some of them, particularly Ibn Bajja. He also refers to al-Ghazali and quotes an important passage on *skepticism*: "If I [al-Ghazali] did nothing but to make you doubt your inherited faith that would be beneficial enough. For he who does not doubt has not looked, and he who has not looked does not see, and he who does not see remains blind and confused." Al-Ghazali then quotes an Arabic poem: "Take only what you see and discard everything you have heard about from others. . . ." Consult the Arabic text of *Hayy Ibn Yaqzan*, ed. Jamil Saliba and Kamil 'Ayyad, 15, or 'Abd al-Karim al-Yafi's edition, 63. The English translation is rendered by me. Cf. Lenn Evan Goodman's translation of Ibn Tufayl's *Hayy Ibn Yaqzan: A Philosophical Tale* (New York: Twayne Publishers, 1972), 101.

30. Dawkins' slide about the Arabs taking their gods with them to battle is rather inaccurate. The ancient Arabs were very irreligious. Some tribes used to make their gods out of dates. Whenever they were hungry they ate them. But the people of the Old Testament had a very different relationship with their God who went with them to battle. The other images: the suicide bomber and Rushdi with the Iranian clerics (never mind that there is no clergy in Islam) were exclusively treated as part and parcel of Islam as a religion which allegedly encourages Moslems to kill innocent people and have a blind faith in authority and scripture. Unfortunately, these images along with many others have become associated with all Moslems (and who ever looks like them; i.e., a person with a beard and dark skin) in the eyes of many westerners. After September 11, 2001 many visible and not so visible Moslems were spat at and insulted in the streets of so many western cities. On the contrary, the image of the American Evangelist Graham projected by Dawkins is certainly not associated with all Americans. No body insults Americans abroad because Graham is one of them. Cf. my Arabic article, "'I am Spanish,' Said the Frightened Lebanese Woman: The Aftermath of September 11, 2001 in Australia." *Al-Mustaqbal* (Beirut), 20 January 2002.

31. Notice that the philosopher Ibn Bajja, or Avempace, who was greatly admired by Ibn Tufayl, uses a similar metaphor in his treatises on physics. According to him there is one Supreme Mover of the universe. See *Kitab tadbir al-mutawahhid* (*Guide of the Solitary*), edited and introduced by Ma'n Ziyada (Beirut: Dar al-Fikr & Dar al-Fikr al-Islami, 1978), 11–13. See also note 13, page 34. Note that the science of mechanics was also used by Ibn Rushd, or Averroes, for instance, in his at-

tempt to explain the conditions of health and disease. Consult his *Kitab al-Kulliyat*, ed. and introduced by Muhammad Bin 'Abd al-Jalil Balqziz. (al-Dar al-Bayda': Al-Najah al-Jadida Press, 2000).

32. According to Dawkins all religions have something very harmful in them. It is not the manipulation of certain men which is responsible so much for the trouble we have today, but rather the ideas propounded by these religions. During the Seminar with Dr. Dawkins and two other professors that took place on Friday, November 21, 2003 at Wiener Auditorium in John F. Kennedy School of Government at Harvard University, Professor Steven Pinker, Johnston Family Professor of Psychology at Harvard observed that religious beliefs exploit our emotions, and that the group tends to control the individual. In describing religious rituals, he spoke about what he called the 'solidarity' phenomenon in such a frightening manner, i.e., engaging in their rituals makes individuals susceptible to group psychology. Again there was no differentiation between fanatics and ordinary pious people. One of his many examples was the Moslems' bowing all at once towards Mecca. He did not elaborate or explain how such an act could harm an individual. It was left for us to speculate the consequences. Feeling no pity for ordinary people who do not share their conviction that religion is harmful, Dawkins and Pinker differ drastically from Ibn Tufayl.

33. Baumer, *Modern European Thought*, 141.

34. See Briefing at the Foreign Press Center, also participating, Air Force General Richard B. Myers, chairman, Joint Chiefs of Staff. News Transcript on the web: http://www.defenselink.mil/news/Jan2003/t01232003 t012, 1.

35. See "US.: Rumsfeld's 'Old and 'New' Europe." Radio Free Europe. http://www.rferl.org/nca/features/2003/01/2401200317, 2. See also the *Washington Post.* January 24, 2003, A20.

36. See BBC News. "Belgium to block US Nato request." http://news.bbc.co.uk/1/hi/world/europe/2743185.stm (9 February, 2003).

37. On January 4, 2004 Robert Kilroy-Silk, a former British Labor Party member of Parliament published an anti-Arab column headlined, "We owe Arabs nothing" in the *Sunday Express* tabloid. In the article he described Arabs as "suicide bombers, limb amputators, woman repressors" and questioned the contribution of the Arab world to civilization. His BBC TV talk show was immediately suspended. "This article is indisputably stupid and its main effect will be to give comfort to the week-minded," said CRE [Commission for Racial Equality] Chairman Trevor Phillips. "Given the extreme and violent terms in which Mr. Kilroy-Silk has expressed himself, there is a danger that this might incite some individuals to act against someone who they think is an Arab." See "BBC Talk Show Host Suspended for Anti-Arab Column." CNSNews.com

2

SERVING GOD OR MAMMON?

Echos from Hayy Ibn Yaqzan and Sinbad the Sailor in Robinson Crusoe[1]

CRUSOE'S FOREIGN MODELS

In a lecture delivered on Defoe in Italian at the Universita Popolare Triestina in 1912, James Joyce argued that 'the first English author to write without imitating or adapting foreign works, to create without literary models and to infuse into the creatures of his pen a truly national spirit . . . is Daniel Defoe.'[2] It is a unique and rather extravagant claim to be made in literary history,[3] and perhaps it is surprising that it was made by a writer like Joyce whose style and method, while utterly original, show a myriad of influences and debts which, not always consciously, found their way into his works. What I should like to argue in this chapter is that there were, indeed, 'foreign works' that could have been used in the writing of *Robinson Crusoe*.

My thesis is that two different figures of Arabic literature, both of which were popular in translations in Defoe's lifetime, may have served as models that merged into one composite figure, Robinson Crusoe. This is not an altogether original view; references to one of the models, Ibn Tufayl's *Hayy Ibn Yaqzan* can be found in some scholarly contributions which, however, were largely ignored by English and American critics.[4] The reason for this, it could be suggested, lies in the 'national spirit' which Joyce has identified with Defoe, and which has contributed to a reluctance to acknowledge foreign models and influences. One of my purposes here is thus to redress the critical neglect with which the work of scholars such as Antonio Pastor has been met. At the same time I should like to point out the possibility of another model for Crusoe, namely 'Sinbad the Sailor,' whose influence on Defoe, to my knowledge, has not yet been investigated.

The first model then, I suggest, is *Hayy Ibn Yaqzan*. Written in Arabic by Ibn Tufayl, adviser and court physician of the Sultan Abu Ya'qub Yusuf of Morocco and Spain in the second half of the twelfth century, *Hayy Ibn Yaqzan* is a philosophical novel which was well known relatively early in Western Europe.[5] It was first translated into Hebrew by Moses of Narbonne in 1349, and into Latin by Pico della Mirandola in the second half of the fifteenth century. Another Latin edition appeared in 1671, made from the Arabic by Edward Pococke, son of the well-known orientalist professor at Oxford. The translation was reprinted in 1700.[6] The work then saw several translations into English: by George Keith, a Scotsman and a prominent Quaker, in 1674,[7] by George Ashwell, the Catholic vicar of Banbury, well known for his naturalist theology, in 1686, and by Simon Ockley, a professor of Arabic at Cambridge, in 1708.[8] Ockley's translation was reprinted in London in 1711. Alexander Pope was familiar with the story of Hayy and owned a copy of the English translation.[9] Dutch versions of *Hayy Ibn Yaqzan* also appeared in Amsterdam in 1672 and 1701, prior to the publication of *Robinson Crusoe* in 1719.[10] It was reported that Spinoza, the Dutch philosopher whose family settled in Holland as refugees from the Inquisition in Spain and Portugal, had either translated the Arabic novel or recommended it to be translated into Dutch.[11]

The second model is the story of 'Sinbad the Sailor.' Dating back to the ninth century, Sinbad tales became very popular in eighteenth-century Europe.[12] Jean-Antoine Galland translated the *Voyages of Sinbad* before he was aware of the existence of the *Thousand and One Nights*. Later, his translation of *Les mille et une nuits* appeared in French between 1703 and 1713, 'This in turn, was translated into English in the first decade of the eighteenth century, and, as early as 1715, [the] Grub Street version of Galland's translation had reached its "Third Edition" . . . Among its first English readers were Swift, Addison, and Pope.'[13]

Thus, it is quite possible that when Defoe worked on Robinson Crusoe he may have considered the two models, perhaps among others, for his hero. The solitary savage saint and self-taught philosopher Hayy, and Sinbad, merchant and wanderer at the time of the powerful empire of Harun al-Rashid in Baghdad, both exemplify essential character traits and features of Defoe's hero Robinson Crusoe. The two men, one deeply religious, the other rather materialistic, seem to be contradictory. Yet, both of them together resemble precisely what Defoe had undertaken to achieve—the combination of a pilgrim and a merchant in one character. Defoe seems to have borrowed certain features from the two stories, Anglicized them and infused them with 'Anglo-Saxon spirit,' to use Joyce's terminology. I suggest that a reading of *Robinson Crusoe* that includes a consideration of the two works as possible models will help to explain the perplexity expressed by many critics about the split personality of Cruso as a man. Is he a pilgrim who can be better understood within a Puritan religious tradition? Is he a trader and a colonist setting out to build an empire and subjugate other races? Is he the eternal traveller who can not settle in one place?[14] Some critics maintain that Crusoe ran away from home 'for the classic reason of *homo economicus*.'[15] Others explain that 'the rationale for [Crusoe's] action may be found in [his] personal characteristics: . . . his love of travel.'[16] Yet others feel that Crusoe was a sinful traveller who finally found his way out of the spiritual wilderness to God and even managed to convert another soul.[17]

We may be able to understand Crusoe and his nature much better if we accept that he is neither a pilgrim nor a trader, neither a redeemed sinner nor a restless traveller, but a mixture of all these characters. Sometimes he serves God, and sometimes he serves Mammon.

Crusoe and Hayy Ibn Yaqzan

Ibn Tufayl's and Defoe's works share several characteristic features: both are about man's ability to survive in a natural state, free of society, history and tradition. Both support the empirical method of science and emphasize the power of human reason. The two works affirm the possibility of man's attaining the true knowledge of God and things necessary to salvation without the help of established religious institutions or formal instruction. Human reason, both works stress, may, by observation and experience, arrive at the knowledge of natural things, and from there progress to supernatural and divine matters. Both question traditional doctrines and values, suggest innovations in religious and educational concepts and advocate, to different degrees, religious tolerance, nonviolence, and peaceful coexistence among people who adhere to various sects.

Hayy Ibn Yaqzan, whose Arabic name means the living son of the wakeful, is born on an Indian island situated under the equator 'where Men come into the world, spontaneously without the help of Father and Mother.'[18] The narrator tells us that this is possible because the island enjoys the most perfect temperature on earth and receives its light from the highest possible point in heaven. For sceptical readers, the narrator presents another version of Hayy's birth. A princess who lives on another island marries a kinsman against the will of the king, her brother, and gives birth to a baby boy. Fearing her brother's revenge she puts the baby in a sealed ark and casts him at nightfall into the sea. The current carries the box to another island and places it in a thick grove full of trees, sheltered from wind, rain and sun. Meanwhile, the nails and timbers of the ark have become loose. The hungry baby starts to cry. A doe who has lost her fawn hears the sound and comes up to the ark. She manages to save the baby and becomes his nurse and mother. This is the account of Hayy's origin: a boy who grows up all alone on a remote island.

Obviously, the story of Hayy's birth has nothing to do with Crusoe, who tells us about his parents, his two elder brothers, and how he goes to sea against the will of his family when he is eighteen years old. Hayy is alone on his island for fifty years when he meets Asal, a hermit who becomes his companion. Crusoe is twenty-seven years old when he is cast on the desert island and remains alone for twenty-five years before Friday appears and becomes his companion. The early circumstances of the two characters are quite different. However, both Hayy and Crusoe share a most important feature, namely their triumph over nature. They gradually solve their daily practical problems and eventually occupy themselves with philosophical and spiritual matters. Both begin to think seriously of God at a very similar age: Hayy at twenty-eight, and Crusoe at twenty-seven and nine months, when he becomes very ill. They also go through similar spiritual meditative stages; Hayy attaining the state of highest perfection when he reaches fifty, and Crusoe progressing in grace until the time of his redemption in his fifties.[19]

There are a few things that Hayy and Crusoe share at this early stage, namely goats and articles found in the infant's ark and the wrecked ship. Hayy has no food or tools. As a baby who cannot feed himself, he has no need for such things. His mother, if we accept the second version of his birth, places some feathers in the ark to keep her infant warm. The deer that finds him makes use of the feathers, covering the baby partly with them and partly with her own body. The Quaker George Keith translates the Arabic word 'Zabya,' meaning female deer, as wild goat and surrounds the infant, later the young toddler, with a herd of goats. An illustration in Ockley's translation shows that Hayy has domesticated fowls and goats.[20] The Dutch translation of *Hayy* in 1701 presents a picture of the solitary man with a goat. The accompanying text reads as follows: 'We see before us a half-naked man, clad only in the skins of animals, called Hayy ibn Yaqzan. At his feet lies a goat, opened, indicating the first cause that induced him to seek the nature and characteristics of the animal.'[21] Reference is made here to Hayy's first experiment in anatomy. After the death of his foster-mother the young boy, who has passed his seventh year, dissects her body in search for the vital principle. I think this is important because in the minds of readers the figure of Hayy as the solitary man became associated with a goat as a companion. It is likely that Defoe had seen the illustrated books, or read Keith's translation many years before he embarked on writing *Crusoe* and surrounded him with goats.

Although the desert islands in both books have different geographical locations (Hayy's is in the Indian Ocean, while Crusoe's is in the Caribbean), they do not seem dissimilar. They are both warm, so there is no need for heavy clothing and there is ample food in the form of fresh water, fruit, milk, birds, fowls, goats and fish. Neither of the islands has wild beasts.

Despite the fact that Hayy does not come in contact with other humans when he is growing up on the island, he manages, just like Crusoe who previously lived in society and used many of its tools, not only to survive, but also to invent his own tools. Observing the other animals around him, Hayy realizes he is different, but he learns immensely from them. The little hinds, for instance, get horns; they use them in order to defend themselves. This leads him to understand his own strength, and how he can use his own hands. He makes his first weapon: a club, just as Crusoe does. After the death of his foster-mother the deer, Hayy gradually discovers fire and becomes a fisherman, hunter, and farmer. He clothes himself first with leaves and then with animal skins, uses hair and strings from various plants to sew his clothes and shoes, builds himself a storehouse and a pantry in order to store his food, makes himself a bed and fortifies his dwelling with a door made out of cane. He tames birds of prey to help him in his hunting and keeps tamed fowls and chickens for their eggs. He chooses some wild horses and asses, trains them to be obedient, and succeeds in riding them after he makes saddles and bridles. Crusoe, too, builds a storehouse and a pantry and fortifies his dwelling against possible attacks from wild beasts or men. He makes a table and a chair, clothes himself with the skins of all the creatures he has killed and tames birds and animals. While Crusoe has a dog, a parrot, some cats and a herd of goats, Hayy has horses, tamed birds of prey and chickens. Both men learn not only how to survive in nature, but how to triumph over it. In order to feed and shelter themselves, both solitary men learn how to gather food and how to become hunters, fishermen, farmers, architects and tailors.

Another similarity between the two is their attitude to sexuality. Although both men have observed animals copulating, they themselves do not seem to have any sexual instinct—neither when they are alone on their desert island, nor when they are joined by other men. Hayy has not seen a human being like himself until he reaches his fifties. On his island there are trees that bear women-like fruit.[22] Strangely enough, the self-taught man who has a habit of dissecting animals and plants, and observing the growth, behavior and death of other creatures around him does not investigate these trees. For Hayy, corporeality is something transitory, whereas spirituality is eternal. Crusoe, likewise, is silent on sexual matters. On one occasion and after being on his island for a few years, he writes in his diary: 'I had neither the lust of the Flesh, the lust of the Eye, or the Pride of Life. I had nothing to covet; for I had all that I was now capable of enjoying' (*RC*, p. 128). Some critics have viewed 'Defoe's failure to attend to the psychological implications of Crusoe's totally non-sexual life . . . as inexcusably unrealistic' (*RC*, p. xi).

Having solved their daily practical problems, Hayy and Crusoe become more interested in their island and in preserving its natural resources. Crusoe worries if he kills more flesh than he can eat, 'the Dog must eat it, or the Vermin'; if he sows more corn than he needs, 'it must be spoil'd.' The trees that he cuts down are 'lying to rot on the Ground,' because he can 'make no more use of them than for Fewel.' He concludes 'that whatever we may heap up indeed to give others, we enjoy just as much as we can use, and no more' (*RC*, p. 129). Likewise, Hayy is content with very little; he eats 'no more than just what would satisfie[y] his Hunger.'[23] But he goes further than Crusoe in formulating a thesis about preservation of both plants and animals. He eats the pulp of ripe fruits, always taking care to preserve the seeds; he neither cuts them, nor spoils them, nor throws them in such places as are not fit for plants to grow. When he decides to eat meat, he takes the animal of which there is the greatest number, so as not totally to destroy any species. His respect of, and care for, plants, animals and water is remarkable. He resolves 'to see no Animal or Plant to want thing, or to have any hurt or damage, or impediment that he could remove from them, but to remove it.'[24]

After being occupied with such earthly matters—gathering food, building shelter, preserving natural resources—Hayy and Crusoe begin to turn their gaze toward heaven. The shift from the earthly to the heavenly conception in both men's mind is due not only to solitude and the special traits that both have, such as perseverance and strength of character, but above all to the inner Light which shines on them and helps them see what others may not be able to see in similar circumstances. Crusoe becomes 'a better Christian while in this solitude than ever he was before' (*RC*, p. 231). His arrival on the island, as G. A. Starr observes, 'marks yet another more drastic stage in God's efforts to reclaim him.'[25] Hayy, on the other hand, rec-

ognizes the existence of one true being without the help of prophets or religious institutions and succeeds in having glimpses of the divine world. 'He
even has a "Vision of the Angelic World" in the manner of Defoe's hero,'
exclaims Maximillian Novak, 'so that one is led to speculate as to whether
or not Defoe knew the story of Yokdhan [Yaqzan].'[26]

Once Crusoe and Hayy acknowledge the existence of the divine
world their long solitude is terminated. A male companion is provided on
each island. Crusoe is joined by Friday, a savage whom he saves from the
cannibals; while Hayy is joined by Asal, a civilized hermit who visits the
desert island. Crusoe attempts to impart to Friday the benefits of his own
conversion and teaches him English and the Christian faith. Asal teaches
Hayy, the natural man, his own language 'according to the same method
employed . . . in the case of Friday by . . . Crusoe,'[27] and hopes not only to
impart knowledge to him, but also to convert him to his own religion. To
his surprise, he discovers that Hayy knows more about the divine world
than he does, and can easily play the role of his spiritual mentor.[28]

The four men, Crusoe and Friday, Hayy and Asal, go back to civilization. But the self-taught philosopher, along with his civilized companion,
return to the desert island after Hayy discovers that he cannot be an instrument of other people's salvation. Salaman, Asal's friend and the king of an
inhabited island, frowns on religious speculations. He and a select group of
his people accept the external interpretation of religion. For them, Hayy is
a man who is only interested in pure truth. They withdraw from him, but
still treat him kindly as a stranger. The rest of the islanders seem to be diverted from thinking of God by 'their Merchandize and Trading.'[29] Hayy
realizes now that, although people are endowed with the same reason and
the desire to do good, all are not capable of applying these natural gifts to
the right uses. Finally, he opts for individual responsibility, and comes to the
conclusion that there is no reason to speak any more of pure truth. Fearing
that he may cause more damage than good, Hayy goes back to the king, excuses himself, even tells him that he now thinks the same way as him, and
implores him to adhere to his own religion. Then he bids him farewell and
returns with Asal to the desert island.

Hayy's discovery that only a very select number of people reach spiritual enlightenment is no different from what Crusoe discovers toward the
end of his stay on the desert island. For Crusoe, God has bestowed upon
his creatures:

> the same Powers, the same Reason, the same Affections, the same Sen-
> timents of kindness and Obligation, the same Passions and Resentments

of Wrongs . . . and all the Capacities of doing Good, and receiving Good [but] how mean a Use we make of all these, even though we have these Powers enlighten'd by the great Lamp of Instruction, the Spirit of God, and by the Knowledge of his Word, added to our Understanding; and why it has pleas'd God to hide the like saving Knowledge from so many Millions of Souls (*RC*, pp. 209–10).

Both Hayy and Crusoe reach the conclusion that people are not the same, that the Light shines within each one of them, but some see it and some do not. Through his acute observation, experiences and reflections, Hayy Ibn Yaqzan attains philosophical knowledge that is reserved only to the privileged few. Crusoe, on the other hand, wanders away from home and eventually attains moral and religious knowledge.[30] He may not become a saint like Hayy, but certainly he rises above the average man. Coleridge observes:

> the carpentering, tailoring, pottery, &c., are all just what will answer his purposes, and those are confined to needs that all men have, and comforts that all men desire. Crusoe rises only to the point to which all men may be made to feel that they might, and that they ought to, rise in religion—to resignation, dependence on, and thankful acknowledgment of, the divine mercy and goodness.[31]

Although Novak thinks that the parallels between Crusoe and Hayy are remarkable, he comes quickly to the conclusion that Hayy's story is almost 'the complete reverse.'[32] He speaks of the effect of fear upon the solitary man's efforts at improving the conditions of his life,[33] and argues that 'Crusoe is no longer able to perfect his bread or invent a new type of grindstone; all his labour is directed to the task of preserving his life. . . . Only the arrival of Friday relieves him from his care and returns him to the life of peace and industry.'[34] Novak seems to imply here that in Crusoe's story solitude is a damnation, while in Hayy's story solitude is a bliss. However, solitude, in the case of Crusoe, has both negative and positive aspects; for without it Crusoe may have no time for religious speculation that enables him to make spiritual progress and eventually helps him have a vision of the divine world. Novak also seems to have misunderstood the point in the story of Hayy. The Arabic book does not advocate solitude, nor does it praise loneliness as a blissful condition. After all, Hayy, the wild man, gladly abandons his isolation and forms a kind of society with another 'civilised' man on the desert island at the end of the story. What the Arabic book advocates is religious tolerance. People, we are told, are different. They use various means in search of the ultimate truth. All of them are endowed with the same reason, but only a few are capable of applying this natural gift to the right uses.[35] Hayy, the prototype of the enlightened human, would never have condemned Crusoe for preferring to return to society, although he himself chooses to return to his island. According to him, there is a place for everyone on this earth. Conformity is not recommended, and heated arguments that may lead to violence and endanger the social and spiritual fabric of society are better avoided. Similarly, Crusoe advocates tolerance on his island when he says: 'We had but three Subjects, and they were of three different Religions. My Man Friday was a Protestant, his father was a Pagan and a Cannibal, and the Spaniard was a Papist: However, I allow'd Liberty of Conscience throughout my Dominions' (*RC*, p. 241).

Both Defoe and Ibn Tufayl wrote their allegorical novels when they were in their sixties. Although they lived in different centuries and different countries, adhered to different religions and had different careers and education, both men expressed their anxiety about religious intolerance through their heroes—one a mixture of pilgrim, trader and traveller, the other a saint and visionary. Defoe was a dissenter employed by the Anglican establishment; Ibn Tufayl was a liberal philosopher and a physician employed by a puritan government in Morocco. There was religious fanaticism in both Defoe's and Ibn Tufayl's times. Religion and politics were generally inseparable in seventeenth-century England and the twelfth-century rule of the Almohads in North Africa and Southern Spain. People were persecuted for their dissenting religious views. Ibn Tufayl was lucky, however. His patron, Abu Ya'qub Yusuf was strict with his subjects, but allowed him and other thinkers to indulge in religious speculation and philosophical doubts. Defoe insisted that his 'story, though allegorical, is also historical' (*RC*, p. ix). Ibn Tufayl, on the other hand, remarked in a letter to a friend who asked him to explain the secrets of the illuminative philosophy, that he would make it interesting by telling him an allegorical story that points to a moral.[36]

Hayy the self-taught philosopher may have fascinated Defoe in the same manner that Crusoe fascinated Jean-Jacques Rousseau. The French philosopher wrote in *Émile* of his admiration for the one book that he felt teaches all that books can teach in the education of a young person. Rousseau freely acknowledges the influence of Defoe, yet Defoe himself remains silent about his sources. We do not know whether he did indeed read the story of *Hayy Ibn Yaqzan* in English or Latin translation. Of course, there are plausible reasons for this, including the hostility between Christianity and Islam, and Defoe's own views on Moslems and their religion.[37]

Crusoe and Sinbad

Hayy may have appealed to Defoe the moralist, but not to Defoe the economist. Unlike Crusoe, Hayy chooses to go back with another male hermit to his island—not to exploit its natural resources as a colonizer, but to lead a quiet and spiritual life. His tale is meant to instruct us, not to entertain us.

Defoe may have looked for another model to complement Hayy, the saint. Seven years before the publication of Crusoe, Defoe wrote in his *Review* that 'he who would go about to Reform effectually, the common vices and luxury of the Nation, at the same time begins the Ruin of our trade, and by that Time he has brought us to be a Nation of Saints, will be sure to make us a Nation of Beggars.'[38] It is clear that Defoe did not think that the wealth of nations goes hand in hand with morality.[39] Yet the man who studied once to be a minister and later left his spiritual calling to become a merchant succeeded in solving this paradox of the moralist versus the economist by creating Crusoe, who serves both God and Mammon. His model for the materialistic man is Sinbad the Sailor, a fictitious character who roamed the high seas in search of adventures and wealth, and a popular role model in Defoe's time.[40] Furthermore, Sinbad may have appealed to Defoe, the novelist, as a narrator who used simple language, and as a restless imaginative traveller whose narrative possessed the dream-like quality that fascinated Coleridge in both *The Arabian Nights* and *Crusoe*.

In his miscellaneous criticism, Samuel Taylor Coleridge recognized the affinity between *Robinson Crusoe* and *The Arabian Nights*. Writing about the *Arabian Nights Entertainments* in the nineteenth century, Coleridge argued that:

> In all these [tales and works of the same kind] there is the same activity of mind as in dreaming, that is—an exertion of the fancy in the combination and recombination of familiar objects, so as to produce novel and wonderful imagery. To this must be added that these tales cause no deep feeling of a moral kind—whether of religion or love; but an impulse of motion is communicated to the mind without excitement, and this is the reason of their being so generally read and admired. . . . The charm of De Foe's works, especially of *Robinson Crusoe*, is founded on the same principle. It always interests, never agitates. Crusoe himself is merely a representative of humanity in general; neither his intellectual nor his moral qualities set him above the middle degree of mankind; his only prominent characteristic is the spirit of enterprise and wandering; which is, nevertheless, a very common disposition. You will observe that all

that is wonderful in this tale is the result of external circumstances—of things which fortune brings to Crusoe's hand.[41]

Crusoe is not a pilgrim according to Coleridge. His tale is not a pious tract. There is no moral in it. What makes it attractive is its dream-like quality. Crusoe, an ordinary person, tells in plain language a story that mixes fact and fancy, authentic and imaginative details. Similarly, Sinbad is not a saint. His tale is not a spiritual ascent. There is no didactic lesson to be learned from it. It is a tale of adventure, meant to entertain rather than to instruct. Sinbad is an ordinary man who speaks simple language and knows how to keep his readers in suspense. As a story-teller, he is superb. Although he begins his story with simple and familiar objects and surroundings he manages to change his direction quickly, for he knows how to mix the romantic and the strange with the familiar.

It is not only the new, simple language that Crusoe's and Sinbad's tales share, nor their carefully observed and vividly rendered details, but also the dream-like quality of narrative. In another comment on *Crusoe*, Coleridge observes that the story 'is like the vision of a happy night-mare, such as a denizen of Elysium might be supposed to have from a little excess in his nectar and ambrosia supper. Our imagination is kept in full play, excited to the highest; yet all the while we are touching by, common flesh and blood.'[42] This imagination that ignites the minds of readers everywhere is the essence of both *Crusoe* and *Sinbad the Sailor*.

There are common features to be detected in both tales. Both are narrated in the first person. Their language is lively and simple. The only personal relation described at length in both of them is that between two males: Crusoe and Friday, Sinbad the Sailor and Sinbad the Landman, or the Porter. Crusoe writes a diary about his ordeal on the desert island and later talks to Friday about his past; Sinbad meets the Porter in Baghdad, in his own house, and tells his poor guest about his past adventures.[43] The relationship between the male couples in both stories is that of a master and a servant, although Sinbad the Sailor tends to stress more than Crusoe the brotherhood that exists between him and his underprivileged guest.

Both Crusoe and Sinbad the Sailor are born of merchant families. Both leave their cities for another port in their native country in order to embark on a trading vessel bound to distant shores. The two men are interested in improving their financial situation, but are also condemned to a life of wandering. Both experience many shipwrecks and difficulties on desert islands, spend their first nights in thick bushy trees, and later become involved in making their own escape boats. Once in a while they think of God and profess that they deserve their misfortunes: Sinbad because of his greed for more wealth and his excessively inquisitive nature about other people and their ways of life, and Crusoe because of his disobedience to his father and his dissatisfaction with the station in which God placed him. Providence plays a very important role in Crusoe's and Sinbad's life-every event seems to be predestined. Although both men lose many years of sinful life, they gain an eternity of bliss at the end of their adventures.

Strangely, both men never think of women; neither seems to have any sexual instinct. However, both marry at the end of their voyages, yet we do not know anything about their wives, not even their names. During the seventh journey, Sinbad remains twenty-seven years away from his relatives in Baghdad; Crusoe remains on his desert island for twenty-eight years. Sinbad owns slaves and is a very wealthy man. His wealth is derived from trade in foreign countries. Crusoe has plans to trade in black slaves but his ship is wrecked on the desert island, and his plans come to an end. However, he seems to have done quite well in Brazil before he is cast on the island, for he manages to derive a handsome income, upon his return to society, from the plantation he once owned.

Historically, both characters have particularly appealed to the small shopkeepers, artisans, sailors and children: *Crusoe* attracted the lower classes in eighteenth-century England,[44] and Sinbad along with other characters of *The Arabian Nights* fascinated the uneducated Arab masses in Baghdad during the tenth century. English and Arab readers believed the adventures of both Crusoe and Sinbad to be based on actual accounts of travel. Their preference for entertainment over truth encouraged writers like Defoe and the unknown author of the Sinbad story to create new characters who can easily be identified within their contemporary social environment.

Some of these characteristics shared by Crusoe and Sinbad can perhaps be found in other men of action in adventure stories. Audacity, prudence, courage, sexual apathy, well-balanced piety, self-confidence and tenacity are all human traits which do not have any specific affinity to one race more than the other, as Joyce would like us to believe when he says: 'The whole Anglo-Saxon spirit is in Crusoe.'[45] There are many adventurers throughout human history who can be considered the prototype of Robinson Crusoe, but Sinbad is a prominent one, if only because of his literary voice and simple prose narrative.

Conclusion

William Eddy observes that 'it has even been argued that "Defoe wrote [Crusoe] primarily for the edification rather than for the delectation of his reader." This is, I believe, a mistake, but there can be no question of Defoe's didactic purpose, which is evident at many points in the narrative.'[46] It is this duality of Crusoe, once disguised as a pilgrim, once as a trader and a restless traveller, that seems to confuse some critics and send opposing signals as to the purpose of the novel on the whole. In order to instruct, but also to entertain his audience, Defoe may have created his Crusoe out of two popular figures of his time, one a sophisticated *philosophus autodidactus* and the other an earthly but imaginative merchant and traveller. Both figures represent facets of Defoe's own life: the moralist who wishes to serve God, and the merchant who is intrigued by Mammon. Although he made Crusoe very English, Defoe could not erase all the traces of Crusoe's foreign ancestors, nor could he stifle all the echoes from the threatening, yet very enchanting East.

NOTES

1. *This article has appeared in* Robinson Crusoe: Myths and Metamorphoses, *ed. Lieve Spaas and Brian Stimpson (London; New York: Macmillan Press & Martin's Press, 1996), 78–97. Note that Defoe's text being used here is* The Life and Strange Surprising Adventures of Robinson Crusoe, of York, Mariner, *ed. with an introduction by J. Donald Crowley (Oxford: Oxford University Press, 1972; reprinted 1983). Further references to* Robinson Crusoe *will be cited in the text in parenthesis.*

2. *Trans. from Italian, J. Prescott,* Buffalo Studies *(1964), 7.*

3. *Cf. J. R, Moore,* Daniel Defoe: Citizen of the Modern World *(Chicago: University of Chicago Press, 1958). Moore also implies that Crusoe has no models, citing Coleridge's comment on imagination to assure us that 'nowhere in all literature before Defoe could one anticipate the cry of the Ancient Mariner, "Alone, alone, all, all alone / Alone on a wide, wide sea!"' 227. On the other hand, Pat Rogers points out that 'it cannot be said that there were no fictional models available to Defoe, but they offered little promise of high creative achievement'* Robinson Crusoe *(London: George Allen & Unwin, 1979), 92. Rogers refers only to English models.*

4. See for example, A. Pastor, *The Idea of Robinson Crusoe*, vol. I (Watford: The Gongora Press, 1930). The book does not deal with Defoe or Crusoe. It suggests that there are very few ideas in literature, and that writers use them and reuse them over and over again. One of these ideas, according to Pastor, is the Crusoe idea. Pastor refers to *Hayy Ibn Yaqzan* and other Near Eastern tales that have similar

outlines. Maximillian Novak briefly mentions Pastor's claim in his book *Defoe and the Nature of Man* (Oxford: Oxford University Press, 1963).

In his book *The Sufis* (London: Allen & Co., 1977), I. Shah argues that the story of Hayy Ibn Yaqzan 'is the prototype of Robinson Crusoe, Alexander Selkirk merely serving as the news peg to provide topicality,' 237. Cf. also R. Kocache's Forward to his translation of Ibn Tufayl's *The Journey of the Soul: The Story of Hai bin Yaqzan as told by Abu Bakr Muhammad bin Tufail* (London: Octagon Press, 1982), ix. See also L. M. S. Baeshen, 'Robinson Crusoe and Hayy Ibn Yaqzan: A Comparative Study,' Diss. The University of Arizona, 1986.

5. For the life and works of Ibn Tufayl, consult *The Encyclopaedia of Islam*, vol. II, 424–25; L. Gauthier, *Ibn Thoifail, sa vie, ses oeuvres* (Paris, 1909); Al-Bustani, *Da'irat Al-Ma'arif*, vol. III (Beirut, 1960), 299–307.

6. For the various translations of *Hayy* see *The Encyclopaedia of Islam*, New Edition, vol. III, 330–34.

7. It is known that Defoe had sympathies with the Quakers: he had seen Quaker children put in the pillory when he was ten years old and he had a number of Quaker friends, including William Penn. Samuel Keimer, a Quaker publisher, seems 'to have encouraged Defoe's fantastic reports and he seems to have introduced Defoe to the Quaker persona.' P. R. Backscheider, *Daniel Defoe: His Life* (Baltimore: The Johns Hopkins University Press, 1989), 377. Cf. T. Wright, *The Life of Daniel Defoe* (London: Cassell, 1894), 197; J. R. Moore, *Daniel Defoe Citizen of the Modern World*, 38–39. It is likely that his Quaker friends may have introduced him to *Hayy Ibn Yaqzan*, in which they saw a confirmation of their doctrine of inner light.

8. For details on Ockley (1678–1720) and his times consult A. J. Arberry, *Oriental Essays: Portraits of Seven Scholars* (London: George Allen & Unwin, 1960), 11–47. Ockley disowned the Quakers in the appendix of his translation. 'The romance [Hayy] was a suspect book and it was important to make one's disagreement with its dangerous influence known.' Pastor, *The Idea of Robinson Crusoe*, 239.

9. In a letter dated 13 September 1719 and addressed to Lord Bathurst, Pope referred to Hayy, the self-taught philosopher, along with Alexander Selkirk, a Scottish sailor who had himself exiled in February 1704 to the desert island of Juan Fernandez, and was rescued in January 1709 by Captain Woodes Rogers. See G. Sherburn (ed.), *The Correspondence of Alexander Pope 1719–1728*, vol. II (Oxford: Clarendon Press, 1956), 13.

10. If we are to believe Defoe that he had been 'pretty well Master of five languages' (*Review*, VII, 114, 16 December 1710), then there is no reason to doubt that he could have read the Arabic book in translation. Defoe offers us a portrait of a tutor with an 'unquestion'd reputation for learning and who was himself a critick in the learned languages and even in all the oriental tongues as the Syriac, Chaldee, Arabic, Hebrew [who] gave his pupils draughts of the works of . . . Newton and others, translated' Karl D. Bülbring (ed.), *The Complete English Gentleman* (London, 1890), 218–19. It is highly likely that Defoe is speaking here of his own tutor,

Charles Morton, and referring indirectly to his own education at Newington Green. Morton was himself an Oxford graduate. When he established his academy at Newington Green, possibly around 1673, *Hayy Ibn Yaqzan* had already appeared in Latin at Oxford two years earlier. He may have read the Arabic book either in Arabic, Latin or English, or he may have seen it in the academy library.

11. See O. F. Best's Nachwort in *Der Ur-Robinson* (München: Matthes & Seitz Verlag, 1987), 190–91.

12. As a merchant, Defoe travelled widely in Western Europe, lived in Spain when he was twenty-seven years old, and traded with the Spaniards and the Portuguese. He therefore may have heard of Sinbad and Hayy not only in England, but also in Spain where the Moors had ruled over most of the country for almost 800 years until 1492. Ibn Tufayl was a prominent Neo-Platonic philosopher, astronomer and physician who was born in Wadi Ash, the modern Guadix, forty miles northeast of Granada and who was later known by the Christian scholastic as Abubacer. Sinbad's voyages 'have long been recognized as based upon actual reports of voyages made by Moslem merchants.' Philip Hitti, *History of the Arabs: From the Earliest Times to the Present* (London: Macmillan, 1970), 305.

13. P. L. Caracciolo, *The Arabian Nights in English Literature*, (London: Macmillan, 1988), 2. The story of 'Sinbad The Sailor,' which was orally transmitted in Europe perhaps as early as the thirteenth century, was first serialized in England in 1720, though Defoe is likely to have known the story before then. Martha Pike Conant speaks in her book *The Oriental Tale in England in the Eighteenth Century* (New York: Octagon Books, 1966) of the 'sudden entrance [of the Arabian Nights] into the England of Queen Anne [1702–1714],' 2.

14. W. H. Halewood points out that Crusoe 'is divided between earth and heaven, between accumulation and renunciation, action and contemplation.' 'Religion and Invention in Robinson Crusoe.' in F. H. Ellis, ed. *Twentieth Century Interpretations of Robinson Crusoe: A Collection of Critical Essays* (Englewood Cliffs: Prentice-Hall, 1969), 89.

15. Ian Watt, 'Individualism and the Novel,' in *Twentieth Century Interpretations of Robinson Crusoe*, 41.

16. M. E. Novak, *Economics and the Fiction of Daniel Defoe* (New York: Russell & Russell, 1976), 32.

17. For religious interpretations of Crusoe see, for instance, G. A. Starr, *Defoe and Spiritual Autobiography* (New York: Gordian Press, 1971); J. P. Hunter, *The Reluctant Pilgrim* (Baltimore: Johns Hopkins Press, 1966); F. H. Ellis, 'Introduction,' in *Twentieth Century Interpretations of Robinson Crusoe;* and E. Zimmerman, *Defoe and the Novel* (Berkeley: University of California Press, 1975).

18. S. Ockley, *The Improvement of Human Reason* (1708; Hildesheim: George Olms Verlag, 1983), 25. Because Defoe may have read Keith's or Ockley's translations of *Hayy*, I have used both versions for my quotations. Keith's translation of 'An Account of the Oriental Philosophy in an Epistle of Abi Jaaphar Ebn Tophail, Concerning Hai Ebn Yokdan' is reprinted in Pastor's book *The Idea of Robinson Crusoe*.

I have consulted the Arabic versions of Dar Al-Mashriq, ed. A.N. Nadir (Beirut, 1968); Dar Al-Afaq, ed. F. Sa'd (Beirut, 1980); the 5th edition published by Damascus University, ed. J. Saliba and K. 'Ayyad [Damascus, 1962}; and the French version of Gauthier, and the English translations of L. E. Goodman (New York: Twayne Publishers, 1972) and R. Kocache.

19. Hayy's life is neatly divided into seven-year periods. Each period represents a natural foundation in man's progress and spiritual development. 'By the solitary exercise of reason he [Hayy] rises through the various stages of understanding the universe, each stage taking seven years and having its appropriate form of thought.' A. Hourani, *A History of the Arab Peoples* (London: Faber and Faber, 1991), 196. The division in Crusoe is not as clearly delineated as in *Hayy*.

20. Ockley, 58, Pastor, 157.

21. Pastor, title-page.

22. Fedwa Malti-Douglas argues that 'the absence of the female is essential to the utopian, harmonious elements of Hayy's and Asal's perfect society. Theirs is a world without sexuality.' *Woman's Body, Woman's Word* (Princeton: Princeton University Press, 1991), 83. Also consult 67–110. On the other hand, J. C. Bürgel observes that the presence of the female as represented by the gazelle is essential for Hayy to survive at all. See 'Ibn Tufayl and His *Hayy Ibn Yaqzan*,' in S. Khadra-Jayyusi, ed. *The Legacy of Muslim Spain* (Leiden: E. J. Brill, 1992), 832. It is possible to place Hayy, in particular, in a Platonic tradition where men alone, specifically philosophers with the toughest intellectual training, are supposedly capable of journeying from the materialistic world to that of the soul where they achieve the beatific vision.

23. Ockley, 114.

24. Keith, in Pastor, 339.

25. G. A. Starr, 101.

26. Novak, *Defoe and the Nature of Man*, 24–25.

27. Pastor, 115.

28. Crusoe comes to similar conclusions to Asal's regarding revelation and established religion.

29. Ockley, 156.

30. Cf. Robert W. Ayers, 'Robinson Crusoe: "Allusive Allegorick History,"' *PMLA*, 82.5 (October, 1967) footnote 28, 404–405. Ayers comments on Crusoe's family name 'Kreutznaer.' He makes the connection between Kreu (t) z (the cross) and kreu (t) zen (to cross, or cruise) and suggests that 'in Crusoe's name we may have an etymological intimation that he is to be regarded as the Christian wayfarer, and that his Life and Adventures is to be taken as a spiritual journey.' Although the Crusader in German is Kreu (t) -zer or Kreu (t) zfahrer, and not as Crusoe said 'Kreutznaer,' it is likely that the son of a migrant who grows up in England corrupts the name of his own father, just as the English authorities have done. It is worth noting that the merchants of Bremen, the town where Crusoe's father came from, had organized a hospice for Germans at Acre in Palestine during the time of the Third Crusade.

31. Samuel Taylor Coleridge, *Miscellanies, Aesthetic and Literary: to which is added The Theory of Life*, collected and arranged T. Ashe (London: George Bell and Sons, 1885), 160.

32. Novak, *Defoe and the Nature of Man*, 25.

33. Novak refers here to the effect of the single footprint in the sand on Crusoe's mind. He observes that fear not only terrifies Crusoe but also consumes his time and energy (35–36). When Crusoe saw the foot on the sand he was in his thirties; he became terrified for a long time and could think of nothing else. Similarly, Hayy saw a foot everywhere on his island when he was in his thirties. But it was not a man's footprint, rather the footsteps of the 'Agent' who created the world (see Ockley's translation, 89–90). Hayy too, was very troubled at that time, 'the consideration of this Agent was so fixed in his mind, that it hindered him to think upon other things beside him' (Keith's translation, in Pastor, 331).

34. Novak, 36.

35. Perhaps the issue of tolerance in Hayy is one of the reasons why the Quakers found the book very inspiring.

36. See the Arabic version of Dar al-Mashriq, 25. Ibn Tufayl wrote a brief introduction to his novel, omitted from Ashwell's and Ockley's translations, in the form of a letter to a friend. He explained the reason that made him tell his allegory and discussed the different views held by Moslem exponents of mystic philosophy, such as al-Farabi, Avicenna, Al-Ghazali and Avempace (Ibn Bajja).

37. See Defoe's 'Essay on the Present State of Religion in the World' in *The Works of Daniel Defoe*, vol. III (New York: Kelmscott Society), 110–82. Peter Earle observes that Defoe 'liked to remind his readers of the glories of the past in regions regarded in his day as undeveloped and miserable—Greece, the Middle East and North Africa—"the most delicious countries, formerly flowing with milk and honey," but now turned "into a desolate howling wilderness." Much of the desolation could of course be attributed to the Devil's favourite, Muhammad, and his heirs the tyrannous Turks.' *The World of Defoe* (New York: Atheneum, 1977), 50.

38. *Review*, VIII, 739 (27 May, 1712).

39. Cf. J. R. Moore, 'Mandeville and Defoe,' in *Mandeville Studies: New Explorations in the Art and Thought of Dr. Bernard Mandeville (1670–1733)*, Irwin Primer, ed. (The Hague: Martinus Nijhoff, 1975), 119–25.

40. In *Europe and the Mystique of Islam*, trans. R. Veinus (Seattle: University of Washington Press, 1991) Maxime Rodinson argues that after the publication of Antoine Galland's translation of the *Arabian Nights* 'the Muslim world no longer appeared as the province of the Antichrist, but rather as an essentially exotic, picturesque world where fantastic genies could, at their whim, do good or evil. For a public that had already shown a decided taste for European fairy tales, all of this was pure enchantment,' 44.

41. Coleridge, *Miiscellanies, Aesthetic and Literary*, 153.

42. Ibid., 159.

43. Cf. Richard Burton's translation of Sinbad's Voyages, *The Book of the Thousand Nights and A Night*, vol. VI (London, 1885–1888), and the Arabic text in *Alf Layla wa Layla*, vol. II (Cairo: Bulaq, 1252 H).

44. See Ellis, 'Introduction,' 3–5 and Sutherland, 'The Author of *Robinson Crusoe*,' 25–27 in *Twentieth Century Interpretations of Robinson Crusoe*.

45. James Joyce, 'Daniel Defoe,' *Buffalo Studies* (1964), 24–25.

46. 'Introduction,' *Gulliver's Travels: A Critical Study* (New York: Russell & Russell, 1963), 8. Eddy quotes here W.P. Trent, *Cambridge History of English Literature*, IX, 1913.

3

THE MAN OF REASON

Hayy Ibn Yaqzan and His Impact on Modern European Thought[1]

I

In his English translation of *Hayy Ibn Yaqzan* in 1708, Simon Ockley is very careful to disassociate himself from early translators, such as George Keith, a prominent Quaker and George Ashwell, the Catholic vicar of Banbury, well known for his naturalist theology. Ockley's reason is not only that these two translators are not able to read Arabic, and that they have done their translation out of the Latin text, but mainly because "there has been a bad Use made of this Book before,"[2] and it is imperative for Ockley to make his disagreement with certain views known. In an appendix to his translation entitled *The Improvement of Human Reason Exhibited in the Life of Hai Ebn Yokdhan*, Ockley refers to the dangerous influence of this book and assures his eighteenth century English readers that "it contains several things co-incident with the Errors of some Enthusiasts of these present Times."[3] It is obvious that Simon Ockley, a professor of Arabic at Cambridge at the beginning of the eighteenth century, is very careful not to compromise his position in Anglican England and associate himself with the views of dissenters, particularly the Quakers.[4]

But what is this dangerous book all about? Why it has been considered "suspect . . . and . . . important to make one's disagreement with its dangerous influence known"[5] to use Antonio Pastor's words? *Hayy Ibn Yaqzan* is a philosophical novel written in Arabic by Ibn Tufayl, adviser and court physician of the Sultan Abu Ya'qub Yusuf of Morocco and Spain in the second half of the twelfth century.[6] Why would its ideas be debated freely

—at least among philosophers—in the twelfth century Morocco and Spain, but considered very controversial and dangerous in early eighteenth century England?

My aim in this chapter is to present the main philosophical and religious ideas of *Hayy Ibn Yaqzan* and to suggest that this twelfth century Spanish-Arabic book has a far-reaching influence on Modern European Thought, and on the Enlightenment movement in Europe in particular.

II

Hayy Ibn Yaqzan, whose Arabic name means the living son of the wakeful, is born on an Indian island situated under the equator "where human beings can be formed there without parents."[7] The narrator tells us that this is possible because the island enjoys the most perfect temperature on earth and receives its light from the highest possible point in heaven. For skeptical readers, the narrator presents another version of Hayy's birth. A princess who lives on another island marries a kinsman against the will of the king, her brother, and gives birth to a baby boy. Fearing her brother's revenge she puts the baby in a sealed ark and casts him at nightfall into the sea. The current carries the box to another island and places it in a thick grove full of trees, sheltered from wind, rain and sun. Meanwhile, the nails and timbers of the ark have become loose. The hungry baby starts to cry. A doe who has lost her fawn hears the sound and comes up to the ark. She manages to save the baby and becomes his nurse and mother. This is the account of Hayy's origin: a boy who grows up all alone on a remote island.

Hayy's story is a triumph over nature. The young boy gradually learns not only how to survive, but also how to invent his own tools. Observing the other animals around him, he realizes he is different, but he learns immensely from them. The little hinds, for instance, get horns; they use them in order to defend themselves. This leads him to understand his own strength, and how he can use his own hands. He makes his first weapon: a club. After the death of his foster-mother the deer, the young boy, who has passed his seventh year, dissects her body in search for the vital principle. Gradually, he discovers fire and becomes a fisherman, hunter, farmer, architect and tailor. He clothes himself first with leaves and then with animal skins, uses hair and strings from various plants to sew his clothes and shoes, builds himself a storehouse and a pantry in order to store his food, makes himself a bed and fortifies his dwelling with a door made out of cane. He tames birds of prey to help him in his hunting and keeps tamed fowls and chickens for their eggs. He chooses some wild horses and asses, trains them to be obedient, and succeeds in riding them after he makes saddles and bridles.

Hayy becomes very interested in his island and in preserving its natural resources. He is content with very little; he eats just enough to satisfy his hunger. He formulates a thesis about preservation of both plants and animals. He eats the pulp of ripe fruits, always taking care to preserve the seeds; he neither cuts them, nor spoils them, nor throws them in such places as are not fit for plants to grow. When he decides to eat meat, he takes the animal of which there is the greatest number, so as not totally to destroy any species. His respect of, and care for, plants, animals and water are remarkable. He resolves to help any animal, or plant that has been hurt or injured.

Once he solves his daily practical problems: gathering food and building shelter, Hayy eventually occupies himself with philosophical and spiritual matters. He begins to turn his gaze toward heaven. The shift from the earthly to the heavenly conception in his mind is due not only to solitude and the special traits that he has, such as perseverance and strength of character, but above all to the inner light which shines on him and helps him see what others may not be able to see in similar circumstances. He comes to recognize the existence of one true being without the help of prophets or religious institutions and succeeds in having glimpses of the divine world. Hayy is fifty years old when he attains the state of highest perfection. Soon after that, his long solitude is terminated. He meets a human being for the first time in his life. Asal, a civilized hermit who has come from a populated neighboring island to devote himself to ascetic life on this supposedly 'uninhabited' place, becomes his companion. The role of the teacher/pupil is blurred. Asal, the civilized man, teaches Hayy, the natural man, his own language and hopes not only to impart knowledge to the savage, but also to convert him to his own religion. To his surprise, he discovers that Hayy, the self-taught philosopher, knows more about the divine world than he does, and can easily play the role of his spiritual mentor.

The two men go back to civilization. But they soon return to the desert island after Hayy discovers that he cannot be an instrument of other people's salvation. Salaman, Asal's friend and the king of the inhabited island, frowns on religious speculations. He and a select group of his people accept the external interpretation of religion. For them, Hayy is a man who is only interested in pure truth. They withdraw from him, but still treat him kindly as a stranger. The rest of the islanders seem to be diverted from thinking of God by "their trading and selling" (*HIY* 59). Hayy realizes now that, although people are endowed with the same reason and the desire to do good, all are not capable of applying these natural gifts to the right uses. Finally, he opts for individual responsibility, and comes to the conclusion that there is no reason to speak any more of pure truth. Fearing that he may cause more damage than good, Hayy goes back to the king, excuses himself, even tells him that he now thinks the same way as him, and implores him to adhere to his own religion. Then he bids him farewell and returns with Asal to the desert island.

III

Ibn Tufayl's book which was written in the second half of the twelfth century was first translated into Hebrew by Moses of Narbonne in 1349, and into Latin by Pico della Mirandola in the second half of the fifteenth century. Another Latin edition appeared in 1671, made from the Arabic by Edward Pococke, son of the well-known orientalist professor at Oxford. The translation was reprinted in 1700. The work then saw several translations into English: by George Keith in 1674, by George Ashwell in 1686, and by Simon Ockley in 1708. Ockley's translation was reprinted in London in 1711.[8] Alexander Pope was familiar with the story of Hayy and owned a copy of the English translation.[9] Daniel Defoe must have known the Arabic book when he published *Robinson Crusoe* in 1719.[10] Dutch versions of *Hayy Ibn Yaqzan* also appeared in Amsterdam in 1672 and 1701. It was reported that Spinoza, the Dutch philosopher whose family settled in Holland as refugees from the Inquisition in Spain and Portugal, had either translated the Arabic novel or recommended it to be translated into Dutch.[11] *Hayy* was also translated into French and German among other languages. Gottfried Wilhelm Leibniz, (1646–1716) one of the eminent rationalist German philosophers had known it in Pococke's translation and admired it a great deal.[12] However, it is not my intention to research who read Ibn Tufayl's philosophical novel and who was influenced by it. What I would like to do is to present the modern thoughts prevalent in this twelfth century Arabic-Spanish book in the fields of educational and religious philosophy, psychology of human development, political science, and the application of scientific techniques in explaining the material world with a degree of precision and simplicity. To my mind, it was Ibn Tufayl, the twelfth century Arab Spaniard, along with Avicenna (980–1037), the Persian philosopher and Averroes (1126–1198), the Andalusian scholar, who heralded the modern age in Europe and made it possible for many European philosophers and scientists from the thirteenth till the eighteenth century to break away from Western dogmatic doctrines and Medieval theological ideas about the universe, to question authority of any kind, whether religious, educational, or political, and to have courage to use reason, not faith, in the quest for knowledge. Indeed, Kant's term "*Sapere aude!*"[13] Have the courage to use your own reason, is the summation of what Ibn Tufayl and other Moslem philosophers have taught Europe.

Ibn Tufayl wrote his allegorical novel when he was in his sixties. In it he expressed his anxiety about religious intolerance through his hero, a self-taught man. As a liberal philosopher and a physician employed by a puritan government in Morocco he was weary of religious and political irrationality sweeping through his country.[14] Religion and politics were generally inseparable in the twelfth-century rule of the Almohads in North Africa and Southern Spain. People were persecuted for their dissenting religious views. Ibn Tufayl was lucky, however. His patron, Abu Ya'qub Usuf (1163–1184) was strict with his subjects, but allowed him and other thinkers to indulge in religious speculation and philosophical doubts. But the son of his patron, Abu Yusuf Ya'qub Al-Mansur (1184–1199), proved to be different when he imprisoned the last and most important rationalist Andalusian philosopher, Averroes, for a few years. Ibn Tufayl did not live to see this shameful episode of history. He would have been very sad to learn about his friend's imprisonment between 1194 and 1198, particularly because it was him who had invited Averroes to the Almohads court in 1182 and encouraged him to write books which were eventually studied in European universities till the mid seventeenth century.[15] He also had no idea that his philosophical thoughts along with those of his teacher Avicenna and his protégé Averroes would revolutionize Europe of the Middle Ages and herald a new world in the West, while the East would slumber back under the nonrational forces, abandon reason and regress to a stage of "self-imposed infancy" to use Kant's term.[16]

In the following I will be examining Ibn Tufayl's thoughts in the fields of educational philosophy, psychology of human development, religion, politics and the significance of science in our life.

1. IBN TUFAYL'S EDUCATIONAL PHILOSOPHY: *HAYY IBN YAQZAN* AND THE NATURE OF HUMAN DEVELOPMENT

Hayy's life is neatly divided into seven-year periods. Each period represents a natural foundation in man's progress and spiritual development. "By the solitary exercise of reason he [Hayy] rises through the various stages of understanding the universe, each stage taking seven years and having its appropriate form of thought."[17]

As an infant Hayy passes through the oral sensory stage. He is attached to his mother, the doe who feeds him adequately and stays close to him as much as possible. The infant is not willing to let his mother out of sight without showing extreme anxiety and rage. "If she were a little late in attending him he would cry out and she would at once run to him" (*HIY* 8).

At the age of two, the boy begins to understand a few things about his environment and how to cope with it. For now he accompanies his mother who takes him to places where ripe fruit have fallen from the trees, shows him how to crack the hard shells with her teeth, and leads him to water if he shows any sign of thirst. The boy also learns about heat and cold, for his mother shields him with her body from the hot sun and protects him from cold at night by arranging a pile of feathers that have fallen out of the little box. Although he is still attached to his mother, his social circle widens. The mother's friends, a herd of oryx, become his friends. Other animals get used to him and he to them. He begins to imitate the sounds he hears on his island, but mostly the deer sounds. He discovers memory and recollection. He can, for instance, retain an image of objects that have already disappeared. Gradually he becomes aware of his unique and separate physical entity vis-à-vis the animals on the island. But he has no natural weapon. To his astonishment he discovers that their development is different from his. They have hair or feathers, some get horns, or tusks, or claws. To his frustration, he has to succumb to attacks by other animals, for he is not able to defend himself or run as they do. From infancy to the seventh year, the boy seems to have basic concepts of space, time and causality, but he still has to solve many other problems using logic.

The second stage—between seven and fourteen years of age—the boy compares and contrasts himself with other animals in his environment. After a long wait he realizes that the things he lacks (horns, tusks, claws, etc.) will not grow. So he learns to make sticks from tree branches and use his hand in order to defend himself. He also notices that other animals have tails to hide their private parts. At first he places leaves in front and behind his body and fasten them with a belt made out of grass and palm fibers. But the leaves dry out quickly and fall off. So he considers using the tail and wings of dead eagle for this purpose. As a result he becomes warm but also feared by other animals. With this development his self-esteem increases slightly. Although at this stage the boy still feels a kind of kinship with all deers in particular, he begins to form his own separate identity and stops identifying with his mother, or with other animals.

The death of the doe, while Hayy is still in his seventh year, forces him to "find some cause of her condition, and by removing it, restore her to her usual state" (*HIY* 10). His action leads him by necessity to learn about anatomy and biology and to use logic in order to solve the problem he is facing. One can attain knowledge through various means: either by observing and imitating others, or inventing new things by using one's reason, or discovering something by accident, or experimenting and examining objects, or comparing and contrasting matters, deducing and inducing results, or supposing and doubting theories. Hayy uses all these means. He builds a hut, for instance, for himself after watching the swallow build a nest for itself. He buries his mother after he observes the raven burying the carcasses of other birds it has devoured. He invents his tools, because he needs them; he discovers fire by accident and learns to cook his meat. But unlike other animals around him, he learns how to excel in particular, in experimentation and in giving his own reasoning a scientific and mathematical structure. Indeed, the dissection of his mother's body in search for the vital principle is one of the early experiments in anatomy, motivated by intellectual curiosity and self doubts.

During the third stage of his life, between 14 and 21 years of age, Hayy frees himself from the domination of his immediate perception, learns how to reflect on things and manages to develop his scientific thoughts. "His findings and reflections finally brought him to a level of knowledge equal to that of the highest natural scientists" (*HIY* 16). He discovers "that every animal, although apparently a multiplicity was really a unity if seen in terms of that spirit which emanated from a small place and spread from there to all the other organs. All these organs were merely assistants to it" (*HIY* 16). Thus he concludes that "the animal spirit is one" (*HIY* 16). Hayy's ability to reflect on his own thought processes points out to his gradual intellectual development.

In the fourth stage of his life, between 21 and 28 years of age, Hayy's thoughts take a new direction. He seriously examines all objects subject to creation and decay and concludes that all of them have some qualities in common and some qualities that are specific. The lengthy examination leads him by necessity to become a zoologist, a botanist, a physicist, a chemist, and a geologist. His speculations and experiments force him to believe that "every action must be produced by a cause" (*HIY* 25). He comes to the conclusion that "a Cause exists which has no physical body" (*HIY* 31). In the world of creation and decay he observes that every physical object exists only through form and image that they arise from the action of the Creator, the Permanent Being.

During the fifth stage of his development, Hayy turns his attention to the heavenly bodies. He reflects on the size of the heaven, doubts it is infinite, and borrows his argument from geometry. He observes the sun, the moon and the stars and examines their movement. Gradually, he discovers the science of astronomy and becomes an astronomer himself. His studies lead him to believe that the heavens and all that they contain are "like a single entity connected within itself," and that all the bodies he has considered before, such as earth, air, fire, water, plants and animals are "all within the firmament and not apart from it. In its entirety it . . . [is] not unlike an animal organism, the luminous stars being the creature's senses, its many interconnected orbits corresponding to animal organs and its inherent nature incorporating creation and decay . . . [is] similar to the viscera of an animal within which both decay and new life could arise" (*HIY* 28). He becomes interested in the question of creation. Has the universe come into being from nonbeing? Or is it something that has always existed? The question puzzles him; he considers contradictory concepts and examines their implications. Eventually, he develops the conception of God, the Mover of this universe, and deduces His qualities from the consideration of the beings of nature. He concludes that God has no physical body to be "perceived by any sense or grasped by imagination" (HIY 30). His power is infinite. He is perfect, beautiful, knowing and merciful. One can reach happiness if one succeeds in contemplating this perfect and eternal being.

When he becomes a man of thirty-five years, Hayy loses "all interest in his previous lines of inquiry into created things" (*HIY* 32) and concentrates on the Creator. But the creator cannot be perceived through the senses, rather by something that is nonphysical. Hayy realizes that his own essence that could not decay has "enabled him to glimpse that Being and this strengthened his knowledge of it" (*HIY* 33). Consequently, he struggles against himself and all physical and material things by practicing ascetic morals. He draws a guideline for his life. "He should imitate the animals" (*HIY* 40) in order to survive. He should endeavor to resemble the heavenly bodies and finally "he should try to imitate and come to resemble the Being whose existence is necessary" (*HIY* 40). Eventually, he experiences annihilation, absorption and union with the One, the Truth. However, it is only at the end of the seventh stage when he has reached his fifties, that Hayy is able to travel easily between the world of the senses and that elevated state.

Hayy's recognition of the existence of one true being at the end of the book comes as no surprise. It is the result of the protagonist's own acute observations, lengthy experimentation and logical reflections on the universe.

The Man of Reason 45

Teachers, prophets and religious institutions have played no role in Hayy's awareness of the creator. His own search for the discovery of the truth is based on objective criteria and the methods used by him in every stage of his development are appropriate to his age. Empirical investigations, deductive and inductive reasoning have helped him answer many of his difficult questions. Science and philosophy are not divorced from each other. Hayy has to become an astronomer, a biologist, a mathematician, a physicist, a psychologist, a sociologist, and a physician before he attempts to solve his philosophical problems and is forced to apply analogous techniques to philosophy. He comes to realize that God has bestowed upon him, and not upon the animals or the plants, the power of reasoning. It is up to him to make a good use of his reason. Yet, when he wishes to have a glimpse of the divine world, he recognizes the limitations of reason in this sphere. Intuition guided by the inner light, or reason, can eventually help the seeker of truth to come face to face with the Eternal Being, who is not subject to the universal laws of creation and decay, and grasp the meaning of the illuminating wisdom, the summit of human knowledge.

In short, Ibn Tufayl's book presents to us a new theory of knowledge and new methodology as to how to acquire this knowledge. According to the Spanish-Arab philosopher, there are two kinds of knowledge: material and metaphysical. The material knowledge can be acquired through observation of all natural things. The methods can vary from simple watching to imitating, from inspecting, to chance discovery, from necessity as the mother of all inventions to experimenting, from empirical testing to comparing, from analogy to deduction, from conjecture to the study of behavior of every material body in the universe. Knowledge of nature is acquired and not created. It is not static, but gradual and progressive. It is varied and derivative. One can acquire it via the senses and experiences, and from there progress to a higher rational knowledge based on deduction and the laws of logic. Because he exerted a substantial effort in seeking knowledge, Hayy was able to cover a large number of human and natural sciences; i.e., pedagogy, ethics, mathematics, geography cosmography, astronomy, physics, chemistry, biology, anatomy, medicine, sociology, and psychology.

The second part of knowledge is metaphysical. To acquire knowledge of what cannot be seen or tested by the senses, one needs intuition. But this intuition is always tied to causes and sources.

It is interesting to note that Jean Piaget, a Swiss biologist who began his work on the nature of children's intellectual development during the 1920s and continued it until his death in 1980, had developed a theory about childhood which is not vastly different from that of Ibn Tufayl.[18]

Piaget's thesis is that children at first lack the capacity either to understand their environment or to reason about it coherently, but they gradually acquire these abilities through the informal experiences with the world around them. Piaget, just like Ibn Tufayl, was concerned not only with the extent of children's intellectual capacities at different ages but also with the kind of experiences that lead to intellectual growth. On the other hand, Erik Erikson, an American German psychoanalytic theorist who died in 1979, wrote about the psychology of human development and came close to Ibn Tufayl's description of Hayy's identity construction. Erikson suggests eight stages of personality development, that is, from the oral sensory stage of the first year to maturity. The eight stages are summarized in lifespan psychology. Each age has its particular task which must be negotiated successfully if the child's emotional and mental health are to be maintained.[19]

2. IBN TUFAYL'S RELIGIOUS THOUGHTS: *HAYY IBN YAQZAN* AND THE UNNECESSARY CONVENTIONAL RELIGIONS

The general thesis of *Hayy Ibn Yaqzan* is that since Reason is the central human capacity for truth-seeking, and since each one of us is endowed with this reason, there is no need for prophets, sacred texts, religious mediators, or conventional religions. However, this thesis will be slightly modified when the protagonist moves on temporarily to a human society. Although all men are equal in respect of their rationality, some are more able than others to make use of it. In this case, one can understand the necessity of conventional religions, particularly for those who neglect to use their reason.[20] It is the rational man's duty and moral obligation to help the less rational in reasoning logically. But in case of failure, the rational person must not use violence or dubious means in converting others. Since reason is his only judge and guide he must avoid conflicts by all means. Tolerance is to be extended to others who profess different views, creeds and beliefs from himself.

   Hayy's God is perfect, rational and free. He is the creator and sustainer of the universe. He holds absolute power and knowledge over His creation. But He is innocent of the shortcomings of His creatures. He exists eternally and necessarily. He is self-sufficient. In short, Hay's God is the Absolute Being, the source of existence of every being; He is existence. Man's ultimate goal in life is to emulate God's goodness and perfection. This endeavor will lead to happiness.

Hayy Ibn Yaqzan, the prototype of the Rational Man, has discovered God, or the Mover of this universe, on the basis of reason and evidence, not on the authority of tradition and other human beings. He has no sacred texts to subscribe to, no prophets to follow, no prayers to perform, no fasting, or pilgrimage to undertake, no strict rules to adhere to. He does not waste much of his time thinking about the world whether it is created or has always existed since his reasoning points to the same conclusion, i.e., "a Cause exists which has no physical body; is neither connected nor separated from a body; is neither inside nor outside a body. All such relationships are qualities and properties of physical matter and He is above and beyond all such things" (*HIY* 31).

Light metaphors are abundantly used in reference to this perfect, beautiful, omniscient and omnipotent Being. They are associated with the science of optics. The properties and phenomena of both visible and invisible light are carefully examined. In his yearning to see the divine light, Hayy realizes that reason alone is not enough, but must be supplemented with intuition. It is only when he experiences total annihilation that he sees the highest sphere that has no physical body. "It could be compared to the image of the sun as seen in a polished mirror. It is neither the sun nor the mirror nor is it anything other than them. He saw signs of such perfection, glory and beauty in the essence of that non-material sphere so great as to be beyond description . . . In a state of ultimate pleasure, happiness . . . and joy, his vision showed him the essence of Truth . . ." (*HIY* 48).

Ibn Tufayl's hero is rational and good like the rest of us. His spiritual progress is not an impossible dream. What distinguishes him from many of us perhaps, is that he has made better use of his reason, and that he has endeavored to see the divine light which shines within each one of us. His story shows how an individual can progress to perfection if he so desires.

These views on the enlightened man who is able to care for his body and soul and to use his own understanding of the universe without the guidance of another, have influenced the Quakers in the seventeenth century England and consolidated their belief in inward spiritual experiences rather than specific creeds. George Keith (1638–1716), a Presbyterian Scotsman joined the Religious Society of Friends in 1662.[21] He was still in his early twenties. In 1674 when he was thirty-five years old he translated *Hayy* into English using the Latin version of Pococke. The reason why he translated the book was stated in his "Advertisement to the Reader": "I found some good things, which were both savoury and refreshing. . . . Preach not thou the sweet savour of a thing thou hast not tasted."[22] For him, Ibn Tufayl "showeth excellently how far the knowledge of a man, whose eyes are spiritually opened, differth from that knowledge that men acquire simply by hear-say or reading."[23]

Robert Barclay (1648–1690) a Scot and a known Quaker theologian was influenced by Keith, a friend and fellow-student at Aberdeen.[24] Barclay referred to *Hayy* in his book *An Apology for the True Christian Divinity: As the Same is Held Forth, and Preached by the People Called, in Scorn, Quakers*, printed in the year 1678. The passage reads as follows:

> Yea, there is a Book translated out of the Arabick, which gives an account of one Hai Ebn Yokdan, [Hay Ibn Yaqzan] who, without converse of man, living in an Island alone, attained to such a profound knowledge of God, as to have immediate converse with him, and to affirm, that the best and most certain knowledge of God is not that, which is attained by premisses premised, and conclusions deduced, but that, which is enjoyed by conjunction of the mind of man, with the supream Intellect, after the mind is purified from its corruptions, and is separated from all bodily Images, and is gathered into a profound stilness.[25]

It is not clear why this reference to *Hayy* has been dropped from the following editions of *An Apology*. Joseph Smith in his book *Descriptive Catalogue of Friends' Books* published in 1867 mentions that

> In the year 1779, the Morning Meeting issued the following minute, "Robert Barclay's *Apology* to be reprinted, omitting the account of Hai Ben Yokdan;" and this account has been omitted in most if not all subsequent editions. Respecting the controversy the passage has occasioned, see a circular issued by me in 1862. The title-page of most modern editions is also very much abridged.[26]

Whatever the nature of the controversy is, there is no doubt that the Quakers have been influenced by certain ideas in Hayy's story, particularly those that exalt personal experience above dogmatic, external teaching, emphasize the significance of the Inner Light given as a gift by God to each one of us, Christians, Jews, Moslems, or heathens, and stress the principle of toleration and the futility of hatred and violence.

3. IBN TUFAYL'S POLITICAL THOUGHTS: *HAYY IBN YAQZAN* AND TOLERATION

The principle of religious and political toleration is clearly expressed in the last episode of Ibn Tufayl's book. Upon hearing Asal's description of the people in the inhabited island, and how they behave, Hayy becomes doubt-ful about two aspects of their religion. He questions the "messenger's use of analogies and parables in most of his description of things in the divine world," and believes that this practice has "led the people to materialize the concepts and hence assign to the essence of Truth attributes of which he [He] was totally innocent." (*HIY* 57). The second aspect that puzzles him is the contradictions inherent in this religion. On one hand, the messenger confines duty to the obligatory prayers and rituals, but allows the accumu-lation of wealth and overindulgence in eating. To Hayy's astonishment, the revealed religion gives so much details about human conduct, particularly in the financial realm and warns of punishment. But since Hayy, up to this point, assumes that all human beings are endowed with reason and are ca-pable of using it wisely he tells Asal, his civilized friend, that if people were to understand "the truth of such matters, they would have refrained from such follies . . . and turned instead to the Truth" *(HIY* 57). As a good hu-man being, Hayy feels pity for those people whom he has never met. He wonders whether he "might be the means of their salvation" (*HIY* 58). But Asal discourages him and tries to convince him that people lack the inborn sense of righteousness. Hayy cannot comprehend such nonsense. He is de-termined to offer his help to those who might need it. Finally, Asal agrees to accompany his good friend to the inhabited island thinking of a certain group of people who might be brought to the Truth since they are the "highest in intelligence and understanding" (*HIY* 58).

Hayy begins to teach King Salaman, Asal's old friend, and his com-panions. But "no sooner had his exposition risen above the purely literal level and he began to explain matters they had previously understood dif-ferently, than they recoiled from him in disgust, condemning him in their hearts. If they appeared to accept him in their outward behaviour, this was only because of their tradition of hospitality to strangers and because Hai was a friend of Asal" (*HIY* 59).

Hayy examines all different types of people and attempts to show them the way of Truth, but to no avail. He has two choices: either to correct their beliefs by persuasion, or by compulsion. The second option is re-jected, because he respects private convictions and because he believes in toleration. For him, all People are endowed with reason, but not all can put their reason to good usage. Furthermore, the way of Truth is not one. There may be other ways as well. Finally, he comes to the conclusion that "each sect 'rejoices in that which is with itself'" (*HIY* 60), and realizes that his teaching may cause more discord among them. For this reason, he bids the king farewell and returns with his friend, Asal, to the desert island.

In his article "Toleration As A Moral Idea," Peter Nicholson defines toleration as "the virtue of refraining from exercising one's power to interfere with others' opinion or action although that deviates from one's own over something important and although one morally disapproves of it."[27] Nicholson's central thesis is that toleration is something good and preferable "because of the weight of the reasons against intolerance."[28] In short, toleration is not a necessary evil, "but a positive good, a virtue distinctive of the best people and the best societies."[29] Seen in this light, Hayy Ibn Yaqzan, is the prototype of the tolerant man created by Ibn Tufayl, a philosopher who had formulated the concept of toleration at a critical historical juncture in order to cope with religious fanaticism which was a continuing threat to civil order and personal security in the second half of the twelfth century Morocco and Spain. Hayy's argument remains relevant and of considerable theoretical interest to us to this very day. There is no doubt, that it helped, directly, or indirectly, the major theorists of toleration, such as Spinoza and Locke, to develop their ideas in this respect.

Who is Hayy Ibn Yaqzan, the prototype of the tolerant man? For one thing, he has no nationality. Although he is created by an Arab Spaniard, he himself adheres to no specific national state. He is formed without parents, if we believe the first account of the story. Social classes are foreign concepts to him. He speaks no language. He is neither white, nor black. He has never been to school, and he is not a follower of any conventional religion. Due to his lonely existence on a remote island, he is forced to depend on himself and use his own reason. One of the things he discovers early in his development is the individual differences existing among various beings including himself. He learns how to respect these differences, provided they do not harm others.

The principle of tolerating diversity in nature and the expressed concern over maintaining harmony among the various creatures on the desert island leads Hayy to want more than ever to see toleration as a way of life in human societies. He tolerates opinions and practices different from his own. But if Hayy is a tolerant man, this does not mean that he is indifferent to his fellow human beings. On the inhabited island, he allows people to do and believe what they want. However, he feels a sense of duty and obligation toward them. In order to help them, he uses rational arguments when he talks to them. He never forces them to see what he sees. He never uses violence, or dubious means of division and friction. Once he fails to convince them of his argument, he comes to the conclusion that it is better to leave them alone till they themselves come back to their senses. Now they have a veil on their eyes, he believes. But eventually, the veil will be lifted when they wish to see the light within them and attempt to use their reason, because they are essentially good human beings. In these circumstances, Hayy accepts conventional religion in human society as a means of stabilizing the life of the majority of people. It is better for them to pursue their own way of life rather than having an alien way imposed upon them. As for him, he chooses to go back to his desert island with his new friend, Asal, who has reached similar conclusions about man's happiness and ultimate goal in life using different methods of inquiry than Hayy and attempting to understand the hidden and spiritual contents of the scripture.

The acknowledgment of individual differences whether among humans, animals, plants, or planets, leads us to think that we are not the center of the universe. They are always others who share this world with us. Such an acknowledgment has led Hayy to be one of the early environmentalists in the Middle Ages. Once he moves to a human society, he realizes the significance of social, religious and political toleration. To try to force people to believe in something, or do things they have no desire to do is to cause more harm than good.

Innovation is necessary in any society to progress. But to force this innovation on others, without them being able to see its necessity, or virtue, is not only useless, but could be very harmful and eventually induce discord and violence. For this reason, Hayy apologizes for what he has said concerning his doubts about certain aspects of the islanders' revealed religion, advises King Salaman and his friends who cling to the literal meanings of the scripture and observe faithfully the ritual requirements of their religion to remain within the boundaries of their religious law, to have faith, and to emulate their righteous ancestors. He earnestly warns them from concentrating on the affairs of the world as the large part of their population do, wishes them well in their endeavor, then leaves.

Although the issue of diversity and the necessity of respecting individual differences has been raised all through *Hayy Ibn Yaqzan*, it is only the last five pages of this philosophical novel that deals specifically with questions of social, religious and political toleration. Questions dealing with the definition of toleration and its characteristics are raised here. Is toleration a simple exercise in restraint? Is it the result of thinking that there is no one exclusive truth, and no one exclusive way of finding the truth? Is toleration another name for indifference, to use Somerset Maugham's expression? Or is it a distinctive moral virtue? Are there valid grounds for a policy of toleration? Shouldn't personal choice be respected? If we recognize that others are just as good as we are and capable of reflecting upon their own circumstances won't we be providing a general principle for toleration?

Unfortunately modern theorists on toleration have not been aware of Ibn Tufayl's book whose ideas without any doubt have infiltrated directly or indirectly the minds of Spinoza (1632–1677), John Locke (1632–1704), Pierre Bayle (1647–1706) and others. In summarizing the general arguments on toleration, Prestin King argues that "it is better to permit false beliefs than to persecute people because of them; that to behave morally is more important than to believe correctly; that truth can of its own power free itself from the false; that truth is better established by demonstration than by intimidation. . . ."[30] King observes that some radical arguments "recommended a redefinition of religion (e.g., minimalising its content) or a restructuring of priorities (so that moral behaviour, for example, supersedes the value of theological creed)."[31] Yet other arguments, according to King, have cast doubts on faith itself. If King were aware of Ibn Tufayl's book he would have noticed that all these arguments have been already raised in *Hayy Ibn Yaqzan* in the second half of the twelfth century.

4. IBN TUFAYL'S SCIENTIFIC THOUGHTS: *HAYY IBN YAQZAN* AND THE SIGNIFICANCE OF SCIENCE IN DAILY LIFE

Hayy Ibn Yaqzan could be considered one of the most important books that heralded the beginning of modern science in Europe. Its author emphasized the significance of experimentation in his attempt to understand himself and the universe. At a time when experiment was associated with black magic in people's mind in Europe, the Andalusian physician and scientist, Ibn Tufayl, was already in the second half of the twelfth century advocating the idea that without scientific experimentation we would not be able to prove the existence of God. Doubt became the departure point of his rationalist worldview. This skepticism which challenged people's ability to obtain reliable knowledge and reach the truth was put to the test.

In his book *The Discovery of Quakerism*, Harold Loukes observes that "The seventeenth century saw the beginnings of modern science. Until the accession of Charles II the problems that had excited most attention from thinking men had been philosophical and theological, while science, as we should think of it, had been under a cloud. Experiment was associated in men's minds with alchemy and black magic, and honest astronomy (such as Galileo's) was suspected of impiety, and of tending to upset the proper views of the universe on which satisfactory human behaviour depended."[32] Loukes, who is full of admiration for the Quakers, attributes to them the shift from scholasticism to the modern scientific age in Europe. He argues that the Quakers "went beyond the scientists in bringing the sceptical temper into religion. Their rejection of priests and sacraments, theology and 'notions' came from the same sceptical temper, the same determination *to understand before believing*, that lay behind the scientific movement . . . we must *experiment* in religion . . . instead of tamely accepting what some one tells us is true."[33] Considering that the Quakers had used *Hayy Ibn Yaqzan* as one of their standard books up to the time it was banned, and the reference to it was omitted from Barclay's book *Apology* in 1779, we can only conjecture the significance of Ibn Tufayl's book on modern European thought.

Hayy's experimentation had led him to discover that matter throughout the universe was of essentially the same type; hence there was no difference in principle between terrestrial and celestial phenomena. The self-educated man observed matters as extended substances, examined their length, breadth, height, motion and light. He discovered the theory of gravity and managed to formulate mathematical covering laws of predictive power. His thoughts are to be found in different variations and to different degrees in the books of Roger Bacon (1220–1292), Hobbes (1588–1679), René Descartes (1596–1650), Spinoza (1632–1677) Isaac Newton (1642–1727) and Gottfried Wilhelm Leibniz (1646–1716).

HAYY IBN YAQZAN AND THE AGE OF ENLIGHTENMENT

The end of the twelfth century was perhaps the last period in the history of Southern Spain and North Africa when human omniscience was thought to be an attainable goal. The progress of physics, mathematics and other sciences in the Islamic world had influenced the nature of true knowledge. Since almost everything in the universe moved according to predictable physical laws, Ibn Tufayl attempted to apply these scientific techniques and principles to philosophy. Dogmatic doctrines about the universe had been long discredited, and precise method of discovery and of exposition was utilized. The new science had superseded theological beliefs.

Religion was not rejected altogether. Its value had been questioned and reassessed. People who put their reason to proper use have no need for it. But the majorities, particularly those who neglect to see the inner light within themselves, seem to be better off with conventional religions. Yet, reason is our central capacity. It enables us not only to think, but also to act.

Consequently, beliefs are to be accepted only on the basis of reason, not on the authority of tradition, or sacred texts.

Man is good and rational by nature. It is possible for him to progress to perfection. Although women do not exist in *Hayy Ibn Yaqzan* except as a figment of imagination (trees that bear women-like fruit), one cannot discount the female deer who saves the baby and helps him survive on the desert island.[34] Indeed, the doe in the story represents goodness, if not perfection. Since men are equal in respect of their rationality and goodness, they should thus be granted equality before the law. Tolerance is to be extended to other views, beliefs and ways of life.

Ibn Tufayl's thoughts are echoed in the doctrines of the European Enlightenment during the seventeenth and eighteenth centuries in the works of diverse thinkers such as Descartes (1596–1650), Locke (1632–1704), Newton (1642–1727), Bayle (1647–1706), Voltaire (1694–1778), Rousseau (1712–1778), Lessing (1729–1781), Diderot (1713–1784) and other Encyclopaedists.[35] No matter how much these thinkers differ, it is clear that they have inherited some basic formulations from this Andalusian philosopher. Reason must be acknowledged as the supreme arbiter. The methods of the natural sciences should be those of philosophy. Religious, educational and political authorities must be questioned and examined.[36] The philosopher is always engaged in a fierce battle with traditional religion and despotism. The irony, of course, is that Ibn Tufayl was the personal friend of a powerful king, Abu Ya'qub Usuf, just like Voltaire was a supporter of Frederick II, and Diderot a close friend to the Empress Catherine the Great. But if Ibn Tufayl's fundamental values, such as equality, freedom and toleration, which the thinkers of the European Enlightenment had adopted as theirs, paved the way to the French Revolution, they certainly marked the end of the age of reason in Southern Spain and the rest of the Islamic world. After nine years of Ibn Tufayl's death, his protégé and the most influential Andalusian philosopher Averroes was imprisoned by the King, son of Ibn Tufayl's friend. And within three hundred years the Spanish Inquisition was set up. There was a fierce campaign of forced religious conversion. Arabic books were burnt. Many people were banished from Spanish soil.

According to Lucien Goldmann one of the fundamental ideas of the Enlightenment is "the great importance attached to making knowledge as comprehensive as possible."[37] He argues that for those European philosophers:

> Knowledge, whether of nature or of society, is *autonomous*. Its existence and range depend on the practical experience of the individual; but it is

not regarded as something whose content is determined by the collective action of mankind in history.

Thus human practice is seen as a socially important application of theoretical knowledge and moral principles. It is *not* seen as having an independent existence with the power to alter the content of knowledge and thus to bring about changes in human society. The thinkers of the Enlightenment in general lack all sense of the *dialectical* relation between knowledge and action, between self-awareness and practice.[38]

Goldmann concludes his argument by saying that:

For them [the thinkers] the mission of man, which gives meaning to his life, lies in the effort to acquire the widest possible range of autonomous and critical knowledge in order to apply it technologically in nature and, through moral and political action, to society. Furthermore, in acquiring his knowledge, man must not let his thought be influenced by any authority or any prejudice; he must let the content of his judgements be determined only by his own critical reason.[39]

Goldmann's assessment of the Enlightenment in the eighteenth-century France could be described as a summary of some of the essential ideas of Ibn Tufayl's philosophical novel. Man must think for himself. If he has to depend on himself, he must seek a wide range of knowledge. But Ibn Tufayl differs from Goldmann's thinkers who are accused of lacking "all sense of the *dialectical* relation between knowledge and action."[40] His protagonist, Hayy Ibn Yaqzan, understands the significance of his findings and has a strong desire to bring about concrete changes in human society. His vision of the world is not individualistic as Goldmann might accuse him. At the same time, he is convinced that his findings are not the only exclusive truth. Other people can reach what he has reached by other means. Therefore, he has to tread carefully. Hayy also is very concerned about the consequences of his action. If his crusade to alter society will definitely lead to discord and violence, he will then prefer to retreat and leave people to think for themselves. In this sense, he gives them a chance to reflect on the issues he has raised, encourage them to use their reason and exert an effort to see the hidden light within themselves.

In his essay "An Answer to the Question: What is Enlightenment?" Immanuel Kant (1724–1804) defines the term as follows:

Enlightenment is man's emergence from his self-imposed minority. This minority is the inability to use one's own understanding without the guidance of another. It is self-imposed if its cause lies not in a lack of understanding, but in the lack of courage and determination to rely on one's own understanding and not another's guidance. Thus the motto of the Enlightenment is "Sapere aude! Have the courage to use your own understanding!" Idleness and cowardice are the reasons why so great a part of mankind, after nature has long since released them from the tutelage of others, willingly remain minors as long as they live; and why it is so easy for others to set themselves up as their guardians. It is most convenient to be a minor. If I have a book to reason for me, or a confessor to act as my conscience, or a physician to prescribe my diet, and so on, I need not take any trouble myself. As long as I can pay, I do not have to think. Others will spare me the tiresome necessity. [41]

Whether Kant read *Hayy Ibn Yaqzan* or not, his words about Enlightenment and the Enlightened man describe faithfully Ibn Tufayl's philosophy. Hayy is the prototype of the man who thinks for himself. He is courageous and industrious. However, Kant does not speak here about the unity between thought and action as Goldmann does. He seems to restrict his definition of the enlightened man to the individual who thinks for himself, but has no vision of changing human society. For Ibn Tufayl, the enlightened man does not only think for himself, but he also wishes that others think as well. Hayy, has a social duty to perform. If he rejects to be a minor, to use Kant's term, he encourages others to be independent thinkers like himself. In short, Hayy has journeyed from passive contemplation in his development to active awareness, but then he is confronted with a big question: If one advocates the use of reason and discovers that his attempt to change society will lead to violence how can he harm good and reasonable people like himself albeit they seem not to put their reason to good use at this moment? Hayy's answer is very clear. One should attempt to show others the futility of their superstition and greed, and help them seek the truth, but one should never cause any harm. [42]

Once his attempt has failed, Hayy abandons the inhabited island in order to set up his ideal society based on reason. Another person, Asal, who has found the truth by using different means, joins him on his desert island where man lives in harmony with nature and where private ownership is not known. The door is still open for others who might like to join Hayy and his friend in the future. [43]

In my opinion, this optimistic vision of the world is certainly attainable, but only in fiction. One sincerely wishes that the world is inhabited by good and rational beings. But history tells us another story full of irrational and bloody characters. However, no matter what our critique is of this vision, we cannot deny its importance and influence on the age of Enlightenment.

CONCLUSION

Hayy Ibn Yaqzan is the story of man's ability to survive in a natural state, free of language, society, history and tradition. It supports the empirical method of science and emphasizes the power of human reason. It affirms the possibility of man's attaining the true knowledge of God and things necessary to salvation without the help of established religious institutions or formal instruction. Human reason, the story stresses, may, by observation and experience, arrive at the knowledge of natural things, and from there progress to supernatural and divine matters. The work questions traditional doctrines and values, suggests innovations in religious and educational concepts and advocates religious tolerance, nonviolence, and peaceful coexistence among people who adhere to various sects and who have different interpretations of religion. People, we are told, are different. They use various means in search of the ultimate truth. All of them are endowed with the same reason, but only a few are capable of applying this natural gift to the right uses. Hayy, the prototype of the enlightened human being believes that there is a place for everyone on this earth, whether one chooses to live on a desert island, or with other people. Conformity is not recommended, and heated arguments, or attempts to force others to change their views, may lead to violence and endanger the social and spiritual fabric of society.

This twelfth-century philosophical novel has exerted a great influence on European Intellectual life, particularly during the Enlightenment, although it has not been often acknowledged. Jean-Jacques Rousseau, one of the French Enlightenment thinkers, wrote in *Émile*, for instance, of his admiration for the one book that he felt teaches all that books can teach in the education of a young person. He was referring to Defoe's *Robinson Crusoe* and obviously not aware of the influence of *Hayy Ibn Yaqzan* on *Crusoe*, for Defoe did not acknowledge his debt to the Andalusian Moslem philosopher. On the other hand, we know that Spinoza and Leibniz had read *Hayy*, and that the Quakers, one of the first religious sects in England to question traditional beliefs and doctrines had adopted the book. But whether European thinkers had known the book or not first hand, it is obvious that they were familiar with the issues raised in it, which were considered very dangerous up to the eighteenth century in Europe. There is no doubt that Ibn Tufayl's philosophy was widely disseminated and had played directly, or indirectly a crucial role in heralding the Modern European Age.

NOTES

1. This article has first appeared in *Qurtuba* 2 (Cordoba), 1997.

2. See Ockley's Appendix to his translation of Ibn Tufayl's work entitled *The Improvement of Human Reason Exhibited in the life of Hai Ebn Yokdhan* (London, 1708; rpt. Hildesheim: Georg Olms Verlag, 1983), 168.

3. Ockley's Appendix, 167.

4. Cf. A. J. Arberry, *Oriental Essays: Portraits of Seven Scholars* (London: George Allen & Unwin, 1960), 22.

5. Pastor, *The Idea of Robinson Crusoe* (Watford: The Gongora Press, 1930), 239.

6. For the life and works of Ibn Tufayl, consult *The Encyclopaedia of Islam*, vol. II, 424–25; L. Gauthier, *Ibn Thoifail, sa vie, ses oeuvres* (Paris, 1909); Al-Bustani, *Da'irat Al-Ma'arif*, vol. III (Beirut, 1960), 299–307; Majid Fakhry, *A History of Islamic Philosophy*, 2nd ed. (London: Longman, 1983).

7. Ibn Tufail, *The Journey of the Soul: The Story of Hai bin Yaqzan*, trans. Riad Kocache (London: The Octagon Press, 1982), 3. All subsequent references to *Hayy Ibn Yaqzan* are from Kocache's translation; page numbers will be cited in the text in parenthesis.

I have consulted the Arabic versions of Dar Al-Mashriq, ed. A. N. Nadir (Beirut, 1968); Dar Al-Afaq, ed. F. Sa'd (Beirut, 1980); the 5th edition published by Damascus University, ed. J. Saliba and K. 'Ayyad (Damascus, 1962); the French version of Léon Gauthier (Alger, 1900), and the English translations of L. E. Goodman (New York: Twayne Publishers, 1972), Ockley's translation *The Improvement of human Reason*, and George Keith's "*An Account of the Oriental Philosophy in An Epistle of Abi Jaaphar Ebn Tuphail, concerning Hai Ebn Yokdan*" reprinted in Pastor's book *The Idea of Robinson Crusoe*, 305–66.

8. For the various translations of *Hayy* see *The Encyclopaedia of Islam*, New Edition, vol. III, 330–34.

9. In a letter dated 13 September 1719 and addressed to Lord Bathurst, Pope referred to Hayy, the self-taught philosopher, along with Alexander Selkirk, a Scottish sailor who had himself exiled in February 1704 to the desert island of Juan Fernandez, and was rescued in January 1709 by Captain Woodes Rogers. See G. Sherburn, ed., *The Correspondence of Alexander Pope 1719–1728*, vol. II (Oxford: Clarendon Press, 1956), 13.

10. See my article "Serving God or Mammon? Echoes from Hayy Ibn Yaqzan and Sinbad the Sailor in *Robinson Crusoe*," *Robinson Crusoe: Myths and Metamorphoses*, ed. Lieve Spaas and Brian Stimpson (London & New York: Macmillan & St. Martin's Press, 1996), 78–97.

11. See O. F. Best's *Nachwort* in *Der Ur-Robinson* (München: Matthes & Seitz Verlag, 1987), 190–91.

12. In an Arabic article on "Ibn Tufayl," published in Beirut 1987, 'Abd Al-Rahman Badawi mentioned that Leibniz had written a letter in French to father Nicaise in 1697 in which Leibniz expressed his admiration for Hayy, the self-taught philosopher. According to Badawi, the letter was published with Leibniz's Complete Works in Geneva 1768 (G. G. Leibnitii, *Opera Omnia*, tome II, 245) and edited by Louis Duteus. See *Tadrees Al-Falasafa Wa Al-Bahth Al-Falsafi Fi Al-Watan Al-'Arabi*, 335–66.

13. Kant, "An Answer to the Question: What is Enlightenment?" trans. Lewis White Beck, in *On History*, ed. L. W. Beck (Indianapolis: Bobbs-Merrill, 1963), 3.

14. For further information on the historical period in which Ibn Tufayl lived, consult 'Abd Al-Wahid Al-Marrakushi, b. 1185, *Al-Mu'jib Fi Talkhis Akhbar Al-Maghrib* (Cairo, 1949) and Jamil M. Abun-Nasr, *A History of the Maghrib in the Islamic Period* (Cambridge: Cambridge University Press, 1987), 87–103; Abdallah Laroui, *The History of the Maghrib*, trans. Ralph Manheim (Princeton: Princeton University Press, 1977), 174–92.

15. See Philip Hitti, *The History of the Arabs*, 10th ed. (London, New York: Macmillan & St. Martin's Press, 1970), 582–84. According to Hitti "After being purged of objectionable matter by ecclesiastical authorities, his [Averroes/Ibn Rushd] writings became prescribed studies in the University of Paris and other institutions of higher learning . . . the intellectual movement initiated by ibn-Rushd continued to be a living factor in European thought until the birth of modern experimental science," 584.

16. Kant, quoted by Goldmann & translated by Henry Maas, *The Philosophy of the Enlightenment*, 3. Cf. Beck's translation: "Enlightenment is man's release from his self-incurred tutelage," *On History*, 3.

17. Albert Hourani, *A History of the Arab Peoples* (Cambridge, Mass.: The Belknap Press of Harvard University, 1991), 196.

18. See Piaget, *Judgement and Reasoning in the Child* (1924; London: Routledge & Kegan Paul, 1962); "Piaget's Theory," in *Handbook of Child Psychology*, 4th ed., vol. 1, ed. W. Kessen. (New York: Wiley, 1983); M. A. Boden, *Piaget* (Brighton, New York: Harvester, Viking Press, 1979).

19. See E. Erikson, "Growth and Crisis of the Healthy Personality," *Psychological Issues* (1959) 1: 50–100; *Childhood and Society*, 2nd ed. (New York: Norton, 1963); *Identity in Youth and Crisis* (New York: Norton, 1968).

20. Cf. George F. Hourani, "The Principal Subject of Ibn Tufayl's Hayy Ibn Yaqzan," *Journal of Near Eastern Studies* XV (Jan. 1956), 40–46. Hourani corrects Gauthier's interpretation of *Hayy*. The story is not about harmony between religion and philosophy as Gauthier claims.

21. See *The Oxford Dictionary of the Christian Church*, ed. F. L. Cross (London: Oxford University Press, 1974), 775; E. W. Kirby, *George Keith 1638–1716* (New

York & London: D. Appleton-Century Company, The American Historical Association, 1942). Note that Kirby mistakenly mentioned that the story of "Hai Ebn Yokhdan" which Keith had translated into English "was written in Hebrew by a contemporary of Averroes," 28. Note that Kirby reported too that Keith had stopped at Cambridge in 1674 to see Henry More and give him a copy of his translation of *Hayy Ibn Yaqzan*, 29. Also consult Hugh Barbour & Arthur O. Roberts, ed. *Early Quaker Writings 1650–1700* (Grand Rapids, Michigan: William Eerdmans Publishing Company, 1973), 598–99; Richard Bailey, *New Light On George Fox and Early Quakerism: The Making and Unmaking of a God* (San Francisco, Mellem Research University Press, 1992), 243–46.

22. Keith, quoted by Pastor, *The Idea of Robinson Crusoe*, 207–208.

23. Quoted by Pastor, 208.

24. See *The Oxford Dictionary of the Christian Church*, 131–32. Also consult M. Christabel Cadbury, *Robert Barclay: His Life and Work* (London: Headly Brothers, 1912); L. Eeg-Olofsson, *The Conception of the Inner Light in Robert Barclay's Theology* (Lund: CWK Gleerup, 1954), 47–53; Sydney V. James, *A People Among Peoples: Quaker Benevolence in Eighteenth Century America* (Cambridge, Harvard University Press, 1963). James refers to Barclay's Inner Light in conjunction with the Cambridge Platonists' Reason and Shaftesbury's moral sense, 321–22.

25. Barclay, XXVII, 126.

26. Smith, vol. I (1867; rpt. New York: Kraus Reprint Co., 1970), 182. In Volume II when Smith is talking about Keith's works, he mentions some of the English translations of *Hayy* and notes that "Neither George Keith nor the Friends (as will be seen by the advertisement prefixed to this Translation) approved of everything contained therein, but, say they, receive what is agreeable to thy taste and pass by what is otherwise,'" 20. Also consult Madani Salih, *Ibn Tufayl: Qadaya Wamawaqif*, 2nd, ed. (Baghdad: Wizarat Al-Thaqafa, 1986).

27. Nicholson, in *Aspects of Toleration: Philosophical Studies*, ed. John Horton & Susan Mendus (London & New York: Methuen, 1985), 162.

28. Nicholson, 162.

29. Nicholson, 166.

30. King, *Toleration* (London: George Allen & Unwin LTD, 1976), 111.

31. King, 111.

32. Loukes (London, Toronto: George G. Harrap & Co. Ltd., 1960), 159.

33. Loukes, 161.

34. Cf. J.C. Bürgel "Ibn Tufayl and His *Hayy Ibn Yaqzan*," in S. Khadra-Jayyusi, ed. *The Legacy of Muslim Spain* (Leiden: E. J. Brill, 1992), 832.

35. See "Enlightenment" in Ted Honderich, ed. *The Oxford Companion to Philosophy* (Oxford, New York: Oxford University Press, 1995), 236–37.

36. Unfortunately, scholars who have discussed the rationalist philosophers of the seventeenth century and the age of Enlightenment tend to be oblivious of the influence of Ibn Tufayl, or Ibn Rushd on Modern European Thought. See for instance, Isaiah Berlin's introduction to his book, *The Age of Enlightenment: The 18th*

Century Philosophers (New York: The New American Library, Mentor Books, 1956), 11–29. See also, Martin Hollis, ed. *The Light of Reason* (London: Fontana/Collins, 1973); Tom Sorell, ed. *The Rise of Modern Philosophy* (Oxford: Clarendon Press, 1993); Peter Gilmour, ed. *Philosophers of the Enlightenment* (Totowa, New Jersey: Barnes & Noble Books, 1990); Thomas J. Schlereth, *The Cosmopolitan Ideal in Enlightenment Thought* (Notre Dame & London: The University of Notre Dame Press, 1977). One of the few scholars to mention modern Europe's debt to the Arabs is John Herman Randall in his book, *The Making of the Modern Mind*, 5th ed. (New York: Columbia University Press, 1976). Randall argues that "Unlike the Greeks, they [the Arabs] did not disdain the laboratory and patient experimentation; and in medicine, mechanics, and indeed all the arts, they seem naturally to have bent science to the immediate service of human life, instead of preserving it as an end in itself. From them Europe easily inherited what we like to call the 'Baconian' spirit of 'enlarging the bounds of human empire' over nature," 208.

37. Goldmann, *The Philosophy of the Enlightenment: The Christian Burgess and the Enlightenment*, trans. Henry Maas (London: Routledge & Kegan Paul, 1973), 1.

38. Goldmann, 2.

39. Goldmann, 2.

40. Goldmann, 2.

41. Kant, quoted by Goldmann, 3.

42. Note that Lenn E. Goodman, along with other scholars, seems to believe that Hayy's choice to abandon the inhabited island is a pessimistic gesture and "an expression of disappointment with the human spirit in general." He argues that "Ibn Tufayl, unlike Hayy ibn Yaqzan and Absal [Asal], did not abandon society but continued to live in it, if not wholly of it." See "Ibn Tufayl," in *History of Islamic Philosophy*, Part I, ed. Seyyed Hossein Nasr & Oliver Leamann (London & New York: Routledge, 1996), 327. Goodman's interpretation is very different from mine. For me, Hayy did not abandon society. His intention is to help society use its reason. The few "rare" enlightened "weeds" that Goodman refers to will not be always rare according to Hayy's optimistic vision. Now, a new society is being formed on another island.

43. In his article "Samuel P. Huntington Wa Ibn Rushd: Al-Tanweer Wa Sira' Al-Hadarat," Stefan Wild argues that the strength in Islamic Civilization lies in the fact that it has always encouraged a variety of theological interpretations, so that knowledge is not restricted to a few people. As a result, there is not one single interpretation that can claim to be the only truth. There seems to exist an infinite variety of truths that might be pursued. See *Al-Fikr Al-'Arabi*, No. 81. (Summer 1995), 24–33. In this sense, Ibn Tufayl's Hayy does not claim that his truth is the only truth, and that his method is the only genuine method. Asal too has managed to see the truth using a different method.

4

BEYOND FAMILY, HISTORY, RELIGION, AND LANGUAGE

The Construction of a Cosmopolitan Identity in a Twelfth-Century Arabic Philosophical Novel[1]

I

In his *Politics*, Aristotle argues, "he who is unable to live in society, or who has no need because he is sufficient for himself, must be either a beast or a god."[2] Writing in the second half of the twelfth century, an Arab Andalusian philosopher, Ibn Tufayl, refutes Aristotle's argument by writing a novel in which he creates a fictitious character who has no need to live in society. Ibn Tufayl's hero is born in nature, without parents, and learns how to be sufficient for himself, yet he attempts to live with other human beings when he discovers them at a later stage. However, he then chooses to return to his desert island accompanied by another male hermit. He is neither a beast nor a god. He is simply a rational human being and a visionary who believes in freedom of choice and toleration.

Ibn Tufayl was born in the first decade of the twelfth century in Wadi Ash, the modern Guadix, forty miles northeast of Granada.[3] We know very little about his family and upbringing. Although he was trained in medicine, he was very knowledgeable in philosophy, mathematics, astronomy, physics, other natural sciences and poetry. He first practiced as a physician in Granada, and then became secretary to the governor of the province. In 1154 he was appointed secretary to the governor of Ceuta and Tangier, a son of 'Abd al-Mu'min, the founder of the Almohad dynasty. Between 1163 and 1184 he was appointed as adviser and court physician at the court of Sultan Abu Ya'qub Yusuf of Morocco and Spain. In his sixties, Ibn Tufayl wrote his allegorical philosophical novel, *Hayy Ibn Yaqzan*, which was well known relatively early in Western Europe.[4] One of the basic concerns of Hayy Ibn Yaqzan, as a philosophical novel, is to answer a range of questions on the subject of personal identity: "Who am I"? "What am I?" "What is the self?" "Are persons bodies?" "Do bodies remain the same, or do they change?" "What is the significance of memories? Are they real or invented?" "How can one achieve self-knowledge?" "What does one see, or think of oneself?" "How do others see us?"

The novel suggests that birth, family, blood ties, name, language, history and religion are neither necessary ingredients for the construction of identity, nor are they necessary for man's attainment of happiness. What constitutes personal identity for Ibn Tufayl is the proper usage of reason and inner light by human beings. The bodily criterion is dismissed, for the body eventually perishes, while the self, which strives to progress to perfection and move upwards toward the One, is eternal. What distinguishes a person from another is not reason, for we all are endowed with the same reason, but what we make out of this reason. Many seem incapable of applying this natural gift to the right uses and prefer not to think for themselves. However, the enlightened person who has acquired a wide range of autonomous and critical knowledge may wish to alert others who have not exercised their reason; but he should never cause them any harm. Above all, the enlightened person must understand that people are different, and that they use various means in search of the ultimate truth. It is true that human beings along with animals and plants have some significant commonalities, but the universe is populated with different identities. Ibn Tufayl urges us to respect these differences and warns us that no one can claim that his truth is the only truth, or that his method is the only genuine method. He advocates harmony and peaceful coexistence between people and nature, between people and people, and between people and their Creator.[5]

Individuals and communities have often bound their identities to their families, histories, religions and languages. In their literature, they seem to elaborate concepts of familiarity and strangeness and tend to exclude others who do not share their ethnic, linguistic, or religious backgrounds. On the contrary, Ibn Tufayl had expressed his anxiety about notions that would eventually lead to exclusion, intolerance and fanaticism. The eponymous hero of his novel, Hayy Ibn Yaqzan, may be considered the prototype of the visionary cosmopolitan individual who disregards name, family, history, religion and language as essential ingredients in the makeup of personal identity.

As a liberal philosopher and physician employed by a puritan government in Morocco, Ibn Tufayl was weary of religious and political irra-

tionality sweeping his country. Religion and politics were generally inseparable during the rule of the Almohads in North Africa and southern Spain
in the twelfth century. People were persecuted for their dissenting religious
views. Ibn Tufayl was lucky, however. While his patron, Abu Ya'qub Yusuf
(1163–1184) was strict with his subjects, he allowed him and other thinkers
to indulge in religious speculation and philosophical doubts.[6] This limited
tolerance came to an end under the rule of Abu Yusuf Ya'qub al-Mansur
(1184–1199), who imprisoned the last and most important of the rationalist Andalusian philosophers, Averroes, between 1194 and 1198. Ibn Tufayl
did not live to see this shameful episode of history. He would have been
very sad to learn about his friend's imprisonment, particularly because it was
him who had invited Averroes to the Almohad's court in 1182 and encouraged him to write books that were eventually studied in European universities til the mid-seventeenth century. Ibn Tufayl also had no idea that his
philosophical thought along with those of his teacher Avicenna and his protégé Averroes would herald a new world in the West, while the East would
abandon reason and regress to a stage of "self-imposed infancy" to use
Kant's term.[7]

What I should like to argue in this chapter is that *Hayy Ibn Yaqzan* is
an early example of political philosophy which promotes the notion that
there is no contradiction between the one and the many; that identities
are similar and different, and that it is possible for human beings to co-
exist peacefully side by side in spite of their differences, or to live separately as they choose. Seen from a political perspective, Ibn Tufayl seems
to call for a pluralistic society, not unlike his own in the golden age, where
Arabs, Berbers, Spaniards, other Europeans, Muslims, Christians, Jews and
atheists lived side-by-side, or quite separate, in Muslim Spain.[8] The model
of this society not only exerted a great influence on the European Renaissance, but on European intellectual life generally, and mostly so during the Enlightenment whose thinkers promoted values such as equality,
freedom and toleration.

It is important to note that Ibn Tufayl did not explicitly deal with political philosophy in his novel in an explicit way. When he wrote his book
all signs were pointing to the impending end of tolerance, and the triumph
of the irrational and fanatic forces in society was imminent. Thus, he chose
the form of a philosophical allegory that offered, nevertheless, sufficient
clues to his readers regarding the dangerous time in which they were living
and invited them to interpret his allegory. In his letter to a friend that served
as an introduction to the novel, Ibn Tufayl referred to two different ap-
proaches to Truth, one rational, the other intuitive. But he mentioned that

it would be difficult to define or explain clearly the secrets of *ishraq*—illumination—or the different stages by which one can experience Truth and become unconscious of the self. One of the reasons offered for not being able to write explicitly about this experience is the atmosphere prevailing in Andalusia and the brand of religion practiced there. Ibn Tufayl answers his friend in riddles and symbols. It is up to his friend to understand the meaning of the story of Hayy Ibn Yaqzan.

II

In order to understand the philosophical notion of the one and the many and then attempt to apply it to political philosophy, we must understand something about the society and times in which Ibn Tufayl lived. In 711, Musa ibn Nusayr, the Arab Governor of North Africa under the Umayyads whose capital was Damascus, dispatched Tariq ibn Ziyad into Spain with a few thousand men, most of whom were Berbers. The Visigothic army was defeated, and in a few months Spanish cities fell one by one into the hands of the conquering Muslims.[9] Within a short time the conquered and the conquerors created together one of the most dazzling cultures in the Middle Ages. Although Arabic was the official language and Islam was the religion of the State, a mixture of ethnic groups, religions and languages thrived side by side in a genuine multicultural society. Andalusian cities became the most glamorous cosmopolitan centers of all of Europe.[10] Cordoba, the capital of the Umayyad caliphs, had half a million inhabitants in the tenth century; it received envoys from the Byzantine emperor and the kings of Germany, Italy and France. A German nun visiting the city considered it to represent "the jewel of the world,"[11] a wondrous capital radiating in affluence of all earthly blessings. Under the caliph al-Hakam II, (961–976), a statesman and a scholar, the University of Cordoba became an educational landmark which attracted students from Europe, Africa and Asia. In describing the general state of culture at that time in Andalusia, the Dutch scholar Dozy observed that "nearly every one could read and write."[12] This was in contrast to the rest of Christian Europe where basic learning was restricted to the clergy.

Non-Arabs and non-Muslims were, generally speaking, able to participate in political, cultural and economic life of Muslim Spain. In her book, *The Jews of Spain*, Jane Gerber argues that "the tenth and eleventh centuries would be remembered by Jews as the nation's Golden Age, an epoch in which they enjoyed unusual political power and could participate actively in the dominant culture."[13] Gerber cites many examples, among them Hasdai (the Nasi) ibn Shaprut (915–970), a celebrated physician, translator and courtier of 'Abd al-Rahman, the Umayyad Caliph, and Samuel ibn Nagrela (993–1055), known as Samuel the Nagid, an accomplished statesman and vizier in the kingdom of Granada, as well as a Hebrew poet and a biblical commentator. On the whole, the tolerance practiced in tenth- and eleventh-century Spain "temporarily lowered the boundaries between Jew, Muslim, and Christian."[14] It was reported that Ibn Shaprut, for instance, had written a strongly worded letter to the empress Helena of Byzantium in defense of Byzantine Jewry who were threatened with religious persecution, reminding her "that his Islamic monarch was tolerant of the numerous Christians in Spain."[15]

But with the advent of Berber hegemony during the reign of the Murabits or Almoravids—"originally a religious military brotherhood established in the middle of the eleventh century by a pious Moslem in a . . . fortified monastery, on an island in the lower Senegal"[16]—tolerant Islam in North Africa and Spain began to be threatened by religious fanaticism. Liberal Muslims, Christians and Jews were persecuted; the books of the philosopher/theologian al-Ghazzali (1058–1111) were either banned or burnt in al-Maghrib and Spain. One of the reasons was that Al-Ghazali had rejected the literal interpretation of the Quran, while the Almoravids theological zealots insisted on the literal meaning of the text. Musa Ibn Maymun, or Maimonides, (1135–1204), the Jewish physician and philosopher, who was born in Cordoba, had to leave his home with his family as a result of Almohad persecution. He settled in Cairo about 1165 and became the court physician of Saladin, King of Egypt and Syria. Ibn Rushd, or Averroes (1112–1198), the most famous Muslim Hispano-Arab philosopher, was banished in 1194 to a penal island-colony and persecuted for his philosophical speculations. He was later recalled to his office in Marrakesh, where he died soon afterwards.[17]

In 1062 one of the builders of the Murabit Empire founded the city of Marrakesh which became the capital. In Spain, Cordoba gave way to Seville, which served as a second capital. But the Murabit dynasty in Spain (1090–1147) was short-lived. Another religious movement with the aim to restore Islam to its pure and original orthodoxy was founded by Muhammad ibn Tumart, a Berber who preached the unity of God. His followers were thus called al-Muwahhidun, (the unitarians), or Almohad. In 1146–1147 'Abd al-Mu'min, son of a Berber potter, put an end to the Murabit dynasty and founded his own empire which stretched from southern Spain to the Egyptian boarder. Marrakesh now became the Almohad capital.[18]

Ibn Tufayl had witnessed the Murabit rule and its collapse, then the advent of the Muwahhid dynasty. He seemed to have supported the latter at the beginning of his life, since he served first as a secretary to one of the sons of the founder of the state, then as an advisor and physician to one of its greatest rulers. But later, Ibn Tufayl seemed to have dissented from the founder's doctrines concerning religion and its significance. For Ibn Tumart, the founder of the Almohads, the Quran, the prophetic traditions, and the practice of the prophet's companions constituted the objective sources of Islamic law. Rational deductions and personal subjective opinions were not only rejected, but frowned upon.[19] In his novel, however, Ibn Tufayl created a literary hero who was not only unfamiliar with Islam, the Quran, the prophetic traditions and the practice of the prophet's companions, but who was more knowledgeable about truth and the sources of the universe. No one punished him for his daring speculation, for it was still possible under the reign of his great-learned patron Abu Ya'qub Yusuf to suggest alternative solutions to philosophical questions.

There is no doubt that the times in which Ibn Tufayl lived were troublesome. His monarch was engaged most of his life in either subduing tribal warriors and rebels, or combating Christian forces in Spain. In 1183 the Caliph made a second crossing to Spanish soil with his army to relieve the cities of Cordoba, Malaga, and Granada. But he was attacked by Castile acting in conjunction with Portugal. As a result of wounds sustained in the siege of Santarem defended by the Portuguese, he died there on 22 July 1184. "The true king," as described by the celebrated historian and chronicler 'Abd Al-Wahid Al-Marrakushi in the first half of the thirteenth century, had allowed most of his subjects to enjoy relative freedom, stability and prosperity. His name will always be associated with the greatest philosophers of Islam: Ibn Tufayl known as Abubacer to Medieval Christian scholastics and Ibn Rushd known in Latin as Averroes.

In the distant East, Saladin, King of Egypt and Syria (1169–1193) was fighting against the Crusaders who had been coming to the Middle East since the end of the eleventh century. It was to al-Mansur's court (son of Abu Ya'qub Yusuf whose mother was a Christian slave) that Saladin sent a delegation asking for help. Al-Mansur was reported to have sent 180 ships to assist the Muslims against the Crusaders.[20] The battle between Islam and Christianity was waged in the Middle East and Europe. But while Saladin managed to recapture Jerusalem from the Crusaders in July 1187 (the last Crusader castle was destroyed by August 1291), the Muslims in Spain were defeated at Las Navas de Tolosa in 1212 and eventually expelled.[21]

One must note that in spite of the religious and political wars that raged between Muslims and Christians during the Middle Ages, that it was still possible for both sides to intermarry among each other, to exchange goods and embassies, and to create tolerant societies where people adhered to different religions and philosophies, expressed divergent views and spoke different languages. But gradually "Andalusi society lost its often stressed composite character as an ethnic, religious and to some extent cultural 'mosaic,' which had distinguished it over the first centuries, and rather became a society very markedly Islamised and Arabised. . . . This trend toward cultural uniformity applied to rural and urban areas alike, and it was upon such a culturally homogeneous society that the Christian conquerors of the . . . twelfth and . . . thirteenth centuries advanced."[22]

III

Ibn Tufayl's philosophical novel describes fictional identities. The hero, Hayy Ibn Yaqzan, may not be historically authentic but he can certainly be explained within the sociopolitical context of Muslim Spain during the golden age. As a kind of literary-philosophical model, Hayy may be imagined in a historically verifiable multicultural setting which allowed people belonging to different races, colors, religions, histories, genders and languages to live side by side and to prosper materially and culturally. The possibilities for acculturation, or assimilation, or ethnic and religious autonomy within the Islamic Andalusian polity were equal options open to minorities. Arabs, Berbers, Spaniards, Slavs, other races and nationalities lived together, or quite separate from each other. They were Muslims, Christians, Jews, atheists, and Neo-Muslims. They spoke Arabic, Romance dialects, Latin, Hebrew, Greek, and other languages. Although the state was a Muslim state, the official language was Arabic and the dominant culture was Arabic/Islamic, the different races had by the early eleventh century fused together in a common Andalusian identity characterized mainly by tolerance and love of knowledge and beauty. This "Islamic Multicultural Model" was flexible enough to allow those who did not share the beliefs of the majority to settle wherever they liked and to run their own affairs. When Hayy chose to reside with another man, quite different from himself, on his original desert island, no one tried to hurt him, or persecute him. He too never tried to hurt others. Both sides believed that diversity was desirable and good, and that there was never any contradiction between the "one" and the "many" the "I" and the "other."

But if *Hayy Ibn Yaqzan* can be situated in an Islamic Multicultural Model where tolerance reigns supreme, a contemporary European literary masterpiece, *The Song of Roland*, belongs to an exclusionary European model where strangers are not welcomed. *The Song of Roland*, written between 1125 and 1150 in Anglo-Norman French depicts the wretched relationship between Christian Europe and Islam characterized by ignorance, fanaticism and the desire of Christian Europe to rid itself of barbarism.[23] Roland's literary model suggested in *The Song of Roland* does not only find a political and historical parallel in Christian Europe during the eleventh and twelfth centuries, but also in fanatic Islamic North Africa and southern Spain during much of the reign of the Almoravids and Almohads.

IV

In an essay entitled "The Formation of National Identity," Anthony D. Smith observes that the problem of identity always seems to reveal two concerns, namely the questions "Who am I?" and "What am I?" The first question is supposedly easily answered if one knows his or her genealogy, family status and residence, while the second involves an assertion of distinctiveness through culture and community. For Smith, "identity operates on two levels, the individual and the collective." He argues that "human beings have a wide variety of possible collective affiliations-economic and occupational groups, leisure and welfare associations, age and gender categories, territorial and political organizations, as well as families and cultural communities."[24] If one accepts this assumption as a basis for the study of identity and attempts to apply it to *Hayy Ibn Yaqzan*, one soon discovers that Ibn Tufayl negates the importance of family and name right from the beginning of his story. He gradually develops a thesis in which he demonstrates that language, religion, formal education, history and everything related to cultures and human communities may play no role at all in constructing one's identity. At a time when internal and external forces of the outside world were asserting the opposite, i.e., the distinctiveness and superiority of one's own culture and community, this was a very dangerous thesis indeed.

How can one describe Hayy Ibn Yaqzan? He is born without parents. He is neither white nor black. He initially speaks no language. He has never been to school, and he is not a follower of any conventional religion. He has no concept of social classes. He has no nationality. Due to his lonely existence on a remote island uninhabited by humans, he is forced to depend on himself and on his own reason. One of the things he discovers early in his development is the individual differences existing among various beings including himself. He learns how to respect these differences, and not to harm others.

Ibn Tufayl presents a theoretical model based on the premise that there are places on this earth where human beings can be born and brought up without parents. The narrator of Hayy's story tells us that the boy was born on an Indian island situated below the equator. This is possible, he assures us, because the island enjoys the most perfect temperature on earth and receives its light from the highest possible point in heaven. For skeptical readers, the narrator presents another version of Hayy's birth. A princess who lives on another island marries a kinsman against the will of the king, her brother, and gives birth to a baby boy. Fearing her brother's revenge she puts the baby in a sealed ark and casts him at nightfall into the sea. The current carries the box to a densely wooded grove on another island. The hungry baby starts to cry. A doe who has lost her fawn hears the sound and comes up to the ark. She saves the baby and becomes his nurse and mother. Regardless of whether we accept the first or the second version of Hayy's origin, we realize that whoever his real parents are, they have played no role in forming his identity.

Hayy ibn Yaqzan is not a known Arabic or Andalusian name. It is neither Muslim nor Christian, nor is it Jewish. It simply translates as "the living, or the alive one, son of the wakeful." Thus, the protagonist simply wants to be identified as a being whose father is wakeful. His name sounds "foreign," perhaps to everyone on earth. Yet it is familiar and universal, for we all are alive and share at least one basic characteristic with the human race and other plants and animals.

On the fertile island where the boy grows up there are no wild beasts, only birds, chicken, deer, horses and cows. The temperature is mild. The tenth century Arab historian al-Mas'udi calls the place "The Island of al-Waqwaq." On it there are trees that bear women as fruit. Hayy is the only human being who lives there for at least fifty years. In line with Arab geographers and historians of the Middle Ages, Ibn Tufayl seems to have thought that landscape and environment play some role in the makeup of their inhabitants.[25] Perhaps, for this reason he depicts a paradise-like island in order to create his perfect rational human being.

Hayy's life is divided into seven-year periods. Each period represents a natural foundation in man's progress and spiritual development.[26] At first he identifies with his mother, the doe, and her friends. He begins to imitate the sound he hears on his island, but mostly the deer sounds. He discovers memory and recollection and begins to understand a few things about his environment and how to cope with it. Gradually, he becomes aware of his unique and separate physical entity vis-à-vis the animals on the island. He discovers that their development is different from his. From infancy to the seventh year, the boy seems to develop basic concepts of space, time and causality.

In the second stage—between seven and fourteen—Hayy compares and contrasts himself with other animals in his environment. He invents his tools and learns how to use his hands in order to defend himself. Although at this stage the boy still feels a kind of kinship with all deer in particular, he begins to form his own separate identity and stops identifying with his mother, or with other animals. The death of the doe, while Hayy is still in his seventh year, forces him to "find some cause of her condition, and, by removing it, restore her to her usual state."[27] His action leads him by necessity to learn about anatomy and biology and to use logic in order to solve the problem he is facing.

During the third stage of his life Hayy learns how to reflect on things and manages to develop scientific thoughts. He discovers "that every animal, although apparently a multiplicity was really a unity if seen in terms of that spirit which emanated from a small place and spread from there to all the other organs. All these organs were merely assistants to it" (*HIY* 16). Thus he concludes that "The animal spirit is one" (*HIY* 16). This crucial idea in the natural sciences will eventually lead him to believe that human identities too seem a multiplicity at first, but in reality a unity.

In the fourth stage of his life, between twenty-one and twenty-eight years of age, Hayy's thoughts take a new direction. He seriously examines all objects subject to creation and decay and concludes that all of them have some qualities in common and some qualities that are specific. His speculations and experiments force him to believe that "every action must be produced by a cause" (*HIY* 25). He comes to the conclusion that "a Cause exists which has no physical body" (*HIY* 31). In the world of creation and decay he observes that every physical object exists only through form and image that arise from the action of the Creator, the Permanent Being.

During the fifth stage of his development, Hayy turns his attention to the heavenly bodies. He observes the sun, the moon and the stars and examines their movement. He comes to the conclusion that the heavens and all that they contain are "like a single entity connected within itself," and that all the bodies he has considered before, such as earth, air, fire, water, plants and animals are "all within the firmament and not apart from it. In its entirety it [. . . is] not unlike an animal organism [. . .] and its inherent nature incorporating creation and decay" (*HIY* 28). Eventually, he develops the conception of God, the Mover of this universe, and deduces His qualities from the consideration of the beings of nature.

When he becomes a man of thirty-five years, Hayy concentrates on the Creator. But the Creator cannot be perceived through the senses, rather by something that is nonphysical. Hayy realizes that his own essence which could not decay has "enabled him to glimpse that Being and this strengthened his knowledge of it" (*HIY* 33). Consequently, he struggles against himself and all physical and material things by practicing ascetic morals. He draws guidelines for his life. "He should imitate the animals" (*HIY* 40) in order to survive. He should endeavor to resemble the heavenly bodies and finally "he should try to imitate and come to resemble the Being whose existence is necessary" (*HIY* 40). Eventually, he experiences annihilation, absorption and union with the One, the Truth. However, it is only at the end of the seventh stage when he has reached his fifties, that Hayy is able to travel easily between the world of the senses and that elevated state.

Reason that has been bestowed upon him, and not upon the animals and the plants, has helped him reflect on his own identity and the identity of other objects. Teachers, prophets and religious institutions have played no role in Hayy's makeup, or awareness of himself, or of others around him, or of God. His own search for the discovery of the truth is based on objective criteria and the methods used by him in every stage of his development is appropriate to his age. Empirical investigations, deductive and inductive reasoning have helped him answer many difficult questions. Science and philosophy are not divorced from each other. Hayy has to become an astronomer, a biologist, a mathematician, a physicist, a psychologist, a sociologist, and a physician before he attempts to solve his philosophical problems and is forced to apply analogous techniques to philosophy. It is only when he wishes to have a glimpse of the divine world that he recognizes the limitations of reason in this sphere. Intuition guided by the inner light, or reason, can eventually help the seeker of truth to come face to face with the Eternal Being, who is not subject to the universal laws of creation and decay, and grasp the meaning of the illuminating wisdom, the summit of human knowledge.

V

The principle of diversity and unity in the natural sciences which helps Hayy Ibn Yqzan formulate his philosophical notion of the one and the many is crucial to our understanding of Hayy's identity vis-à-vis other identities and his concern over maintaining harmony between people and nature, people and people, people and God. During the fourth stage of his development he examines "all objects subject to creation and decay—the animals and plants in all their varieties, the metals and rocks and such things as soil, water, steam [. . .] smoke and flames" (*HIY* 17). He concludes:

> all of them had some qualities in common and some qualities were specific. When considered from the viewpoint of their common qualities they were all one. When considered from the viewpoint of their different qualities, they were a multiplicity. If he tried to set out the unique characteristics, those qualities that separated them from others, then the variety of difference was truly enormous and the whole of creation spread out into a multiplicity beyond classification.
>
> When he considered his own being and looked at the variety of his organs, each with a unique function and a specific quality, then his being did indeed seem to be a multiplicity.
>
> On the other hand he could see that his organs, though many, were all interconnected and related and from this point of view his being was a unity. The different function of different organs depended on what reached them of the power of the spirit, the spirit itself being one. From this line of thought he concluded that spirit is a unity in its essence and is the reality beyond the self, all the organs being merely tools. His own self now appeared as a unity. (*HIY* 17–18).

This argument will prove helpful when Hayy moves temporarily from the wilderness to a human society ruled by a king. If there is no contradiction between the one and the many in the natural world, then there is no reason why there should be any contradiction between one personal identity and another in the human world. He extends his line of thought to other human beings when he meets Asal, a hermit who suddenly appears on the uninhabited island. According to Hayy, diversity and unity are two sides of the same coin. Such a belief will eventually lead him to the notion of toleration in human societies.

After having learned Asal's language and familiarize himself with the stranger's religion and customs, he accompanies him to the inhabited, civilized island from which Asal has come. Here Ibn Tufayl depicts a multitude of different identities. Salaman, Asal's friend and the king, for instance, has been shaped by his society and religion. He frowns on religious speculations. He and a select group of his people accept the external interpretation of religion. For them, Hayy is a man who is only interested in pure truth.

They withdraw from him, but still treat him kindly as a stranger. The rest of the islanders seem to be diverted from thinking of God by their merchandise and trading. Hayy realizes that, although people are endowed with the same reason and the desire to do good, all are not capable of applying these natural gifts to the right uses. Finally, he opts for individual responsibility, and comes to the conclusion that there is no reason to speak any more of pure truth. Fearing that he may cause more damage than good, Hayy goes back to the king, excuses himself and implores him to adhere to his own religion. Then he bids him farewell and returns to his island with Asal. His companion has reached similar conclusions about man's happiness and ultimate goal in life by using different methods of inquiry than Hayy, namely by attempting to understand the hidden meanings and spiritual contents of the scripture. The message of the novel is quite clear. People, we are told, are different although they belong to the same species. One must accept their multiplicity and unity at the same time. They happen to use various means in search of the ultimate truth. According to Hayy, there is a place for everyone on this earth. Conformity is not recommended, and arguments that may lead to violence and endanger the social and spiritual fabric of society are better avoided.

VI

If the philosophical message of *Hayy Ibn Yaqzan* is that there is no one exclusive truth and no one exclusive way of finding the truth, then it is possible to argue that there is no one single authoritative definition of personal identity, and that there is no one single exclusive way of discovering what personal identity is all about. Ibn Tufayl depicts several identities in his philosophical novel, but concentrates on one identity in particular. His hero, Hayy Ibn Yaqzan, is not shaped by family, society, history, language, or religion. He is a cosmopolitan personality; a rational free thinker who can function anywhere on this earth. What shaped him is how he has made good use of his reason and intuition. His scientific experiments have helped him see diversity and unity, strangeness and familiarity in a dialectical way. Consequently, his identity has never clashed with other identities. Theoretically, he believes that since everyone is endowed with reason, there is no need for prophets, sacred texts, religious mediators, or conventional religions. However, this thesis is modified when Hayy encounters different personalities on the inhabited island. Only then he realizes that other people may be shaped by conventions and customs; that they tend to rely heavily on social, political, religious and educational authorities, and that they hardly allow their own reason to play any role in shaping their identity. Hayy attempts to convince others of the virtues of autonomous and critical knowledge. He encourages them to think for themselves, but he fails. Since he always wishes to be a good man and is concerned about the consequences of his action, he prefers to tread carefully. If his crusade to alter society will definitely lead to discord and violence, he will then retreat and leave people time to think for themselves.

This courageous, tolerant and rational identity cannot only be considered as the isolated product of Ibn Tufayl's philosophical and literary imagination. Indeed, it has its historical roots during the golden age of Muslim Spain. The Andalusian society had diverse people: different races, languages, histories, bodies, memories, landscapes, environments, and religions. People were able to live side by side in a relatively tolerant society, but they were also able to live separately. The mind was free. Rational thinkers wrote and spoke freely about their philosophical speculations without being afraid to be punished.

But with the new emphasis on race, ethnicity, religion, history, language, "we" versus "them," "diversity," versus "unity," "rationality" versus "irrationality," "tolerance," versus "fanaticism," the golden age began to wither. It was the task of the philosopher and freethinker to recreate and reinvent the identity of Hayy Ibn Yaqzan who was able to see the danger inherent in conformity and similarity when others preferred to remain blind.

NOTES

1. This article has first appeared in *Adventures of Identity: European Multicultural Experiences and Perspectives*, eds. John Docker & Gerhard Fischer (Tübingen: Stauffenburg Verlag), 75–89.

2. Aristotle, *"Politics,"* in Richard McKeon, ed. *The Basic Works of Aristotle* (1941; New York: Random House, 1966), 1130.

3. Cf. Madani Salih, *Ibn Tufayl: Qadaya wa-Mawaqif*, 2nd ed. (Baghdad: Wizarat al-Thaqafa, 1986), 13–14. Salih uses the account of Ibn al-Abbar, a contemporary of Ibn Tufayl, who mentions that the Andalusian philosopher was born near Wadi Ash in Barshana, a fortified town.

4. For the life and works of Ibn Tufayl, consult *The Encyclopaedia of Islam* 1927, vol. ii, 424–25; L. Gauthier, *Ibn Thoifail, sa vie, ses oeuvres* (Paris, 1909); Al-Bustani, *Da'irat al-Ma'arif*, vol. iii (Beirut, 1960), 299–307.

5. For the various translations of *Hayy* see the *Encyclopaedia of Islam*, New Edition, vol. iii, 330–34. I have consulted the Arabic versions of Dar al-Mashriq, ed.

A. N. Nadir (Beirut, 1968); Dar al-Afaq, ed. F. Sa'd (Beirut, 1980); the 5th edition published by Damascus University, ed. J. Saliba and K. 'Ayyad (Damascus, 1962), and the English translations of L. E. Goodman, *Ibn Tufayl's Hayy Ibn Yaqzan* (New York: Twayne Publishers, 1972) and R. Kocache's *The Journey of the Soul: The Story of Hai bin Yaqzan* (London: The Octagon Press, 1982). All subsequent references to *Hayy Ibn Yaqzan* are from Kocache's translation; page number will be cited in the text in parenthesis.

6. See my article "Serving God or Mammon? Echoes from Hayy Ibn Yaqzan and Sinbad the Sailor in Robinson Crusoe," in Lieve Spaas and Brian Stimpson, eds. *Robinson Crusoe: Myths and Metamorphoses*, ed. Lieve Spaas and Brian Stimpson (London, New York: Macmillan Press & St. Martin's Press, 1996), 78–97. For more details on the life of Yusuf, Ibn Tufayl's patron, consult Ibn Khallikan's *Wafiyat al-A'yan wa-Anba'Abna'al-Zaman*, ed. Ihsan 'Abbas (Beirut: Dar al-Thaqafa, n.d.), 130–38.

7. See my article "The Man of Reason: Hayy Ibn Yaqzan and His Impact on Modern European Thought," in *Qurtuba estudios andalusies* 2 (Cordoba 1997): 19–47.

8. For the ethnic and religious composition of Muslim Spain see Pierre Guichard, "The Social History of Muslim Spain from the Conquest to the End of the Almohad Regime (Early Second/Eighth–Early Seventhh/Thirteenth Centuries)," 697–723, and Mahmoud Makki, "The Political History Of Al-Andalus 92/711–897/1492," 3–87 in Salma Khadra Jayyusi, ed. *The Legacy of Muslim Spain*, (Leiden: Brill, 1992). Cf. also Thomas F. Glick, "Ethnic Relations," in *Islamic and Christian Spain in the Early Middle Ages* (Princeton: Princeton University Press, 1979), 165–93.

9. For more details on the political history of Muslim Spain, see Philip Hitti. *History of the Arabs*, 10th ed. (London, New York: Macmillan & St. Martin's Press, 1970), 493–556. Cf. also Anwar G. Chejne, *Muslim Spain: Its History and Culture* (Minneapolis: The University of Minnesota Press, 1974), 3–109.

10. See Hitti, *History of the Arabs*, 526–27.

11. See Hrotsvitha in *Scriptores rerum Germanicarum; Hrotsvithoe opera*, ed. Paulus de Winterfeld (Berlin, 1902), 52, l. 12. Quoted by Hitti, *History of the Arabs*, 527.

12. Quoted by Hitti, *History of the Arabs*, 531. Cf. Lévi-Provencal (ed.), *Histoire des Musulmans*, vol. ii (Leyden, 1932), 184; Reynold A. Nicholson, *Literary History of the Arabs* (Cambridge, 1969), 419; Rafael Altamira in *The Cambridge Medieval History* (New York, 1922), vol. ii, 434.

13. Jane S. Gerber, *The Jews of Spain* (New York: The Free Press, 1994), 28. Cf. Hitti's reference to "Hasday ben-Shaprut, the Jewish minister and physician who translated into Arabic, with the collaboration of a Byzantine monk Nicholas, the splendid illustrated manuscript of the *Materia medica* of Dioscorides, which had been sent as a diplomatic present to Abd-al-Rahman III from the Byzantine Emperor Constantine VII." *The History of the Arabs*, 577. Also see Hitti, 524 and 543.

14. Gerber, 52.

15. Gerber, 49.

16. Hitti, *History of the Arabs*, 541.

17. See Hitti, *The History of the Arabs*, 582. Cf. Antoine Sayf, "Introductory Remarks," Seminar on Ibn Rushd, *Al-Fikr al-'Arabi* 81 (Summer 1995): 5–7.

18. For more information on this historical era consult Hitti, *History of the Arabs*, 541–49.

19. Consult Jamil M. Abun-Nasr, *A History of the Maghrib in the Islamic Period* (Cambridge: Cambridge University Press, 1987), 87–89.

20. See Hitti, *History of the Arabs*, 548.

21. See Hitti, 549.

22. Pierre Guichard, "The Social History of Muslim Spain," in *The Legacy of Muslim Spain*, 702.

23. See *The Song of Roland*, trans. Dorothy L. Sayers (1957; Harmondsworth: Penguin, 1967.

24. Anthony D. Smith, "The Formation of National Identity," in Henry Harris (ed.), *Identity: Essays Based on Herbert Spencer Lectures Given in the University of Oxford*, (Oxford: Clarendon Press, 1995), 130. On the other hand, Terence Cave, a literary critic, argues that "the history of identity is a good deal more visibly and coulourfully exhibited in fiction than in philosophy as such." He believes that there is "a delicate and difficult balance in the construction of individual identity: the balance between internal and external co-ordinates or criteria; between personal identity as individual differentiation and personal identity as constituted by belonging to one or more groups (family, gender, social status, national allegiance, ethnic affiliation, language, colour, and so on)." See Terence Cave, "Fictional Identities," in *Identity: Essays Based on Herbert Spencer Lectures*, 105. When speaking about 'personal identity' modern philosophers debate theories of the body, the brain, the physical, the memory and psychological continuity. Some philosophers support the theory of the 'bodily criterion' that advocates "personal identity is no different from the identity of material objects in general." Others reject such a view and argue that with a possible brain transplant in the future, the person will not be the same as he was before. Yet others refute the 'brain criterion' of personal identity and argue that the human brain has two very similar hemispheres with independent functioning and different roles. Both hemispheres are not necessary for survival. Indeed, one can survive having only part of the brain of the original person. For other philosophers, personal identity is constituted by psychological factors. Memory seems to be crucial to personal identity. Others again insist on psychological continuity and attempt to define personal identity over time. On the other hand, Derek Parfit, one of the modern philosophers, argues that "identity is not what matters in survival." For a discussion of modern philosophical definitions of 'personal identity' see Sydney Shoemaker and Richard Swinburne, *Personal Identity* (Oxford: Basil Blackwell, 1984); Harold Noonan, *Personal Identity* (Dartmouth: Dartmouth Publishing Company, 1993); Andrew Brennan, *Conditions of Identity: A Study in Identity and Survival* (Oxford: Clarendon Press, 1988); C. J. F. Williams, *Being, Identity and Truth*, (Ox-

ford: Clarendon Press, 1992); Charles Taylor, *Sources of the Self: The Making of the Modern Identity* (Cambridge: Cambridge University Press, 1989); C. Fred Alford, *The Self in Social Theory: A Psychoanalytic Account of its Construction in Plato, Hobbes, Locke, Rawls, and Rousseau* (New Haven & London: Yale University Press, 1991).

25. Cf. Abu-al-Qasim Sa'id al-Andalusi (1029-70), *Tabaqat al-Umam* (*Classification of Nations*). Sa'id thought, for instance, that "because the sun does not shed its rays directly over their [the Nordic people] heads, their climate is cold and atmosphere clouded. Consequently their temperaments have become cold and their humours rude, while their bodies have grown large, their complexion light and their hair long. They lack withal sharpness of wit and penetration of intellect, while stupidity and folly prevail among them." Quoted by Hitti, *History of the Arabs*, 526–27. For Abu-al-Qasim Sa'id in English translation see *Science in the Medieval World: Book of the Categories of Nations* (trans. and ed. Sema'an I. Salem & Alok Kumar), Austin: University of Texas Press, 1991.

26. See my article "*The Man of Reason: Hayy Ibn Yaqzan and his Impact on Modern European Thought*," *Qurtuba* 2: 25–30.

27. Ibn Tufayl, *The Journey of the Soul: The Story of Hai bin Yaqzan*, trans. Riad Kocache (London: The Octagon Press, 1982), 10. All subsequent references to *Hayy Ibn Yaqzan* are from Kocache's translation; page numbers will be cited in the text in parenthesis.

5

THE BOOK THAT LAUNCHED A
THOUSAND BOOKS

Hayy Ibn Yaqzan is an optimistic treatise on human nature. Man is both body and soul. He is different from animals, for he can control his passions if he wishes. Humans are endowed with reason and free will. If they use their rational capacity wisely they will be able to have power over nature. Everything could be learned by experience. Science is the key that signifies certainty of demonstration. Mathematics, geometry and physics help solve everyday problems. Some bodies are in constant motion. The principle of mechanical cause and effect is of paramount importance. In short, material knowledge can be acquired through observation and experimentation. It is possible for man to control his universe and to progress to a higher rational knowledge. Yet, there is another dimension to man's greatness, that is, his capacity to attain metaphysical truth.

Hayy's basic thesis proves to be accurate in a natural state where a wild boy could change and be changed through different experiences and even surpass his original condition by making use of his inborn reason and intuition. Human nature at this juncture is supposed to be uniform. Although man is motivated by self-interest at first in order to survive in the wild, he quickly comes to the conclusion that it is in his own interest too to think of the general good. For this reason, for instance, Hayy is most concerned about the survival of other species on his island.

But since Hayy has lived only in nature he has no idea about human societies. His thesis must be tested in a political state that is essentially a body and moved by natural desires of men. Does human nature change according to time and place? How do men live in society, or ought to live?

What laws regulate human actions? And how does one solve the conflict between what is and what ought to be? In his attempt to apply mathematical reasoning and psychology to social and political phenomena Hayy discovers that not all men are willing to use their rational power in order to control their passions, or to seek pure truth. But there is no reason to believe that they cannot, or will not change in the future, for men have great potential in themselves. To build a rational society is not a dream. Every one of us possesses reason and free will. But in order to succeed we must only activate these valuable traits and use them wisely. Reason will eventually liberate man and show him the path to happiness. The antagonism between science and theology will cease to exist. Orthodox, or traditional religion, as we know it, will eventually diminish in status. But in the meantime the prince ought to be pragmatic, keep peace at any cost for the general good of humanity and avoid violence and bloodshed.

The notion of the greatness of man with emphasis on his significant rational power and empirical ability was one of the favorite themes in the Renaissance and seventeenth-century Europe. The image of the self-made man was glorified. Leonardo Da Vinci (1452–1519) who was born in a small town in north Italy, then moved to Florence which was ruled by the Medici family, then to Milan, represents the emergence of this modern man. During his lifetime, *Hayy Ibn Yaqzan* was translated into Latin by Pico Della Mirandola, one of the most illustrious men of the Renaissance.[1] Like Hayy, Leonardo became interested in both man and nature. In Florence he studied anatomy and dissected bodies. The detail fascinated him. He wished to observe more and understand the meaning and function of each member. His search for the vital principle evokes Hayy's dissection of the deer, his mother. "And I [Leonardo] made an autopsy in order to ascertain the cause of so peaceful a death, and found that it proceeded from weakness through failure of blood and of the artery that feeds the heart and the other lower members, which I found to be very parched and shrunk and withered. . . ."[2]

Like Hayy, Leonardo also looked for the cause and mechanism that moved animated bodies: "Instrumental or mechanical science is the noblest and above all others the most useful, seeing that by means of it all animated bodies which have movement perform all their actions; and the origin of these movements is at the center of their gravity, which is placed in the middle with unequal weights at the sides of it, and it has scarcity or abundance of muscles and also the action of a lever and counter lever."[3] Leonardo did not turn to the Greek masters for his science. He never believed in authority. Like Hayy, the wild boy in nature, he observed, discovered, and invented. The result of his work shows that man has an incredible ability and unlimited potentialities. Hayy's notion of the one and the many in the natural world is echoed in Leonardo's writings. The Italian artist shows how one can discover the great structure, or design of things through the minute detail. Bronowski and Mazlish attribute this great discovery to Leonardo. They observe: "This is the discovery at the base of modern science, all the way from atomic structure to genetics. In the nature of things, this discovery had to be made by an artist. . . . What Leonardo did was to take this discovery from the studio into laboratory. He made the artist's eye for meaningful detail become part of the essential equipment of the scientist."[4] One wonders how much Hayy, the child who was born from the soil of a desert island and proved that he was capable of becoming a genius, had influenced Leonardo Da Vinci and his contemporaries.

In the seventeenth–century Europe, the theme of the greatness of man became more recognizable. The emphasis was on man's rational power and ability to control nature. Hayy's manuscript was in vogue. Edward Pococke's Latin translation appeared in 1671 followed by other translations in English and Dutch. Francis Bacon, Spinoza, Leibniz, Locke and others emphasized the significance of human power and portrayed man as a rational being. Some believed that men are capable of even attaining metaphysical truth. Others insisted that men are capable of controlling their passions and consequently will be able to build a more rational society. The exalted view of man also appeared in the works of Descartes who differentiated sharply between men and animals and spoke of the freedom of the mind. Many ideas were discussed, accepted or discarded. Is man nothing but a machine? How can one solve the dichotomy of mind and body? Is there a relationship between freedom and determinism? How can one explain the imperfection and limitation of human nature? Some, like Hobbes, adopted mathematics and geometry as their scientific method and attempted to apply it to politics. Others like Leibniz made mathematics the basis for their political projects in the hope that they would discover universal characteristics in man and be able to eradicate conflicts.

The metaphor of Leviathan, or commonwealth, suggested by Hobbes, evokes Hayy's description of man's organs and its interconnected relation not only within a single body, but also within other bodies in nature.[5] Motion and the mechanical cause and effect govern everything in the universe. The state and nature are juxtaposed in both Ibn Tufayl's and Hobbe's works. But while Hobbes clearly depicts the Leviathan as a giant whose body consists of smaller bodies of men and who enjoys a soul, reason and will, Ibn

Tufayl leaves it to his intelligent reader to apply what is in nature to the state and to make the link between the two. In his attempt to make a connection between physics, politics and psychology, Hobbes likens the body politics to an engine continuously moving by means of springs and wheels. The suggestion is that the state is a rational being made by men. Ibn Tufayl, on the other hand, does not elaborate on this issue, but he makes it abundantly clear that the state visited by his protagonist Hayy Ibn yaqzan is a rational construct meant to check men's greed and desires by rational means.[6] Hayy's state consists of many bodies which shun the inner light and empirical knowledge at the present time. Nevertheless, it is one body if we consider Hayy's theory of the one and the many in the natural world. The state is ruled by a sovereign and a selected circle of men who are more rational than the majority of their citizens, but still adhere to conventional religion, believe in revelation and discourage any religious speculation. This is not an ideal situation. But in order to have a relative peace and avoid war at any cost, a contract between the ruler and the ruled is established. Human beings join together in the formation of a state whereby individuals surrender some of their interests for the sake of security and basic existence. The sovereign, on the other hand, maintains peace and stability and ensures the welfare of his people.[7] It is worth mentioning that the problem of body and soul in this state is quite pronounced. It is only when men fully use their reason, derive their knowledge from science and overcome their excessive desires, that this problem can be solved.[8]

Ibn Tufayl, the creator of Hayy, was a physician. He made his protagonist a physician first at an early age. Physical objects can be examined; their functions and activities be described and explained using mechanistic terms. The same thing applies to the state that is a physical object as well. But as long as men do not recognize their ability to use their reason in order to examine their actions, it is better to leave them alone. Force will lead only to disastrous results. Hayy's model is there for all to see and emulate if they wish.

The stage for the notion that conventional religion is unnecessary if man uses his reason is now set. By not adhering to any specific orthodox religion Hayy can be considered one of the early promoters of secularism. Science has won the battle against theology. European thinkers have developed these ideas after hundreds of years. But with Darwin's appearance on stage in the nineteenth century followed by other scientists, the notion that the unknowable existence of the Ultimate Cause, or Great Mover of the universe is carried to its ultimate conclusion. For many Western scientists and philosophers the world begins to look chaotic with no design, or God.

Like Ibn Tufayl, Darwin (1809–1882) studied medicine and was very much interested in the natural world. One wonders if he ever saw, or heard of *Hayy Ibn Yaqzan* at the University of Edinburgh, or later at Cambridge, or through his association with the naturalists. He is described as the father of evolutionary biology and is well known for the process designated as "natural selection." In his theories on evolution, Darwin stresses the notion that evolutionary change does occur but only after thousands of years. The survival or extinction of a species depends on its ability to adapt to its environment.[9] Hayy could easily be used as an example to illustrate Darwin's ideas. Born from the soil of an island, the boy came spontaneously into being.[10] But the process took thousands of years before the soil was ready to give birth to a human being who considered himself an animal among animals for some years of his life. Ibn Tufayl describes at length his protagonist's struggle for life and eventual survival. But whereas Darwin's concept of the "survival of the fittest" has come to acquire a racist and sinister overtone,[11] Ibn Tufayl's concept of survival illuminates the possible ways of how one can avoid harm to oneself, but also to others as well. Darwin's vision of the natural world is frightening and brutal. Competition is the essence of everything in life. Self-interest guides all species on earth. But Ibn Tufayl's vision of nature is quite different. True there is competition here as well. The notion of one's struggle for life is highly significant. However, human reason can create a balance between the self and the other. The state of continuous warfare is not difficult to be checked. Harmony and peace can be established on earth.

It is not surprising then for Darwin to see the human world in a constant war with itself. In his autobiography, Darwin associates the French Revolution with violence. Describing a horrid event he witnesses once in Cambridge where a crowd attacks two prisoners, he likens the scene to the French Revolution.[12] For Ibn Tufayl, the human world can be a battleground too if people do not use their reason, and if the sovereign of a state does not strive to keep peace and order. Hayy is created as a model for us to examine and comprehend. In the early years of his life he thinks of himself as an animal. He imitates what he sees in nature. But once he discovers that he is different, and that unlike other animals he can use his reason, not only for his own benefit, but also for the benefit of others, he begins to see the world differently. This optimistic vision of the world contrasts sharply with that of Darwin.

In a shocking passage from *Voyage of the Beagle*, Darwin describes the destructive consequences of the encounter between different species of men. He observes that "Wherever the European has trod, death seems to pursue the aboriginal. We may look to the wide extent of the Americas, Polynesia, the Cape of Good Hope, and Australia, and we find the same result. Nor is it the white man alone that thus acts the destroyer; the Polynesian of Malay extraction has in parts of the East Indian archipelago, thus driven before him the dark-coloured native. The varieties of man seem to act on each other in the same way as different species of animals—the stronger always extirpating the weaker."[13] This argument would be abhorrent to the ears of Ibn Tufayl, the philosopher. His protagonist, who managed to survive in the most difficult circumstances, would never see himself, or be seen by others, as a destroyer of life. The Europeans have forced the natives wherever they went to adopt alien ways of thinking and behavior. This is very foreign to Hayy's philosophy. Realizing the danger of friction and conflict which his presence may cause among others, Hayy leaves the inhabited island knowing quite well that sooner or later people will use their reason wisely and without interference from anyone else.[14]

Darwin's frightful world seems to have neither a Mover, nor a Cause. In a passage where the scientist confesses his apathy toward the existence of a personal God he observes that "The old argument of design in nature . . . which formerly seemed to me so conclusive, fails, now that the law of natural selection has been discovered. . . . Everything in nature is the result of fixed laws."[15] In his journal he once wrote that while "standing in the midst of the grandeur of a Brazilian forest 'it is not possible to give an adequate idea of the higher feelings of wonder, admiration, and devotion which fill and elevate the mind.' I well remember my conviction that there is more in man than the mere breath of his body. But now the grandest scenes would not cause any such convictions and feelings to rise in my mind."[16]

Describing his fluctuating religious beliefs Darwin argues that when he wrote the *Origin of Species* he had to look for "a First Cause having an intelligent mind in some degree analogous to that of man; and I [Darwin] deserve to be called a Theist."[17] But this condition does not last for long. His convictions become weaker. He poses a question: "But then arises the doubt—can the mind of man, which has, as I fully believe, been developed from a mind as low as that possessed by the lowest animal, be trusted when it draws such grand conclusions? May not these be the result of the connection between cause and effect which strikes us as a necessary one, but probably depends merely on inherited experience? . . . The mystery of the beginning of all things is insoluble by us; and I for one must be content to remain an Agnostic."[18]

On the contrary, Ibn Tufayl's tone is quite different. There is no apathy, or sarcasm. Through his protagonist Hayy, the Arab philosopher does not only attempt to prove the existence of the Mover of the universe by means of logical reasoning, but also he goes a step further. There is no reason for the existence of the Cause, for He is the Ultimate Cause. Hayy, who is given not only reason, but also intuition can strive to behold this eternally existing Being who transcends physical attributes. "Passing through a deep trance to the complete death-of-self . . . , he saw a being corresponding to the highest sphere, beyond which there is no body, a subject free of matter, and neither identical with the Truth and the One nor with the sphere itself, nor distinct from either—as the form of the sun appearing in a polished mirror is neither sun nor mirror, and yet distinct from neither. The splendor, perfection, and beauty he saw in the essence of that sphere were too magnificent to be described and too delicate to be clothed in written or spoken words. But he saw it to be at the pinnacle of joy, delight, and rapture, in blissful vision of the being of the Truth."[19]

Being aware of the existence of the Mover of the universe, or being able to see a glimpse of that other world imposes an important responsibility on the individual. Hayy realizes that he is "the ideally balanced animal . . . a species set apart from all other animal species, created for a different end than all the rest, dedicated to a great task which no animal could undertake."[20] The notion of the greatness of man must be translated into action. Responsibility is not only toward oneself, but also toward others including animals and plants and the whole of creation. Man must strive to be a perfect creature. It is not an easy task, but it is possible.

Some European philosophers opt for Ibn Tufayl's optimistic vision of the world and the innate goodness of man. The image of the child who not only survives the horrid experience of birth in nature, but is also transformed into a man of reason, begins to surface more strongly in their work. Rousseau's *Émile* (1762), for example, emphasizes the significance of the child's education and the discovery of man's natural self.[21] The benefit, he reckons, will be for both individual and society. Like Ibn Tufayl, Rousseau believes that education begins at birth. The infant needs to stretch and move. Constraining the newborn child is to deprive him of his inalienable right to be free. But while Ibn Tufayl's infant is born in nature and nursed by a doe, Rousseau's child is born in eighteenth-century Paris where fashionable women were not only reluctant to breast-feed their children, but also to bestow love on them. Hayy's mother, the doe, is fat and has plenty of milk. She feeds the infant for two years and takes care of him. Only when she has to graze she leaves him alone. He cries if she is late. But once he learns how to walk he follows her everywhere. She teaches him how to crack the hard-shelled fruit since he has teeth now. He also begins to learn her language and that of the other deer. During this early stage of his life Hayy gradually becomes able to stand on his own in nature. His relationship with the doe is very strong. Once she becomes old he takes care of her and feeds her. And when she dies he is only seven years old. Nevertheless he manages to survive. What Hayy has learned from his own experience as a child is not only how to depend on himself, exercise his senses and use his own reason, but also how to love and pity others. His mother loves him dearly and pities him as a weak infant. He in turn loves his mother and pities her as a weak old creature. These qualities learnt in nature will help him later on in his life.

Similarly, Rousseau advocates that parents should not only feel pity toward their infants, but also strive to make them independent. The child must learn how to observe, invent and discover. But above all, he must also learn how to be responsible for his own actions. Nature teaches him what pain and suffering mean. In this way he gradually gets to know himself, how to live and how to achieve happiness. Due to his suspicion of authority Rousseau does not wish Émile to read books. But there is one exception. The irony is that the book he recommends is most likely based on *Hayy Ibn Yaqzan*. He observes:

> Since we must have books, there is one which, to my mind, furnishes the finest of treatises on education according to nature. My Émile shall read this book before any other; it shall for a long time be his entire library, and shall always hold an honorable place. It shall be the text on which all our discussions of natural science shall be only commentaries. . . . What wonderful book is this? Aristotle? Pliny? Buffon? No; it is *Robinson Crusoe.*
>
> The story of this man, alone on his island, unaided by his fellow-men, without any art or its implements, and yet providing for his own preservation and subsistence, even contriving to live in what might be called comfort, is interesting to persons of all ages. It may be made delightful to children in a thousand ways. Thus we make the desert island, which I used at the outset for a comparison, a reality.[22]

Rousseau is not only aware of Defoe's *Robinson Crusoe*, but he is also knowledgeable about Hobbe's argument on human nature and Locke's maxim as how important to use reason with children. Although he may differ from other philosophers, nevertheless he seems to be acquainted with their philosophy. He observes, for instance, that "Man is naturally disposed to regard as his own whatever is within his power. In this sense the principle of Hobbes is correct up to a certain point; multiply with our desires the means of satisfying them, and each of us will make himself master of everything. Hence the child who has only to wish in order to obtain his wish, thinks himself the owner of the universe. He regards all men as his slaves. . . ."[23] On the other hand, Locke's maxim that one ought to use reason with children is questioned by Rousseau. According to the French philosopher reason comes quite late in a child's development. He tells us that "Nature intends that children shall be children before they are men. If we insist on reversing this order we shall have fruit early indeed, but unripe and tasteless, and liable to early decay. . . ."[24]

In Book I and II Rousseau treats early infancy and childhood respectively. Then he turns his attention to the youth between the ages of twelve and fifteen in Book III. This is a very important period in the boy's life. During this stage the youth studies what is useful to him. He observes natural phenomena, makes his own instruments and invents what he needs. Robinson Crusoe here is his ideal. Rousseau stresses the fact that "The thing is, not to teach him [the youth] knowledge, but to give him a love for it, and a good method of acquiring it when his love has grown stronger. Certainly this is a fundamental principle in all good education."[25] Learning by oneself is emphasized and praised. On the contrary, depending on authority is condemned. Émile might have very little knowledge at this stage, but it is all his own. When he reaches his fifteenth birthday he becomes an independent person and capable of reflecting on his own thought processes. Rousseau's three stages differ slightly from those of Hayy. The age variation might be attributed to the fact that Émile grows in civilization, while Hayy grows in nature. The wild boy becomes a doctor when he is only seven years old, while Émile is not meant to be one at a very early age.

Ibn Tufayl did not have to flee his country after he wrote his book *Hayy Ibn Yaqzan* in the twelfth century. No one accused him of atheism.[26] He was a respected physician, scientist and philosopher and was supported by his king and nation. But Rousseau, the Swiss French author, had to flee France in 1762 after the publication of *Émile*. The book was condemned for propagating natural philosophy in lieu of revealed religion. The Archbishop of Paris, Christophe de Beaumont, considered it to be a very dangerous work, and formally refuted *Émile* as a deviation from Christian teaching. There was a warrant issued by the Parliament of Paris for the author to be arrested, and the book was burnt.

In *Confessions*, which was posthumously published in 1782, Rousseau wrote that he had abandoned his five children to orphanages despite the objection of his partner and later wife Thérèse Levasseur. For someone who advised other people about the upbringing of their children, who emphasized the notion of pity in his philosophy, this revelation is quite shocking. But we know that Rousseau had a troubled life. He spent most of it in exile. After the publication of *Émile* he dressed as a modest Armenian, perhaps to differentiate himself from the fashionable society of his time, but also to avoid the authorities that persistently pursued him. Yet, unlike Voltaire, and Diderot he was never imprisoned. What made him happy was his close relationship to nature. "Rousseau recorded the ecstasy he felt on rare occasions in his life and attempted to recapture the bliss of these privileged moments. Botanizing and assembling herbaria in Switzerland emerge as special earlier pastimes that had restored tranquillity to his sometimes tortured spirit."[27]

Rousseau's role in contributing to the French Revolution was quite remarkable. His book *The Social Contract* became one of the most important texts not only in France, but also in the Western world. Revolutionaries were especially attracted to its basic message, namely, the call for establishing a republic of virtue within which freedom is achievable. Rousseau observes that "Man is born free, and yet we see him everywhere in chains."[28] This is the problem that the French philosopher sets out to solve. Hayy Ibn Yaqzan is confronted with the same issue once he moves on to society, but unlike Rousseau he neither discusses the problem in depth, nor does he consider its ramification. Yet both arrive at a similar conclusion. A wise group of men working with a wise sovereign will be able to improve this wretched situation. For Hayy Ibn Yaqzan, King Salaman and his friends are not tyrants. They are ruling the island through popular consent and thus are able to enforce the law. His problem lies somewhere else. As a man of nature, Hayy does not see the relevance of any revealed religion. But once he comes into contact with other men in society, he realizes that a revealed religion is perhaps the lesser evil. For Rousseau, tyranny and inequality are burning issues in eighteenth-century France as reflected in his *Social Contract*. Democracy must be established. Social classes must be abolished. Religious tolerance must prevail and "all religions that tolerate others ought to be tolerated, so long as their dogmas discover nothing contradictory to the duties of a citizen."[29] In describing the ideal state, Rousseau could be easily speaking for Hayy Ibn Yaqzan as well: "it is the best and most natural rule that the wisest should govern the multitude, when there is an assurance that they will govern for its welfare, and not for their own."[30] It is clear that Rousseau's sovereign must not only have political power, but a moral one as well. The image of the bodies within one body is evoked in his book. In order to be protected, the citizens will have to surrender their individual wills to the common interest of the community.[31]

At the end of his novel Ibn Tufayl speaks of a fleeting glimpse that he offers his readers, of a veil that can easily be pierced by someone who really wants to see.[32] But Rousseau speaks directly and clearly about man's bondage in society and how to achieve ultimate freedom. He differentiates between the state of nature and the political state. "Adam was sovereign of the world, as Robinson Crusoe was of his island, because he was its only inhabitant; and the happiest circumstance attending the empire was that the monarch was secure in his throne, having nothing to apprehend from rebellion, wars, or conspiracies."[33] But once man is in society with other men the story is quite different. Unlike Ibn Tufayl, Rousseau highlights the notion of force that leads to slavery and subjugation. In a nutshell he describes the situation of man as follows: "'When a people is constrained to obey, and does obey, it does well; but as soon as it can throw off its yoke, and does throw it off, it does better: for a people may certainly use, for the recovery of their liberty, the same right that was employed to deprive them of it: it was either justifiably recovered, or unjustifiably torn from them.' But the social order is a sacred right that serves for the basis of all others. Yet this right comes not from nature; it is therefore founded on conventions."[34]

For Hayy Ibn Yaqzan, man's greatness lies in his natural makeup if only recognized by himself. Each one of us is endowed with reason and free will. It is important to see the difference between us and other animals. But this does not mean that we will live in a condition of war with all of them and at all times. On the contrary, we must strive to create a harmonious world that will benefit us all. Conflicts, frictions and wars in both nature and society can be avoided. Man should not be a destroyer. It is against reason and common sense. All of us are born free. We have no right to usurp other people's freedom. There is no contradiction between the one and the many. This simple message has spread like fire from Moorish Spain to the rest of Europe. The messenger was forgotten and the message was interpreted in different ways, but nevertheless disseminated widely and even reached the shores of the New World.

NOTES

1. The date of Pico's translation of *Hayy* is not certain. But we do know that Pico, the son of a wealthy Italian prince, was born in 1464, and that he died young in 1494. As a young boy he studied in Bologna for two years, then drifted through the major universities of Italy and France for seven years. In his early twenties he came to Rome to participate in a debate that never took place. *The Oration on the*

Dignity of Man written in 1486 was to be his keynote address. Pope Innocent III banned the debate. Only one year before his death, Pico Della Mirandola was exonerated of suspicions of heresy. The theme of the greatness of man seems to have haunted Pico. He states: "I have read in the records of the Arabians, reverend Fathers, that Abdala the Saracen, when questioned as to what on this stage of the world, as it were, could be seen most worthy of wonder, replied: "There is nothing to be seen more wonderful than man." Trans. Elizabeth L. Forbes (Lexington, KY: Anvil Press, 1953). Quoted in *Symposium Readings: Classical Selections on Great Issues: Human Nature*, 2nd ed., compiled and edited by Julius A. Sigler et al. (Lanham, Maryland, University Press of America, 1997), 248. Pico argues that only man in all creation can fashion himself the way he wishes, for he is given freedom of choice by God. "We can become what we will," Pico says encouraging men to recognize their ability to choose freely, 249–50. Also see the brief introduction on Pico, 247. Cf. Bacchelli, F. "Pico della Mirandola: traduttore di Ibn Tufayl," *Giornale Critico della Filosofia Italiana*, 72i (1993), 1–25.

Note that many encyclopedias and books on Pico fail to mention his translation of *Hayy Ibn Yaqzan*. One wonders why. See for instance *The New Encyclopaedia Britannica*, 15th ed., vol. 5, 2002, or Dora Baker's book, *Giovanni Pico della Mirandola: Sein Leben und sein Werk* (Dornach, Schweiz: Verlag am Goetheanum, 1983), or the introduction of Paul J. W. Miller to Pico Della Mirandola: *On the Dignity of Man, On Being and the One, Heptaplus*, translated respectively by Charles Glenn Wallis, Paul Miller, Douglas Carmichael (1965; Indianapolis: Hackett Publishing Company, Inc., 1998).

2. *Extracts from Leonardo Da Vinci's Note-Books*, ed. Edward McCurdy (London, 1908), 78–79. Quoted by Jacob Bronowski & Bruce Mazlish, *The Western Intellectual Tradition from Leonardo to Hegel* (New York: Books for Libraries A division of Arno Press, Inc, 1979), 13. Cf. *The Notebooks of Leonardo Da Vinci*, 1952, selected and edited by Irma A. Richter (Oxford: Oxford University Press, 1980), 151. "I have dissected more than ten human bodies, destroying all the various members and removing the minutest particles of the flesh which surrounded these veins, without causing any effusion of blood other than the imperceptible bleeding of the capillary veins. And as one single body did not suffice for so long a time, it was necessary to proceed by stages with so many bodies as would render my knowledge complete; this I repeated twice in order to discover the differences."

3. *Extracts from Leonardo*, ed. Edward McCurdy, 79. Quoted by Bronowski and Mazlish, *The Western Intellectual Tradition*, 13.

4. Bronowski and Mazlish, *The Western Intellectual Tradition*, 18.

5. See Thomas Hobbs, *Leviathan*, 1651, ed. Richard Tuck, revised student edition (Cambridge: Cambridge University Press, 1996). Note that "The Introduction" sets the tone for the whole book. Hobbs observes that "NATURE (the Art whereby God hath made and governes the World) is by the *Art* of man, as in many other things, so in this also imitated, that it can make an Artificial Animal. For seeing life is but a motion of Limbs, the beginning whereof is in some principall part within;

why may we not say, that all *Automata* (Engines that move themselves by springs and wheeles as doth a watch) have an artificiall life? For what is the *Heart*, but a *Spring*; and the *Nerves*, but so many *Strings*; and the *Joynts*, but so many *Wheeles*, giving motion to the whole Body, such as was intended by the Artificer? *Art* goes yet further, imitating that Rationall and most excellent worke of Nature, *Man*. For by Art is created that great *Leviathan* called a *COMMON-WEALTH*, or *STATE*, (in latine CIVITAS) which is but an Artificiall Man; though of greater stature and strength than the Naturall, for whose protection and defence it was intended; and in which, the *Soveraignty* is an Artificiall *Soul*, as giving life and motion to the whole body. . . ." 9.

6. Contrast Ibn Tufayl's social contract with that of Rousseau. See *Discourse on Inequality* (1755), trans. with an introduction and notes by Maurice Cranston (New York: Harmondsworth, Middlesex, Penguin Books, 1984). According to Charles Mills "Rousseau argues that technological development in the state of nature brings into existence a nascent society of growing divisions in wealth between rich and poor, which are then consolidated and made permanent by a deceitful 'social contract.' Whereas the ideal contract explains how a just society would be formed, ruled by a moral government, and regulated by a defensible moral code, this nonideal/naturalized contract explains how an unjust, exploitative society, ruled by an oppressive government and regulated by an immoral code, comes into existence." *The Racial Contract* (Ithaca and London: Cornell University Press, 1997), 5.

7. Compare what Hobbes says about the condition of man and the necessity of having a sovereign with Ibn Tufayl's general thesis. See *Leviathan*, chapter XIV "Of the first and second Naturall Lawes, and of Contracts" 91–100 and chapter XVIII "Of the Rights of Soveraignes by Institution," 121–29. Hobbes argues that the condition of man is a condition of war, everyone against everyone else. But reason tells us to strive for peace. Therefore individuals agree among themselves to be governed by a sovereign who will protect them. But in return they have to surrender some of their rights. The covenant cannot be broken. Both parties are obliged to adhere to its rules. It is important to note, however, that Ibn Tufayl's sovereign is not a tyrant, nor his citizens are slaves. The covenant in the Arabic book is certainly of a different nature than that of Hobbes.

8. Ibn Tufayl's position is quite clear here. It is understood that when human beings begin to emerge from their "self-imposed minority," to use Kant's term, and show their courage in using their own understanding, then there will be no need for a state, or a contract of any kind. (The reference here is made to Immanuel Kant's essay, "An Answer to the Question: What is Enlightenment? (1784)." See Kant, *Practical Philosophy*, trans. & ed. Mary Gregor, 11–22.

Unlike Ibn Tufayl, many Western theorists saw danger in unregulated state of nature and envisioned only chaos and savagery. It is interesting to see how Kant in his *Anthropology From a Pragmatic Point of View* read and understood Rousseau. In a revealing passage on "The Character of the Species" Kant argues: "One certainly need not accept the hypochondriac (ill-tempered) picture which Rousseau paints of the human species. It is not his real opinion when he speaks of the human species as daring to leave its natural condition, and when he propagates a reversal and a return into the woods. Rousseau only wanted to express our species' difficulty in walking the path of continuous progress toward our destiny. . . . Rousseau wrote three works on the damage done to our species by 1) our departure from Nature into culture, which weakened our strength; 2) civilization, which resulted in inequality and mutual oppression; and 3) presumed moralization, which caused unnatural education and distorted thinking. I say, these three works, which present the state of Nature as a state of innocence . . . should serve only as preludes to his *Social Contract*, his *Émile*, and his Savoyard Vicar so that we can find our way out of the labyrinth of evil into which our species has wandered through its own fault. *Rousseau did not really want that man go back to the state of nature, but that he should rather look back at it from the stage that he had then reached. He assumed that man is good by nature* . . . , but he is good in a negative way. *He is good by his own decision and by intentionally not wanting to be evil.* He is only in danger of being infected and ruined by evil or inept leaders and examples. Since, however, good men, who must themselves have been trained for it, are required for moral education, and since there is probably not one among them who has no (innate or acquired) depravity himself, the problem of moral education for our species remains unsolved." See Kant's *Anthropology*, trans. Victor Lyle Dowdell, revised and edited by Frederick P. Van De Pitte (Carbondale and Edwardsville, London and Amsterdam: Southern Illinois University Press, 1978), 243–44. Emphasis is mine.

9. See Charles Darwin, *On The Origin of Species By Means of Natural Selection*, ed. Joseph Carroll (Peterborough, Ont.; Orchard Park, NY: Broadview Press Ltd., 2003).

10. In his book *Islamic Naturalism and Mysticism*, Sami Hawi discusses the relationship between Ibn Tufayl and Darwin. He argues that the spontaneous generation of Hayy suggests four propositions which Ibn Tufayl must have considered: "a) nonliving matter can be transformed into living matter . . . that bio-/genesis is possible; b) all elements that constitute organic bodies are found in the inorganic world; c) organic compounds must have preceded the phenomenon of life; d) inorganic elements must undergo a slow process of transformation "over many years" which ultimately leads to a spasmodic emergence of life." See Hawi, 107. According to Hawi, modern scientists have confirmed these propositions, a matter that places Ibn Tufayl squarely "in the heart of the naturalistic tradition," 107. Hawi also discusses at length Hayy's struggle for existence. See 118–24. He concludes that "one can still infer with a fair amount of confidence that Ibn Tufayl believed in the slow generation of life from inorganic matter, the notion of struggle for existence, and the necessity of adaptation of the organism to the environment, all of which are evolutionary Darwinian concepts. Through Hayy Ibn Yaqzan, he tried indirectly to force these views on a reluctant world hostile to non-Islamic concepts such as these." 124. Hawi does not discuss the implications and consequences of Ibn Tufayl's, or Darwin's theories. Also, Hawi's terminology that Ibn Tufayl indirectly tries to force

these views on other Moslems is quite misleading. After all, Ibn Tufayl presents two views on birth, one traditional, the other is not. He does not support any of them. It is up to the reader to make his final judgment.

11. Diane S. Paul shows how Darwin's ambiguous language has contributed to the diverse readings of Darwinism. Many thinkers, including Marx, have hailed Darwin's book, *On the Origin of Species by Means of Natural Selection*. By the 1890s, Paul argues that German Darwinism "was most often read to imply the necessity of competitive struggle, especially among groups, and linked to racism, imperialism and suppression of working-class demands." See Diane B. Paul, "Darwin, Social Darwinism and Eugenics," in *The Cambridge Companion to Darwin*, ed. Jonathan Hodge and Gregory Radick (Cambridge: Cambridge University Press, 2003), 233. Note that Paul also refers to a recent and different reading of Darwin by Peter Singer in his book, *A Darwinian Left: Politics, Evolution and Cooperation* (London: Weidenfeld and Nicolson, 1999). She writes: "The philosopher Peter Singer has recently called for a new Darwinian Left, which 'takes seriously the fact that we are evolved animals.' It should acknowledge that there is a real human nature, which constrains our behaviour. This nature includes competitive but social and cooperative tendencies on which the Left can build. [Singer also hopes that recognition of our continuity with other animals will make us less likely to exploit them]," 236.

12. See Darwin's *Autobiographies*, ed. Michael Neve and Sharon Messenger (London: Penguin, 2002) 34–35. "I once saw in his [Professor Henslow] company in the streets of Cambridge almost as horrid a scene, as could have been witnessed during the French Revolution. Two body-snatchers had been arrested and whilst being taken to prison had been torn from the constable by a crowd of the roughest men, who dragged them by their legs along the muddy and stony road. They were covered from head to foot with mud and their faces were bleeding either from having been kicked or from the stones; they looked like corpses, but the crowd was so dense that I got only a few momentary glimpses of the wretched creatures. Never in my life have I seen such wrath painted on a man's face, as was shown by Henslow at this horrid scene. He tried repeatedly to penetrate the mob; but it was simply impossible. He then rushed away to the mayor, telling me not to follow him, to get more policemen. I forget the issue, except that the two were got into the prison before being killed."

13. Darwin, "Appendix B: From Voyage of the Beagle: Excerpts from Journal of Researches into the Geology and Natural History of the Various Countries Visited by H. M. S Beagle (1839; 2nd ed. 1845)" in *On the Origin of Species*, 460.

14. Note that Hayy is an intruder in a sense on the inhabited island. Normally an intruder who intrudes upon a community upsets the status quo and may cause a destructive revolution in the country. But Hayy is different from all intruders. See for instance my study, *The Intruder in Modern Drama* (Frankfurt am Main: Lang, 1981).

15. Darwin, *Autobiographies*, 50.

16. Darwin, *Autobiographies*, 52–53.

17. Darwin, *Autobiographies*, 53.

18. Darwin, *Autobiographies*, 54.

19. Ibn Tufayl, *Hayy Ibn Yaqzan*, trans. Lenn Evan Goodman (New York: Twayne Publishers, Inc., 1972), 152. Cf. the original Arabic manuscript, ed. Jamil Saliba and Kamil 'Ayyad (Damascus: Damascus University, 1962), 79.

20. Ibn Tufayl, *Hayy*, trans. Goodman, 141. Cf. the Arabic version, ed. Saliba, 67.

21. Jean Jacques Rousseau, *Émile: Or Concerning Education*, trans. Eleanor Worthington (Boston: D. C. Heath & Co., 1883).

22. Rousseau, *Émile*, Book III, 147.

23. Rousseau, *Émile*, Book II, 48–49.

24. Roussea, *Émile*, Book II, 52.

25. Rousseau, *Émile*, Book III, 131.

26. Note that many European thinkers who expressed different views on religion during the seventeenth and eighteenth centuries were persecuted and had to flee their countries. In Hobbes's case, for instance, a bill was "introduced into the House of Commons [October 1666] which would have rendered Hobbes liable to prosecution for atheism or heresy." See "Principal events in Hobbes's life" *Leviathan*, lix. See, for example, what Hobbes says about religion, or the question of the authority of the Holy Scriptures. *Leviathan*, 75–86; 33–34.

27. See the entry "Rousseau, Jean-Jacques" written by John C. O'Neal in *Encyclopedia of the Enlightenment*, vol. 3, ed. Alan Charles Kors (Oxford: Oxford University Press, 2003), 480.

28. Rousseau, *The Social Contract*, an eighteenth-century translation revised and edited by Charles Frankel (New York: Hafner Publishing Company, 1947), 5.

29. Rousseau, *The Social Contract*, 125.

30. Rousseau, *The Social Contract*, 62.

31. Note that Rousseau differs from Hobbes who highlights the political power of the sovereign, or the assembly of men on one hand, and the citizen's obligation to obey the laws on the other. See for instance chapter XIV "Of the First and Second Naturall Lawes, and of Contracts," "Part 2" "Of Commonwealth," chapter XVIII "Of the Rights of Soveraignes by Institution" in *Leviathan*, 91–100, 117–29.

32. See the Arabic version of *Hayy*, ed. G. Saliba, 92–93. Cf. Goodman's English translation, 165–66. Note that Ibn Tufayl speaks through his protagonist in detail about the state of nature. We have sixty-five pages in the Arabic text on Hayy in nature. In contrast there are only ten pages on Hayy in society.

33. Rousseau, *The Social Contract*, 8.

34. Rousseau, *The Social Contract*, 5–6.

6

THE EXTRAORDINARY VOYAGE

In his book *The Extraordinary Voyage in French Literature Before 1700*, Geoffroy Atkinson argues "Translations and analyses of the Hayy ben Yaqdhan, although known in France before 1700, seem to have had no influence on the French novel until after the end of the century."[1] Earlier in his introduction Atkinson defines what he means by extraordinary voyage: "A fictitious narrative purporting to be the veritable account of a real voyage made by one or more Europeans to an existent but little known country— or to several such countries—together with a description of the happy condition of society there found, and a supplementary account of the travelers' return to Europe."[2] The term "extraordinary" is borrowed from M. Gustave Lanson who considers this type of voyage "as a manifestation of the rationalistic spirit of the seventeenth and early eighteenth centuries of French Literature."[3] Atkinson distinguishes between the extraordinary voyage and the utopia of Thomas More and other fantastic imaginary journeys. For him, the extraordinary voyage has a realistic setting and a didactic content. Three obscure French novels are studied and analyzed as examples of this type. They are: *La Terre Australe Connue* of Gabriel Foigny, 1676; *L'Histoire des Sévarambes* of Denis Vairasse d'Alais, 1677–1679; and *Les Aventures de Télémaque* of Fénelon, 1699. All three novels share at least one thing, namely the contrast between two different states, one ideal, the other is pragmatic.

Fénelon's novel, however, illustrates most of the significant characteristics of this genre. The ideal state is associated with a primitive society on a desert island. Everything in it seems to be desirable. The climate is moderate all year round. No one uses money. There is no war. Conventional religions are not known. The inhabitants are cut off from the rest of the world. They are free, equal and happy people. No one has ever attacked them, or occupied their island. They have no cities, no trade, and no material attachment. They are either shepherds, or tillers of the soil. Nature has helped them attain this perfection. The pragmatic state, on the other hand, is associated with a highly civilized society and is facing many social, political, religious and economic problems. It is supposed to symbolize troubled France during the seventeenth century. The need for reform is emphasized. An established and civilized state cannot progress unless practical reforms are carried out. Conventional religion is disregarded. Extravagant luxury is frowned upon. Education and morals are promoted. The return to nature is encouraged. M. Lanson points out that Mentor, or Minerva in Fénelon's novel symbolizes Reason rather than being just a Greek goddess. Reason can bring happiness to people as in the case of the ideal state. It is therefore of utmost importance to reform the other state by means of rational thinking.[4]

Atkinson argues that the Extraordinary Voyage is a product of at least three factors. The first is an interest, particularly after 1650 in the vast literature on newly discovered lands, or actual voyages made in different parts of the world. The second is the increasing importance of rationalist thought. And the third is the rapid development of Deism in Europe. Writers used the novel as a vehicle to promote their rationalistic philosophy, to criticize European societies and attack religious and political authorities.[5]

It is extraordinary that Atkinson fails to see how these French writers utilize Ibn Tufayl's basic framework of ideal and pragmatic states and fill it with their own detail. According to him, the only novel from this period to resemble *Hayy Ibn Yaqzan* is the first part of *Le Criticon* of Baltasar Gracian that appeared in France in 1696. Originally written in Spanish and published in 1650, *El Criticon* tells the story of the only survivor of a shipwreck and his arrival at the island of Saint Helena of Critilo.[6] His encounter with Andrenio, the counterpart of Hayy Ibn Yaqzan, is the beginning of a relationship between the two men. Once Andrenio learns how to speak he relates the stages of his discovery of God.[7] The emphasis in the story is on the moral aspect rather than the philosophical one. Again Atkinson claims that no influence is exerted on the seventeenth century French writers after the appearance of this translation. But he reports a strange happening in the year 1708. A French novel resembles the story of *Robinson Crusoe* of later years is published under the title *Les Voyages et Aventures de Francois Leguat et de ses Compagnons*. It is translated into English and published in London the same year. The British museum has both versions. Atkinson concludes his argument by saying that the translation of both *Hayy* and *Le Criticon* have definitely influenced French and English literature of the eighteenth century, but not before.[8]

The Extraordinary Voyage attempts to prove that a new type of novel is created in France during the seventeenth century, and that it has nothing to do with *Hayy ibn Yaqzan*, or any other book similar to it. This novel is somewhat philosophic in nature and has a realistic setting. Its significance, however, is recognized once Defoe publishes *Robinson Crusoe*. According to Atkinson "The London correspondent of the *Nouvelles littéraire* of Amsterdam, in December 1719, found the then recently published story of *Robinson Crusoe* to be a novel *dans le gout de l'Histoire des Sévarambes et de Jacques Sadeur*."[9] Thus, the French have known this type of novel forty years at least before the publication of *Crusoe*.

Literary influence takes different shapes. A writer might paraphrase another work, just like the case of the anonymous author of *The Life and Surprising Adventures of Don Antonio Trezzanio* that was published in London in 1761. The book is a similar version to Ockley's translation of *Hayy Ibn Yaqzan*. Another writer opts for the imitation of a small, or a large part of another book, such as the case of the Jesuit Baltazar Gracian in his work *El-Criticon*, or Daniel Defoe in his novel *Robinson Crusoe*. In both cases, Hayy Ibn Yaqzan is the obvious model. Yet other writers prefer to borrow the structure, or the frame of another writer along with a few ideas here and there. This will definitely be the case of the French authors in the seventeenth century studied by Atkinson in his *Extraordinary Voyage*. There is a myriad of ways in which a writer borrows from other writers and appropriates their works. Many questions ought to be asked, particularly when new literary forms appear in a nation that never used them before.

Ibn Tufayl's model of the two distinctively different states has been framed in order to create a philosophical tale. The frame is primarily used as a critical means of the highly civilized, but corrupt state. On the other hand, the study of nature and the use of reason are associated with the ideal and primitive state. Only men who use their reason can know the meaning of happiness. This simple model has been borrowed throughout the seventeenth and eighteenth centuries in Europe. It is invented and reinvented hundreds of times, but its traces are still clear to the critic's sharp eyes. The details, of course, always remain different, but the main structure on the whole is the same. At times borrowing occurs directly from the original model, but most of the time indirectly from other and even remote versions. One should always remember that many printed books in Paris, for instance, were immediately translated into English, or Dutch and became available to other European readers. Although many of these books were popular in their time, they were completely forgotten in later years. Their authors failed as literary artists who could not mold together the adventurous, social and philosophical parts of their stories. But there were other writers who became part of canonical French and English literature.

Ibn Tufayl's ideal state has a specific geographical location. It is an island off the coast of India below the equator. There is no excessive cold, or heat there. The weather is moderate during the whole year. The sunlight is perfect. It streams down on earth. Many geographers believed that an island like this could not be inhabited because of its excessive heat. They basically repeated what other geographers said in the past, but never investigated the matter themselves. As a scientist, Ibn Tufayl presents his theory and attempts to prove it. He does not ridicule his opponents. His aim is to show them the truth. The other point, which he seems to be at odds with the majority of people, is the origin of life. He believes that it is possible for a human being to be spontaneously generated. Indeed, he tells us that out of a pocket of the soil and over many years a mass of clay was blended in a proper way, and then fermented. Only the middle part of it was suitable to survive and become a human. And thus Hayy Ibn Yaqzan was born without a father or mother. But Ibn Tufayl is cautious to mention the other traditional and more acceptable version of the origin of life. In this case the story begins with the strange adventure of an infant who has a father and mother. Due to difficult circumstances his mother puts him inside a tightly sealed ark and casts him into the sea. A strong current carries the boat and wrecks it on the shore of another island. This traditional version of the origin of life is mentioned in order to accommodate other beliefs. Not everyone accepts the scientific spontaneous generation theory in explaining the origin of life. Many people adhere to the story of creation as described in their scripture. But the task of the scientist is to explain his theory and show proofs in order to demonstrate his thesis. As a rational man he does not ridicule current ideas. He states them side-by-side along his theory and leaves the final judgment to each one of us.

On this island, we are told there are no humans, only birds, deer, and a variety of animals. There are no beasts of prey, such as leopards. The island is very fertile. It has plenty of trees, pasture and brooks. The sea is full of fish. A doe adopts the boy with no name and becomes his mother. For many years of his life, Hayy considers himself an animal among animals. He has to use his hand and invent tools in order to defend himself. But once he discovers that he is different from the animals, and that he is endowed with reason he manages to transform the island into a harmonious and peaceful place. He builds a hut for himself, domesticates animals, eats just enough to survive and takes care of his environment. His extensive study of nature leads him not only to discover many things about the universe but also to gain an insight into its Mover. And this is how Hayy attains happiness and peace of mind. On his island there is no money, no religious, or political institutions. The place hardly changes when a civilized man joins Hayy although the newcomer has different food, clothes and ways of thinking. Since both men exalt reason their path to happiness is already charted.

In contrast the pragmatic state has political and religious institutions. People own property and are greedy to amass lots of fortune. Buying and selling are the major activities in their cities. Here passions control men's lives. No one is interested in learning or using one's reason. Everyone is seeking pleasure, or satisfying some lust. Religion is literally understood, and religious rites are mechanically performed. Neither Hayy, nor Asal, his civilized friend attempts to incite a revolution in order to transform the pragmatic state into an ideal one. In describing civilization there is no sarcasm or satire in Hayy's language as one will find in many European novels that imitate the basic model, only astonishment and disbelief that men who are born to be good don't think rationally of what is best for them and for others as well. The prospect of war here is possible, but could be avoided. Reform cannot be enforced on people if they do not wish it, or work for it. A revealed religion, even in the way it is understood by the majority of people, serves a good purpose. It constantly reminds them to be good and decent with each other. The process of rationalism is the only way forward. Wars and conflicts subjugate human beings to their destructive passions.

The seventeenth century French novels that opened wide possibilities for writers in the centuries to come use Ibn Tufayl's basic model modifying it a great deal and injecting in it a satirical spirit. Its aim is to instill and develop the rational process in French and other European societies. If one examines certain critical passages in Atkinson's book without referring to the name of the French writer one is immediately reminded of *Hayy Ibn Yaqzan*. In his discussion of Foigny, for instance, Atkinson observes that the French writer "rebels against the current ideas of geography. . . , against current ideas of climate and the influence of the sun's proximity on weather. . . . In religious matters, he rebels against revealed religion, the authority of the Old Testament, the missionary spirit of the times, and against the constant agitation of religious problems and discussion of them. Rationalism is the characteristic of the entire book as far as the thought contained in it is concerned."[10] On the other hand, Vairasse's novel *L'Histoire des*

Sévarambes evokes the issue of a newly acquired language. Atkinson observes that "The language of the country is a 'created' language, and is based on logical principles rather than on tradition."[11] The religion of the natives is Deism. Yet Fénelon's *Les Aventures de Télémaque* further advances Ibn Tufayl's model. Commenting on the novel, Atkinson maintains that "Not only is it the thesis of this book that a virtuous people must be of necessity a simple people, but it is also contended that by taking a people used to living in luxury in a city, it is possible to reform them and bring them happiness and contentment by causing them to return to Nature. In this setting forth of a remedy for existing conditions, The *Aventures de Télémaque* contains the idea (if not the term) 'progress.'"[12]

Ibn Tufayl's book along with other oriental tales seem to have become central to Voltaire (1694–1778) at some point in his life. The realistic setting and the fantastic imaginary voyage become fused together. Surprisingly however, the outcome of this fusion of rational and irrational is very sensible and even leads to some philosophical notions. In his introduction to *Zadig, or Destiny: An Oriental Tale* (1747) Voltaire addresses the fictitious Sultana Sheraa to whom he dedicates his epistle and tells her that Zadig

> was written first in ancient Chaldean. . . . It was translated into Arabic to amuse the famous Sultan Ulugh Beg. This was in the time when the Arabs and the Persians were beginning to write *The Thousand and One Nights*, *The Thousand and One Days*. . . . Ulugh preferred to read *Zadig*; but the sultanas preferred the *Thousand and Ones*.
>
> "How can you prefer," said the wise Ulugh, "stories that make no sense and mean nothing?"
>
> "That is precisely why we like them," replied the sultanas.
>
> I flatter myself that you will not be like them and that you will be a true Ulugh. I even hope that when you grow tired of general conversations, which are like the *Thousand and Ones*, except that they are less amusing, I may have a minute to have the honor of talking sense with you.[13]

This dedication sets the tone to the voyage of Zadig whose Arabic name, Sadiq means the man who never lies. The senseless and the sensible, the imaginary and the philosophical, the amusing and the didactic are fused together. The author's aim is to instruct and to entertain. Indeed the borderline between reality and illusion is somehow blurred.

In many ways Zadig is represented as a comic and distorted *philosophus autodidactus*. He is naive and simple. Only reason and doubt guide him.[14]

His good nature is strengthened by good education. He is able to control his passions and never insists that his own ways are always right. He cares about others and respects "human frailty."[15] His knowledge of physical principles and metaphysics puts him above the average man. According to Ibn Tufayl, a man like that will find happiness. Many contemporaries of Voltaire also agree with this view. But in order to refute them all, particularly Leibniz, the German philosopher who seems to have adopted Hayy Ibn Yaqzan, Voltaire proves that his protagonist has experienced nothing but misfortunes.[16] Unlike Hayy who goes through trials and always triumphs at the end of each ordeal, Zadig is punished when he ought to be praised and rewarded when he ought to be penalized. His adventures and voyages bring no happiness, only disaster. His studies of the properties of animals and plants prove no uniformity, only differences.

"The Hermit," title of the twentieth chapter of *Zadig* satirizes the notion of providence and the current philosophy championed by Leibniz in particular. Apparently Voltaire was inspired by Thomas Parnell's poem, "The Hermit," published in 1721 and based on a short verse from the *Quran* that became very popular in Europe from the thirteenth century onward.[17] What Zadig finally learns is that "no evil out of which some good is not born. . . ." and that "frail mortal" should "cease to argue against what . . . [he] must worship."[18]

Voltaire's *Conte Philosophique* entertains and instructs. Like the *Voyage Extraordinare* in seventeenth-century France it compares and contrasts many lands and makes the reader laugh a great deal. Martha Pike Conant situates it within a new genre that specializes in observing manners and behavior. She argues that "By the time *Zadig* appeared, the European critic of manners and thought in the disguise of an Oriental had become a conventional type in the oriental tale. *Zadig* is a variant on the theme of the *Lettres Persanes*. Voltaire is a more subtle satirist in that he does not locate his Oriental in Paris, but in Babylon. Hence, like Swift's satires, Voltaire's criticisms of European customs, because ostensibly remote and not aimed at Europe, are the more penetrating."[19]

In writing *Zadig*, Voltaire may have wished to parody a book that many thinkers of his generation have admired. The naive figure who grows up in nature appears several times in many of Voltaire's tales. The voyage here comes to assume a new comical dimension. Hayy is replaced by Zadig, or Ingenuous, or Candide. Everything is questioned and fiercely satirized. Orientals, Europeans, savages are all tossed together in a tale which is very intricate in design. In chapter 14 of *Ingenuous*, for instance, written in 1767 and attributed falsely and on purpose to Father Pasquier Quesnel (1634–1719) a Jansenist leader, the narrator observes that:

> Ingenuous Was Making rapid progress in all kinds of knowledge, and especially in the knowledge of man. The cause of the rapid development of his mind was due to his savage education almost as much as to the temper of his soul. For having learned nothing in his childhood, he had learned no prejudices. His understanding, not having been warped by error, had remained in all its rectitude. He saw things as they are; whereas the ideas we are given in childhood make us see things all our lives, as they are not.
>
> "Your persecutors are abominable," he said to his friend Gordon. "I pity you for being oppressed, but I pity you for being a Jansenist. Every sect appears to me a rallying point for error. Tell me whether there are any sects in geometry?"[20]

Like Hayy, Ingenuous too grows up not knowing any father, or mother. He has never read any Scripture. Yet his knowledge is far superior to that of his friend Gordon, or Asal in the story of *Hayy*. "What!" Gordon exclaims at one point in the narrative, "I have consumed fifty years in learning, and I fear I may never attain the natural good sense of this almost savage lad! I tremble lest I may have laboriously strengthened my prejudices; he listens only to the voice of pure nature."[21] But if Hayy returns to his desert island with his friend Asal, Ingenuous becomes an officer and lives with the good Gordon for the rest of his life! The hilarious motto is reiterated again: "misfortune is good for something."[22] Ibn Tufayl's philosopher and natural man has now changed his name in Voltaire's work and has become a warrior.

Voltaire's naïve young man also appears in *Candide, ou L'Optimisme* published in 1759. Fearing persecution the French author attributes his new story to a certain German by the name of Dr. Ralph. Again the young man's upbringing is considered. We are told how nature has bestowed upon him a gentle character. His judgment is sound. His name fits his personality. No one knows for sure his origin, or his parents. There are speculations and rumors about that. Candide is not the only one who borrows a few traits from Hayy, but also Pangloss, the optimistic tutor who proves "admirably that there is no effect without a cause."[23] Both disciple and tutor travel from place to place after having lived briefly in an earthly paradise, the castle of a German Lord. Their adventures are horrific. They witness shipwreck, earthquake and many other disasters. The same questions are asked over and over again: Is it possible that man is born good? What is the function of his will? Do men help or massacre each other? Can one ignore evil in the world and still be an optimist? The disciple and the tutor get separated during their adventures. Candide meets Martin, the poor scholar who believes that the world is manipulated by evil spirits. Both men travel together. On the other hand, Pangloss who is supposed to be hanged or burnt, miraculously escapes and the two philosophers meet again. Candide asks his tutor whether after this horrible ordeal he is still optimistic, Pangloss replies: "I am still of my first opinion . . . for after all I am a philosopher, it is fitting for me to recant, for Leibniz cannot be wrong, and besides, pre-established harmony is the finest thing in the world, like the plenum and subtle matter."[24]

But the questions that have plagued human beings remain unanswered. Why are we born? What is the origin of evil? What is the nature of the soul? For Martin, the scholar, "man was born to live in the convulsions of anxiety or the lethargy of boredom."[25] Candide does not like the idea, but he is not sure what to say. Pangloss, the optimist likes to believe that the world is wonderful, but finds it now very hard to believe. No one has the answer to the human riddle. It seems that even the dervish who ought to know the answers does not know. When the two philosophers and the scholar go to meet him in Constantinople he slams the door in their faces. But finally they meet a happy Turk who tells them about the secret of his happiness. In many ways this man represents one facet of Hayy's complex life. He lives in nature, cultivates his own garden and never meddles with public affairs. For him "work keeps away three great evils: boredom, vice and need."[26] Both Candide and Pangloss embrace this suggestion, although the latter modifies his philosophy. "You are right," Pangloss addresses his pupil, "for when man was put in the garden of Eden he was put there . . . to work; which proves that man was not born for rest." Tired of reasoning and rational thinking, Martin, the scholar exclaims: "Let us work without reasoning . . . it is the only way to make life endurable."[27]

The fiction ends on a similar note to that of *Ingenuous*. A new society is formed. Everyone has a function in it. The goal is to cultivate the common garden and live in peace. Never tired of argumentation, Pangloss reminds Candide that everything is related and linked together in this world. If the expulsion from the castle had not taken place, and if all the other events and adventures had not materialized the good natured man would not be enjoying now the fresh air and "eating candied citrons and pistachios."[28] But Candide has become a very pragmatic man. For him the most important thing now is to cultivate one garden.[29]

The notion that the world is a wonderful place, and that people are responsible for creating good, or evil is questioned several times by Voltaire
throughout his work. Leibniz who admired Hayy Ibn Yaqzan's thesis and
extensively elaborated on it in his philosophy is now on trial.[30] But the
judges and the spectators are akin to clowns. A very serious charge is not
dealt with in a solemn court, but rather in a circus. In this way human suffering can become bearable. The final verdict is that total optimism is an illusion.[31] Yet human beings must entertain some hope to go on living. A
limited optimism is permissible, and a practical solution is found. Schopenhauer, the nineteenth-century German philosopher is reported to have said:
"I can see no other merit in Leibniz's *Theodicy* except that of having fur-
nished the great Voltaire with the occasion of his immortal *Candide*."[32] It
seems that Schopenhauer, who once considered Gracian's *El-Criticon* which
borrowed heavily from *Hayy* as one of the most important books, makes a
definite distinction between its philosophy and that of Leibniz.

Voltaire might have borrowed his naive man directly or indirectly from
Hayy Ibn Yaqzan, but he was certainly more preoccupied with the pragmatic
state. The Andalusian philosopher had delineated a brief outline of such a
state, but never described its problems in detail. Voltaire's state, on the other
hand, is plagued with chronic wars and afflicted with religious, social, and
economic woes. People living in it are neither free, nor happy. Reform is
desperately needed. Part of the solution is found in Ibn Tufayl's philosophy.
Reason can bring happiness, or relative happiness to individuals and societies. Ernst Cassirer sums up the problem and its solution. He observes that
"In *Candide* . . . in which Voltaire pours out all his scorn for optimism, he
does not deviate from this basic attitude. We cannot avoid evil and we cannot eradicate it. We should let the physical and moral world take their
course and so adjust ourselves that we can keep up a constant struggle
against the world; for from this struggle arises that happiness of which man
alone is capable."[33] But we must always remember that we have to work together. Like Hayy, Candide too comes to realize that the state is like a body.
All its members are interrelated, and each one of them has a specific function to perform. This is the only way that the state can be held together,
and that relative happiness can be achieved.

Martha Pike Conant refers to the similarities and differences between
Voltaire's *Candid* and Johnson's *Rasselas*. Both books were published in
1759. She quotes Boswell, Johnson's biographer as saying: "I have heard
Johnson say, that if they [the books] had not been published so closely one
after the other that there was not time for imitation, it would have been in
vain to deny that the scheme of that which came latest was taken from the

other."[34] It is obvious that both French and English writers are using directly, or indirectly various Arabic models, including Ibn Tufayl's philosophical novel, and inventing their own narratives and viewpoints. Although Voltaire contrasts sharply with Johnson, both writers have created two opposing states: One idealistic, the other realistic. Their protagonists are naive and hopeful. However, the hero's voyages from land to land always prove that the search for the ultimate happiness is quite futile. The differences lie in the final interpretation of the book, the style used by the author and the overall tone of the narrative.

Johnson replaces Ibn Tufayl's ideal island and Voltaire's castle with a palace in the Happy Valley. His hero, Rasselas, prince of Abissinia is confined in a palace surrounded by mountains. Once he reaches his twenty-sixth year his contemplative nature leads him to ask a very significant question. One is reminded by Hayy when he sees Rasselas watching the goats and comparing them to himself. During the same stage in his life, Hayy too examines the qualities he shares or does not share with other animals. Rassela's question is brief and to the point

> "What," said he, "makes the difference between man and all the rest of the animal creation? Every beast that strays beside me has the same corporal necessities with myself; he is hungry and crops the grass, he is thirsty and drinks the stream, his thirst and hunger are appeased, he is satisfied and sleeps; he rises again and is hungry, he is again fed and is at rest. I am hungry and thirsty like him, but when thirst and hunger cease I am not at rest; I am, like him, pained with want, but am not, like him, satisfied with fulness. The intermediate hours are tedious and gloomy. . . . Man has surely some latent sense for which this place affords no gratification, or he has some desires distinct from sense which must be satisfied before he can be happy."[35]

Thus begins his wondering and search for happiness. Accompanied by his sister Nekayah and two others, Rasselas journeys to different places and meets a variety of people. But happiness is nowhere to be seen. We learn that "Human life is everywhere a state in which much is to be endured, and little to be enjoyed."[36] Rasselas resolves to go back to his native country. Free choice seems to be an illusion. The only consolation to man is to fill his time with work, to be patient, honest and courageous. Seeking knowledge helps him attain some happiness and serenity. Although the philosophic tale ends with a chapter entitled "The conclusion, in which nothing is concluded" a few observations remain with us. One of them is that "All that virtue can afford is quietness of conscience, a steady prospect of a happier state; this may enable us to endure calamity with patience; but remember that patience must suppose pain."[37]

Johnson's somber tone is radically opposed to the mockery and wit of Voltaire. Nevertheless, his biting satire at some point alleviates the unbearable gloom that pervades his work. The philosopher is not only rejected by Johnson's hero, but also satirized.

> "Sir, ..." [said Rasselas], "Let me only know what it is to live according to nature."
>
> "When I find young men so humble and so docile," said the philosopher, "I can deny them no information which my studies have enabled me to afford. To live according to nature, is to act always with due regard to the fitness arising from the relations and qualities of causes and effects; to concur with the great and unchangeable scheme of universal felicity; to co-operate with the general disposition and tendency of the present system of things."
>
> The prince soon found that this was one of the sages whom he should understand less as he heard him longer. He therefore bowed and was silent, and the philosopher, supposing him satisfied, and the rest vanquished, rose up and departed with the air of a man that had co-operated with the present system.[38]

Johnson's tale is dotted with many satirical passages. Yet the overall effect on the reader is despair. The glimmer of hope is dispersed in the text, never highlighted. Voltaire concludes his *Candide* with the notion that one should cultivate one's garden for his own benefit and for the benefit of others. Johnson repeats the same idea, but he hides it in the middle of his essay-like tale. In chapter XXVIII, Rasselas and Nekayah continue their conversation. Now that they have experienced many things themselves they can sit together and compare notes. The cultivation of one's garden is expressed in this way: "We will not endeavour to modify the motions of the elements, or to fix the destiny of kingdoms. It is our business to consider what beings like us may perform; each labouring for his own happiness, by promoting within his circle, however narrow, the happiness of others."[39] The effect of such a passage is blurred. There is too much human rambling and the conclusion unfortunately does not conclude anything.

NOTES

1. See G. Atkinson, *The Extraordinary Voyage in French Literature Before 1700* (New York: AMS Press, Inc., 1966), 141.

2. Atkinson, *The Extraordinary Voyage*, ix.

3. Quoted by Atkinson, *The Extraordinary Voyage*, xi. Cf. G. Lanson. *Manuel bibliographique de la littérature française moderne*. Paris, 1914 and "Origines et premieres manifestations de l'esprit philosophique. . . . " *Revue des Cours et Conférences*, December, 1907.

4. Atkinson, *The Extraordinary Voyage*, 144–61.

5. See Atkinson's "Conclusion," *The Extraordinary Voyage*, 162.

6. Note that *El-Criticon* was "considered by the nineteenth century German pessimistic philosopher Arthur Schopenhauer one of the most important books ever written." See the *New Encyclopaedia Britannica*, 15th ed., vol. 5 (2002), 402.

7. In her article "European Influence of Hayy ibn Yaqzan," Dorothy Rundorff cites the argument of the Spanish scholar Garcia Gomez regarding *El Criticon*. Gomez maintains that the Jesuit Baltazar Gracian is more likely to have heard of Hayy's story from Aragonese moriscos than to have read or used Ibn Tufayl's polished manuscript. It is also worth mentioning that Gomez considers *El Criticon* a premature, but still a precursor to Rousseau's concept of "the child brought up outside the influence of society." Voltaire's *L'ingenue* is also mentioned in this regard. See *Islamic Literature*, 4 (1952): 277–81.

8. See Atkinson, *The Extraordinary Voyage*, 140–43.

9. Quoted from W. E. Mann, *Robinson Crusoe en France*, Paris, 1916, 14. See Atkinson, *The Extraordinary Voyage*, 165.

10. Atkinson, *The Extraordinary Voyage*, 85–86.

11. Atkinson, *The Extraordinary Voyage*, 139.

12. Atkinson, *The Extraordinary Voyage*, 161.

13. Voltaire, Zadig, in *Voltaire's Candide, Zadig and Selected Stories*, trans. with an introduction by Donald M. Frame (Bloomington: Indiana University Press, 1961), 103–104.

14. Note that Roger Pearson in *The Fables of Reason: A Study of Voltaire's "Contes Philosophiques"* (Oxford: Clarendon Press, 1993) observes, "Doubt is what marks Zadig out for angelic enlightenment. If we will but abandon our blind faith in easy explanation and dare to doubt, then we may be enlightened by *Zadig*." 93.

15. Voltaire, *Zadig*, 104.

16. Cf. "Voltaire against Leibniz" in the introduction to *Candide*, trans. Daniel Gordon (Bedford, Boston & New York: St. Martin's, 1999), 18–24.

17. Voltaire, *Zadig*, 164–70.

18. *Zadig*, 169.

19. Martha Pike Conant, *The Oriental Tale in England* 1908 (New York: Octagon Books, 1966), 134. One reference here is made to Montesquieu's *Les Lettres Persanes* (1721). Two Persians traveling in Europe write letters back home in which they satirize the social, political, religious and literary fabric of the French society at the time. The other reference is made to Jonathan Swift, most probably to his *Gullivers Travels*.

20. See *Ingenuous*, in *Voltaire's Candide, Zadig and Selected Stories*, trans with an introduction by Donald M. Frame (Bloomington: Indiana University Press, 1961),

296. Note that Voltaire attributes this tale to Father Quesnel who provoked the religious authorities by publishing a book entitled, *Réflexions morales sur le Nouveau Testament*. The book was condemned by the Pope in 1713. See Frame's note, page 255.

21. Voltaire, *Ingenuous*, 289. Note that Roger Pearson in *The Fables of Reason: A Study of Voltaire's "Contes Philosophiques"* considers *L'Ingénu* "a politically radical text because it seeks to wean us—both intellectually and emotionally—from slavish dependence on the power of the book." 193.

22. Voltaire, *Ingenuous*, 318.

23. Voltaire, *Candide*, 4.

24. Voltaire, *Candide*, 95.

25. Voltaire, *Candide*, 99.

26. Voltaire, *Candide*, 100.

27. Voltaire, *Candide*, 101.

28. Voltaire, *Candide*, 101.

29. A sensible interpretation of *Candide* is offered by Roger Pearson in *The Fables of Reason: A Study of Voltaire's 'Contes Philosophiques'* (Oxford: Clarendon Press, 1993), 110–36. Pearson makes the connection between Voltaire and Locke when he argues that: "At the end of *Candide* . . . retrospect should suggest not the absurd chain of events described by Pangloss but the Lockian 'steps by which the mind attains several truths.' Movement through time means movement toward increased knowledge and wisdom. It remains to be seen whether the lessons learnt by Candide in the final chapter can be regarded as at all conclusive. For the moment, however, it is important to note how the replacement of providence by the order of education is accompanied at the narrative level by the underpinning of the entertaining spoofs of chivalric romance and the picaresque novel with a symbolic order of a more serious kind. Candide's voyage of reason is represented as a journey from one Garden of Eden to another via Eldorado, or from falsity to reality via the ideal." 119.

30. For a comparison of the philosophies of Leibniz and Voltaire see the study of Richard A. Brooks, *Voltaire and Leibniz* (Geneve: Librairie Droz, 1964).

31. Note that Voltaire expresses the same views over and over again. In his philosophical letter "On Mr. Pope" published in 1756, he observes that "The *Essay on Man* of Pope seems to me the most beautiful, most useful, most sublime didactic poem ever written in any language. It is true that the whole groundwork of it is to be found in Lord Shaftesbury's *Characteristics*, and I do not know why Mr. Pope gives the honor solely to Lord Bolingbroke, without saying a word about Shaftesbury, the pupil of Locke.

Everything related to metaphysics has been thought in all periods and among all peoples who cultivate the mind, and this system much resembles that of Leibniz, which maintains that, of all possible worlds, God must have chosen the best, and that in this best it was necessary that the irregularities of our globe and the stupidities of its inhabitants should have their place. . . . Optimism leads to despair. It is a cruel philosophy under a consoling name." See Voltaire's *Philosophical Letters*, translated with an introduction, Ernest Dilworth (New York: The Bobbs-Merrill Company, INC, 1961), 147–50.

32. Quoted by J. G. Weightman, "The Quality of Candide" in *Essays Presented to C. M. Girdlestone* (Durham, 1960), 335–47; reprinted in Voltaire's *Candide*, 2nd ed. Trans. Robert M. Adams (New York, London: W. W. Norton & Company, 1991), 153. Note that Theodor W. Adorno clarifies the issue in his *Kant's Critique of Pure Reason* (1959), ed. Rolf Tiedemann, trans. Rodney Livingstone (Oxford: Polity Press in association with Blackwell publishers Ltd., 2001). Adorno writes: "Kant is enlightened in the sense that he is a critic of dogmatism. It must be pointed out, however, that the concept of dogmatism undergoes a curious enlargement at his hands. Whereas the older Enlightenment and the Western Enlightenment mainly used the term to refer to theology proper, Kant uses the term . . . to apply also to metaphysics. This, too, is a feature that Kant shares with the mature Enlightenment. Those of you who have studied French will be aware that one of Voltaire's chief works, certainly the book that is best known in Germany, is his *Candide. Candide* is an attempt to expose the dogmatic character not so much of theology as of German metaphysics, namely, Leibniz's theodicy. To a degree, then this critique of the dogmatic side of reason is to be found among the themes of the *Critique of Pure Reason* . . . nothing should be accepted without questioning it, neither theology nor metaphysics and the allegedly eternal truths of reason, nor even, as Kant would doubtless have said, the empirical objections that have been advanced against a rationalist metaphysics. *It is this refusal to accept statements unquestioningly that marks the rather more incisive version of Enlightenment thought in Kant in which reason broadens its critical, anti-dogmatic activities to embrace everything that is not completely transparent and self-evident*" 59. The emphasis is mine. Of course, Adorno does not seem to be aware of the origin of Kant's enlightened ideas.

33. Ernst Cassirer, *The Philosophy of the Enlightenment*, trans. from the German Fritz C. A. Koelin and James P. Pettegrove (Princeton: Princeton University Press, 1951), 148.

34. Quoted from Boswell, *Life of Johnson*, ed. G.B. Hill, Vol. I., 342 in Martha Pike Conant, *The Oriental Tale in England in the Eighteenth Century*, 144.

35. Samuel Johnson, "The History of Rasselas Prince of Abyssinia" in *Rasselas and Other Tales*, ed. Gwin J. Kolb (New Haven and London: Yale University Press, 1990), 13.

36. Johnson, *The History of Rasselas*, 50.

37. Johnson, *The History of Rasselas*, 102.

38. Johnson, *The History of Rasselas*, 87–89.

39. Johnson, *The History of Rasselas*, 103.

7

A PHILOSOPHICAL LETTER, AN ALLEGORICAL VOYAGE, OR AN AUTOBIOGRAPHY?

Hayy Ibn Yaqzan *as a Model in Modern European Literature*

No one seems to be sure as how to describe the genre of *Hayy Ibn Yaqzan*. Is it a romance, or a philosophical novel? *The Encyclopedia Britannica* refers to *Hayy Ibn Yaqzan* as "a philosophical romance in which he [Ibn Tufayl] describes the self-education and gradual philosophical development of a man who passes the first fifty years of his life in complete isolation on an uninhabited island."[1] A. M. Goichon in *The Encyclopedia of Islam* calls it a philosophical allegory[2] and discusses it in relation to another work by Ibn Sina, or Avicenna (980–1037). Goichon explains that *Hayy Ibn Yaqzan*, the title shared by both books, is "the proper name of the active Intellect, 'living,' since Ibn Sina places perfection in life in intelligence and action, 'son of the wakeful one,' because he [Hayy] emanates from the penultimate pure Intelligence which knows neither sleep nor inattention. This name is closely connected with the theory of creative emanation professed by Farabi (d. 950) and Ibn Sina. The active Intellect is also, through knowledge surpassing the perceptible world, the soul's guide towards its prime principle, the Being that shines forth over all others."[3] On the other hand, Christoph Bürgel rejects the formula 'philosophical novel' and observes that "given the fact that the hero reaches his goal not in the realm of reason but in the vision of God and the mystical union with the highest being (without, however, forswearing the use of his rational faculty), one could perhaps rather call it an initiational tale."[4]

Literary terms, such as romance, novel, philosophical allegory, or autobiography are extensively defined and discussed in many books and dictionaries. Romance, for instance, is described as "Very loosely, a narrative characterized by exotic adventure rather than by the realistic depiction of character and scene usually associated with the novel."[5] There are three types: The Greek romance whereby lovers are separated by shipwrecks and wars, but miraculously reunite at the end; the chivalric adventures of the late middle ages which emphasize the power of love and the significance of specific virtues, such as honor, loyalty and courage; and the exotic novels of some of the nineteenth century English and American literature. Surely, *Hayy Ibn Yaqzan* does not belong to any of these types. But if one accepts the general definition of romance as "a narrative characterized by exotic adventure" one may classify *Hayy* as a romance. The birth episode, for instance, would appear as a fantastic happening to many readers although it is meant to be a scientific presentation of a current theory. Otherwise it is not very easy to apply the term romance to the book.

On the other hand, a novel is defined as "a fictional prose narrative of considerable length."[6] In this sense *Hayy Ibn Yaqzan* fits this definition. Also the setting and the character if not totally realistic are certainly not far-fetched. But the novel has many types. Hayy seems to belong to more than one. In one sense, it can be considered a *Bildungsroman*, or an *Erziehungsroman*. After all, its primary aim is to demonstrate the upbringing, initiation and development of a child and his education.

Hayy may also be considered as a philosophical novel written in a letter-form. A man writes a long letter to his friend telling him about the spiritual journey of another man, or possibly his own alter ego. An epistolary novel is described as "a narrative in the form of letters. Popular in the eighteenth century. . . . The form enabled [Samuel] Richardson conveniently to reveal his heroine's private thoughts and feelings while advancing the plot."[7]

As an epistolary novel, *Hayy* consists of three distinct parts. The first part is the introduction: a letter to a friend acquiescing to his request to help him understand the secrets of the illuminative philosophy as mentioned by Avicenna. Then comes a brief survey and evaluation of three Moslem philosophers: Ibn Bajja, or Avempace (d. 1139), Al-Farabi (d. 950), and Avicenna (980–1037). The introductory letter is written in the first person singular, but the philosophical survey is related in the first person plural.

The second part, which makes the bulk of the novel, is the story of Hayy Ibn Yaqzan. The narrative is in the third person. Ibn Tufayl as an author/and a writer of a long letter, or epistle utilizes the form to reveal his protagonist's inner thoughts and feelings, but at the same time constructing a very tight plot. At some points, he discreetly comments on his protagonist using verses from the Quran, or quotations from some mystics. At other points, he explains some scientific facts or experimentations and gives proofs from mathematics, or other sciences. However, the reader does not feel the intrusion of the author. One must read the text several times in order to distinguish between the protagonist and the narrator. Toward the end of part two when Hayy "saw what no eye had seen, or ear had heard"[8] the narrator shifts to the first person addressing his friend, "Listen now with your heart. Stare with your mind to what I shall tell you. Perhaps you will find guidance on your path. Don't ask me now to explain to you more than I have already in this letter."[9] The story of Hayy and Asal on the inhabited island is again introduced briefly by the first person narrator, but the narration quickly shifts to the third person.

The third and last part of the long letter is mainly narrated in the first person singular, but in a few sentences the plural is also used. Here the narrator ties up the introduction and the conclusion together. The secret cannot be concealed, but at the same time, it cannot be revealed. To capture the detail of the experience is almost impossible. Ibn Tufayl presents the mystery in the form of a veil. He who uses his reason and intuition can see through it and possibly even lift it. But he who does not will be plunged into darkness, and the veil will appear to him very thick and prohibiting. The letter is meant to encourage man to seek the truth and strive in order to find it.

Although Ibn Tufayl, as a narrator, does not clearly side with his protagonist within the second part of the book, it is clear to the reader, particularly from the introduction and the conclusion of the letter, that he sympathizes and perhaps even identifies with the wild boy who seeks the truth and finds it at the end.[10] In this regard, he is different from Scheherazade who tells the stories of many degenerate men and women without commenting on their action. But it is the task of the reader to reexamine the original frame, namely the beginning and end of *One Thousand and One Nights* in order to realize that the narrator is very different from the characters depicted in the various stories. Unlike her many heroes and heroines, Scheherazade is the model of virtue and knowledge.[11]

But if Scheherazade is a fictitious character Ibn Tufayl is a real person who lived in the twelfth century. His letter to an unnamed friend suggests that he may be writing his own autobiography and telling bits and pieces about the difficulties faced by philosophers and scientists during his own life. The secrets that he refers to at the end of his letter are not only meant to be understood in the realm of the personal sphere, but also in the public one as well. Religious intolerance was rife among certain groups during his time. Philosophers needed the protection of enlightened kings. But if autobiography is defined as "a continuous narrative of the major events (and sometimes the minutiae of . . . [the author's] past"[12] it could be argued that Ibn Tufayl's autobiography is also concealed behind a veil.

> Allegory is defined as:
>   An extended narrative that carries a second meaning along with the surface story. The continuity of the second meaning involves an analogous structure of ideas or events (frequently historical or political). . . . Landscapes and characters in allegory are usually incarnations of abstract ideas. . . . It is often said that allegory 'both conceals and reveals.' In political allegory, the author may disguise his criticism or satire for fear of reprisal, but perception of the analogy between the narrative and contemporary events reveals the intended meaning. . . . Allegory is not only a literary mode but, by extension, a method of critical analysis as well. Thus critics sometimes interpret works allegorically where they perceive coherent analogies between characters and abstract ideas.[13]

Since the information we have on the Andalusian philosopher is very scanty we can assume from what we know about him that as a scientist Ibn Tufayl has passed through most of the stages of his protagonist in the state of nature. The political state, however, seems to resemble the Andalusian society of his time. Although King Salaman in the story espouses orthodox religion and approves of its outward manifestation for the benefit of his own people, he is tolerant toward Hayy and Asal who are quite different from his subjects. In this sense, Salaman is similar to Ibn Tufayl's king, Abu Ya'qub Yusuf who protected philosophers and made sure they were not harmed. But the real king even went further than the fictitious one in participating in the actual religious and philosophical speculations. The encounter between Ibn Tufayl's king and Ibn Rushd, or Averroes is vividly described in Arabic sources. The king asked the philosopher who was introduced to him by Ibn Tufayl whether the universe had always existed, or whether it was created from nothing. Averroes wished to avoid these questions. He was probably afraid. The king did not rebuke him. On the contrary, he started discussing these issues with Ibn Tufayl. He seemed to be knowledgeable about Aristotle, Plato and other Moslem philosophers. As a result Averroes was encouraged and participated in their discussion. He realized that he would be able to air his views freely without being afraid of punishment. The significance of such an encounter cannot be underestimated. Without it Averroes would not have written his extensive commentaries on the works of Aristotle and Europe's Renaissance would have been delayed. Dante's "famed commentator" who escaped the Inferno and was placed in Limbo with other great Greek philosophers and scientists in *The Divine Comedy* owed it not only to his genius, but also to the tolerance of his great king who encouraged him to ask forbidden questions and investigate issues that normally lead many to their sure death.

Many critics wrote about *Hayy Ibn Yaqzan* as an allegory, but they emphasized the philosophical or religious aspect rather than the political one. Hayy represents the active intellect. His name is borrowed from Avicenna's book. The story describes the progress of the soul and the eventual discovery of the ultimate truth. One critic, however, situates *Hayy* in a different realm. In his article "The Political Thought of Ibn Tufayl," Hillel Fradkin examines the political state in *Hayy*, the orthodox religion practiced in it, and its citizens' attachment to corporeality. He argues that in this community "man's access to truth—except in the case of very superior human beings—must take the form of images of the truth."[14] It is the task of the just king to balance and regulate the desires of men. Absolute happiness will not be achieved in this state. But everything is relative. And for the citizens to practice the apparent manifestations of their religion is better than to neglect them. For neglecting them may lead to extreme moral, social and political chaos. In order to situate *Hayy* in the realm of politics, Fradkin accepts the second version of Hayy's birth which identifies the boy's parents, and links it to the last few pages of the book. The conclusion raises the question whether there is a contradiction between the depreciation of corporeality advocated in the natural state for man to reach happiness and the significance of corporeality in the political and social state. The author argues that there is no contradiction. Human beings are created by God, religion cannot deny their fundamental nature. The only way out is to "adapt the truth to it . . . present images of the truth as if they were the truth itself and regulate men's corporeal affairs as if these concerns were not in themselves ultimately inferior. . . ."[15] Fradkin asserts at the end of his article that there is a "relationship between mysticism and social life and there-with, of political life as well."[16] In this light, *Hayy Ibn Yaqzan* can be read as a political allegory in which man journeys not in order to find the ultimate truth, but an acceptable image of it, not total perfection, but practical and possible. It is a journey to earth, not to heaven. In this political state there is no room for tyranny, or gross injustice. The king who is presumably chosen by his subjects understands the human dilemma and differentiates between the pure truth and its diverse images, but opts to be pragmatic and above all a peacekeeper not a cause for division, friction and violence among his own people. In this sense, St. Augustine's heavenly and earthly cities will not grow apart. The city of man will not be in a chronic condition of civil war. On the contrary, both cities will flourish and the gap between them will narrow as long as the just and virtuous king wisely steers the helmet.

If Scheherazade has provided Western literature with a variety of narrative modes since the translation of *One Thousand and One Nights* into European languages, there is no doubt in my mind that Ibn Tufayl too has influenced many European writers directly or indirectly not only in the content of his spiritual epistle, but also in its form.[17] Defoe who is held as the father of the English novel, particularly for his book *Robinson Crusoe* has modeled his hero on characters from the Moslem East, namely, Sinbad the Sailor and Hayy Ibn Yaqzan. Part of his narrative which has a "dream-like quality," to use Coleridge's terminology, is borrowed from *The Arabian Nights*,[18] while the other part which conceals and reveals certain glimpses of his hero's spiritual progress is borrowed from *Hayy Ibn Yaqzan*. Some critics fail to see the autobiographical elements in *Robinson Crusoe* and think that Crusoe has nothing to do with Defoe, his creator.[19]

In the eighteenth century, the epistolary novel became very popular in Europe.[20] Samuel Richardon wrote such a novel in 1740. Its title was *Pamela*. Soon it was followed by *Clarissa* in 1748. The reader as a voyeur could detect the shifting points of view. But the pseudo-letter form was mainly utilized by various writers in order to depict two different countries and to satirize the manners and customs of Europeans by contrasting them with the real, or imaginary customs of the protagonist's native land. The aim is not only to instruct as in the case of *Hayy Ibn Yaqzan*, but also to entertain as in the case of "Sinbad the Sailor." Contemporary European societies, morals, religion, politics and political institutions were exposed and satirized, and the various oriental tales, which were less serious than *Hayy*, were also parodied and criticized as well.

But not all letters were written to form a novel. Voltaire (1694–1778), for instance, opted to have his letters express directly philosophical, religious, social and political issues of his time. The aim is to compare and contrast two distinct societies: one is quite liberal and advanced on many fronts; the other is conservative and backward. The tone is hardly serious. Even in the most polemical issue the reader detects irony and is never sure what to make out of the text. *Lettres Philosophiques*, or *Letters Concerning the English Nation*, which were published in England first in 1733, were later condemned in France. The book was burnt and a warrant to arrest its author was issued. There are twenty-four miscellaneous letters, plus the "Anti-Pascal." Seven of them deal with religion and religious toleration. The diversity of sects and religions in England seemed to have fascinated

Voltaire.[21] In his "Sixth Letter" he observed that "If there were only one religion in England, there would be fear of despotism; if there were but two, the people would cut one another's throats; but there are thirty, and they all live happy, and in peace."[22] The Quakers who openly admired *Hayy Ibn Yaqzan* were themselves admired by Voltaire but only for a while.[23] They were the first sect in England to be influenced by certain ideas in *Hayy*, namely the significance of the inner light which is a gift from God to humanity and the notion of toleration.

Other letters exalt Bacon as "the father of experimental philosophy,"[24] or describe Locke as the most "exact logician."[25] Yet others deal with institutions, or literature and art. Voltaire seems to be immersed in oriental lore, even in Arabic science. His "Eleventh Letter: Inoculation" tells the hilarious story of how Lady Mary Wortley Montague has learnt about the curious smallpox inoculation during her visit to Constantinople, the capital of the Ottoman Empire. She has a hard time convincing her chaplain of the need to have her child inoculated. For the chaplain believes "that this practice was not Christian, and could only be expected to succeed with infidels."[26] Upon her return to England she informs the Princess of Wales about this medical advancement in the Islamic empire. As a result and after testing the inoculation on four criminals, the princess and all her children are inoculated. Then all of England follows suit. The irony, of course, is that the rest of Europe, and France in particular, remains behind, for inoculation is considered not Christian. Voltaire is attributing the discovery of such an inoculation to the Circassians and for reasons that have little to do with science. But when he is corrected he makes fun of the whole issue and says, "There are some who pretend that the Circassians formerly learned this custom from the Arabians. We will leave this point in history to be elucidated by some learned Benedictine, who will not fail to compose several large volumes upon the subject, together with the necessary proof."[27]

In his *Guide to French Literature*, Anthony Levi observes "In religion Voltaire prefers the Quakers although, having used them as a stick with which to beat other Christian bodies, he then holds them up to ridicule themselves. It is here that his religious position clearly emerges as dominated by a hatred of rites because they lead to superstition, and a hatred of dogmas, because they lead to intolerance. . . . At this date the Quakers seemed to offer Voltaire the best balance between tolerance and minimal dogmatic commitment on the one hand, and the institutional organization of Christianity to guarantee the fabric of society on the other. The *Lettres* contains more than one echo of Fénelon."[28]

Voltaire, however, does not only use his *Conte Philosophique* as a vehicle to criticize both Oriental and European customs and beliefs, but he also utilizes dramatic narratives which have not been popular in the Arab and Moslem East during the Middle Ages. In writing his play, *Mahomet the Prophet, or Fanaticism: A Tragedy in Five Acts* (1741), Voltaire depicts Muhammad as the symbol of aggression, and deceit. In appropriating Ibn Tufayl's philosophy which stresses the significance of reason, the various paths to truth, the importance of pity and the necessity to avoid violence, Voltaire uses Muhammad as a stick to beat other Christian bodies, but also to ridicule the prophet as an immoral character. The play that claims to portray the historical Muhammad is dedicated to Pope Benedict XIV. Voltaire seems to parody Ibn Tufayl's ideas and to suggest similarities between all religions. Toward the end of the play, Palmira, who is supposedly a slave of Mahomet, discovers that her master is nothing but a "blood-smeared impostor." She exclaims: "May religion, the source of deceit, be henceforth held in scorn by the human race!"[29] At another point Mahomet himself explains how he detests the name Seid, a supposed slave of his. Seid, or rather Sa'id, in Arabic means "the happy person." "You know" Mahomet addresses his follower Omar "that in this pit of iniquity I seek a throne, an alter and victims. . . . We must deliberate what best will serve my interests . . . and religion to which all must submit, and necessity, the mother of all evil."[30] Voltaire attacks obedience and ridicules the slave who is meant to be happy according to his name, but fails to think for himself. Seid is asked to commit a crime. At the beginning he hesitates, and even questions the authority of the prophet. "Is terrible Mahomet really God's sole interpreter?"[31] the slave cries in agony. Here religion seems to be a horrible thing, for it stands in sharp contrast to reason and morality. The conflict between authority and man is finally resolved. Having a feeble will the slave totally surrenders to his assailant. "If it is heaven's wish," Seid says, "I shall obey. But the cruel obedience! Oh heaven! At what a price!"[32]

Pious Moslems will, of course, dismiss Voltaire's interpretation of their prophet as nothing but a crusading spirit and a false presentation of the historical Muhammad and his moral character. But the sensible among them will read beneath the surface and realize that Voltaire is mainly satirizing fanatic Europe during his lifetime and fanaticism in general. Knowingly, or unknowingly, Voltaire had used the basic assumptions of Ibn Tufayl, a Moslem philosopher who was particularly popular in England during the eighteenth century. He interpreted his ideas and reached specific conclusions. But if he used Muhammad, a figure who was and still is a target of fanatics, orientalists, and evangelicals, he was perhaps very concerned about his own safety in fanatic Europe and wished to locate fanaticism in remote regions and precisely among the people who taught Europe the meaning of tolerance. Of course it is difficult to strip the play from its historical protagonist and the religion he espouses.[33] But if one attempts to change the names of the characters, the locale and the supposedly historical details, one finds that the basic conflict revolves around authority versus individual. The questions asked are very simple. Should we, or can we use our reason? If we do and our reason clashes with that of authority what do we do then? Do we challenge authority and fear the consequences? Or do we surrender? Voltaire's vision is very pessimistic and unlike that of Ibn Tufayl. The French philosopher is proposing here that authority always wins, that the Machiavellians of this world will never let us use our reason, that this talk about free will is nothing but an illusion, and that history is a big lie.

In his introduction to *Mahomet The Prophet*, Robert L. Myers argues "Voltaire's investigations into man's cultural and political history led him to the unhappy conclusion that of all the causes of man's sufferings none perhaps could equal religious fanaticism. His now dusty epic poem, *La Henriade* (1723), is a description in verse form of the horrors of the religious wars of sixteenth-century France."[34] Myers speaks of Voltaire's persecution and imprisonment for standing against authority in general. But he highlights the profound influence exerted by what he calls the new English "revolutionary thinkers" on Voltaire and other French philosophers, particularly after 1726 when Voltaire chooses to go into exile to England.[35] Myers, however, does not make the connection between England and Moorish Spain and the role of *Hayy Ibn Yaqzan* in particular in helping create those innovative thinkers. One does not know for sure whether Voltaire has read Hayy, or heard of him. But one is certain that Voltaire has used Hayy's ideas that have been prevalent in England during his stay there, not only among the Quakers, but also among the English thinkers he has befriended and admired.

In his book *The Fables of Reason*, Roger Pearson wonders whether Locke has made Voltaire think narratively. He observes, "Jacques Van den Heuvel has made the valuable point that Locke's philosophical method in the *Essay Concerning Human Understanding*, which so influenced Voltaire, is itself essentially narrative. Locke speaks of this method as being 'historical' and 'plain': 'historical' because ideas are not innate but arrived at by stages ('the steps by which the human mind attains several truths') and 'plain' because, in its uncorrupt state, the mind is untrammelled by prejudice and preconception."[36] Of course, it does not occur to Pearson that both Locke and Voltaire have a common source in *Hayy Ibn Yaqzan* in which storytelling is central to the philosophical letter sent to a friend by the Andalusian philosopher Ibn Tufayl. Pearson can only think of Western models some of which have also used Hayy. "Did Voltaire invent the *conte philosophique*?" Pearson asks. His answer is expected. "In using fictional narrative for the illustration and discussion of philosophical and moral issues, Voltaire was following a well-established tradition stretching back to Lucian, though his immediate precursors included Montesquieu, Swift, Tyssot de Patot, Cyrano de Bergerac, and Rabelais."[37] It is important to note, however that Ibn Tufayl's narrative is meant to enlighten and instruct his own friend. Voltaire's narrative, on the other hand, is similar to that of *Crusoe*. It is meant not only to instruct, but also to entertain. Hayy happens to be one model. There are others as well: *The One Thousand and One Nights* and the numerous Oriental Tales.

NOTES

1. See *The New Encyclopedia Britannica*. 15th ed., vol. 6 (2002), 226. Cf. Henry Corbin, *Histoy of Islamic Philosophy* (1964), trans. Liadain Sherrard with the assistance of Philip Sherrard (London: Kegan Paul International, 1993), 237–42. Corbin describes *Hayy* as a "philosophical romance, or more accurately, . . . 'recital of initiation,'" 239.

2. *The Encyclopedia of Islam*. New edition. Vol. III. Ed. B. Lewis et al. (Leiden, London: E. J. Brill, Luzac & Co., 1971), 330.

3. *The Encyclopedia of Islam*, 331. Note that T. J. De Boer, for instance, sees *Hayy* as a romance and an allegory. In *The History of Philosophy in Islam* 1903; trans. Edward R. Jones (Richmond, Surrey: Curzon Press, 1994) De Boer observes that "With Ibn Sina the character of Hai represents the Superhuman Spirit, but the hero of Ibn Tofail's romance seems to be the personification of the natural Spirit of Mankind illuminated from above; and that Spirit must be in accordance with the Prophet-Soul of Mohammed when rightly understood, whose utterances are to be interpreted allegorically." 185. De Boer does not describe *Hayy* as an autobiography, but he makes a very brief reference to Ibn Tufayl's life and suggests a vague connection between the book and its author. "It is true that this condition [perfection of man] is attained only in mature age, in which, besides, a human friend has been met with; and attention to what is material, and to the arts and sciences, forms the natural preliminary stage of spiritual perfection. *Thus Ibn Tofail is permitted to look back without regret or shame upon his life spent at court*" 185. The emphasis is mine.

4. See J. Christoph Bürgel, "Symbols and Hints: Some considerations Concerning the Meaning of Ibn Tufayl's *Hayy Ibn Yaqzan*." In Lawrence I. Conrad, *The World of Ibn Tufayl: Interdisciplinary Perspectives on Hayy Ibn Yaqzan*, 132.

5. See Karl Beckson and Arthur Ganz, *Literary Terms: A Dictionary*, 2nd ed. (New York: Farrar, Straus and Giron, 1975), 214.

6. Beckson & Ganz, *Literary Terms*, 164.

7. Beckson & Ganz, *Literary Terms*, 72.

8. Ibn Tufayl, *Hayy*, Saliba's Arabic edition, 76; Goodman's English translation, 149

9. Ibn Tufayl, *Hayy*, Saliba's Arabic edition, 76. Goodman's English translation, 149.

10. This identification, or perhaps strong empathy with the protagonist led many critics to confuse Hayy's voice with that of the narrator. In his article "Through the Thin Veil: On the question of Communication and the Socialization of Knowledge in *Hayy Ibn Yaqzan*" Lawrence I. Conrad complains that "Modern discussions . . . have tended to embrace rather simplistic comparisons between Ibn Tufayl's famous hero and the author himself." In *The World of Ibn Tufayl: Interdisciplinary Perspectives on Hayy Ibn Yaqzan*, 238.

11. See my article with G. Fischer, "Promiscuity, Emancipation, Submission: The Civilizing Process and the Establishment of A Female Role Model in the Frame-Story of *1001 Nights*," *Arab Studies Quarterly*. 13, No. 3 & 4 (Summer/Fall 1991):1–18.

12. Beckson & Ganz, *Literary Terms*, 20

13. Beckson & Ganz, *Literary Terms*, 8–9. Cf. J. A. Cuddon, *A Dictionary of Literary Terms and Literary Theory*, 4th ed. Revised by C. E. Preston (Oxford: Blackwell, 1998), 20–23. "The term [allegory] derives from Greek *allegoria*, 'speaking otherwise.'"

14. See Hillel Fradkin, "The Political Thought of Ibn Tufayl," in *The Political Aspects of Islamic Philosophy: Essays in Honor of Muhsin Mahdi*, ed. Charles E. Butterworth (Cambridge: Center for Middle Eastern Studies, 1992), 237.

15. Fradkin, "The Political Thought of Ibn Tufayl," 238.

16. Fradkin, "The Political Thought of Ibn Tufayl," 245.

17. Note that in 1771 the American writer, Benjamin Franklin, began writing his autobiography that ranks with Rousseau's as the best example of the genre during the Enlightenment. "Dear son," he began casting his narrative as a letter to William, whom he had not seen for several years. Franklin described himself as a self-made man reminding his son and reader of his humble origin. One critic suggested that "the closest model that [Franklin] had, in terms of narrative style, was one of his favorite books, John Bunyan's allegorical dream, *A Pilgrim's Progress* that he had read at fourteen." See Franklin, "The Autobiography" in *A Benjamin Franklin Reader*, ed. and annotated by Walter Isaacson (New York: Simon & Schuster, 2003), 401. But Franklin also referred to other books, such as *Robinson Crusoe* and *Pamela* in his autobiography. The technique of mixing narration and dialogue had fascinated him. Although he never mentioned Ibn Tufayl, Franklin, who was born in Boston in 1706, was likely to have been familiar with the story of the self-made man, *Hayy Ibn Yaqzan*. He would have been introduced to it either at home through the Quakers in New England, or Philadelphia, or abroad during his journeys to Holland, Scotland, England and France.

18. Note that Pat Rogers observes that "Strangely—as some might think—it was the Romantic movement which lifted prosaic old Daniel Defoe, controversialist and compiler, to the status of a major artist" Like other English and American critics, Rogers never sees the connection between Defoe's plain, rambling prose in *Crusoe* and Sinbad's diction, nor makes a link between Coleridge's remark about *Crusoe* and the *1001 Nights*. See *Robinson Crusoe* (London: George Allen & Unwin, 1979), 141.

19. See for instance what Manfred Weidhorn says in his brief note on "Autobiographical Impulse" in *Dictionary of Literary Themes and Motifs*, ed. Jean-Charles Seigneuret, vol. 1 (New York: Greenwood Press, 1988), 135–42. Speaking about *Crusoe*, Weidhorn observes, "The feigned autobiographer (Defoe) simply writes a work of fiction in the first person, a confession of an individual who never existed and who has nothing in common with the author." 136. Many of Defoe's critics share these views. But in Cuddon's *Dictionary of Literary Terms and Literary Theories* published by Blackwell in 1998 these views seem to be changing. Under the item "Autobiography" the author states that "During the 18th c. we find there is some connection between autobiography and the then relatively new form of the novel. For example, Defoe's *Robinson Crusoe* (1719) and Sterne's *Sentimental Journey* (1768) are taken to be a kind of autobiographical fiction, or fictionalized autobiography" 65.

20. Consult Martha Pike Conant, *The Oriental Tale in England in the Eighteenth Century*, 1908 (New York: Octagon Books, Inc., 1966). Conant lists many such works in both English and French literature. But the most outstanding works are: Goldsmith, *The Citizen of the World, or Letters from a Chinese Philosopher Residing in London to His Friends in the East* (1762); Montesquieu, *Les Lettres Persanes* (1721).

21. For more detail on Voltaire's life in England consult J. Churton Collins, *Voltaire, Montesquieu and Rousseau in England* (London: Eveleigh Nash, Fawside House, 1908). Rpt. (Folcroft Library Editions, 1980).

22. Voltaire, "Sixth Letter: On The Presbyterians," in *Voltaire: Candide and Other Writings*, 1956 (New York: Modern Library, 1984), 327.

23. See Voltaire's first four letters "On the Quakers" in *Letters Concerning the English Nation*, ed. Nicholas Cronk, 1994 (Oxford, New York: Oxford University Press, 1999), 9–25.

24. See the "Twelfth Letter: On Lord Bacon," in *Voltaire: Candide and Other Writings*, 337. Cf. Voltaire's *Letters Concerning the English Nation*, 49–53.

25. "Thirteenth Letter: On Locke," in *Voltaire: Candide and Other Writings*, 340. Cf. Voltaire's *Letters Concerning the English Nation*, 54–60.

26. "Eleventh Letter: Inoculation," in *Voltaire: Candide and Other Writings*, 334. Cf. Voltaire's *Letters Concerning the English Nation*, 44–48.

27. Voltaire, "Eleventh Letter: Inoculation," 334.

28. Anthony Levi, *Guide to French Literature Beginnings to 1789* (Detroit, London & Washington DC: St. James Press, 1994), 905.

29. Voltaire, *Mahomet the Prophet*, trans. Robert Meyers (New York: Frederick Ungar Publishing Co., 1964), 57–58.

30. Voltaire, *Mahomet*, 27.

ence, have obviously accepted the thesis that there is a distinction between the Orient and the Occident, and that they are mostly interested in defining the West as a separate entity with its own ideas, experiences and achievements. If further developed, Said's thesis will certainly shed more light on the historical relationship between East and West. Quoting Harry Bracken's article on "Essence, Accident and Race," Said makes the connection between some English thinkers in the seventeenth century and racial theory. He argues that "as Harry Bracken has been tirelessly showing— philosophers will conduct their discussions of Locke, Hume, and empiricism without ever taking into account that there is an explicit connection in these classic writers between their 'philosophic' doctrines and racial theory, justifications of slavery, or arguments for colonial exploitation. These are common enough ways by which contemporary scholarship keeps itself pure."[17]

Of course, Said is not aware of the influence of Ibn Tufayl on these "classic writers" because of his exclusively Western education. Had he known about the impact of *Hayy Ibn Yaqzan* on Europe throughout the seventeenth and eighteenth centuries he might have reached different conclusions. Why Alexander Pope, for example, exalts all men, while Cromer exalts only Westerners? Said poses this question. He observes: "In Cromer's own case as an imperial administrator the 'proper study is also man,' . . . When Pope proclaimed the proper study of mankind to be man, he meant all men, including 'the poor Indian'; whereas Cromer's 'also' reminds us that certain men, such as Orientals, can be singled out as the subject for *proper* study. The proper study—in this sense—of Orientals is Orientalism, properly separate from other forms of knowledge, but finally useful (because finite) for the material and social reality enclosing all knowledge at any time, supporting knowledge, providing it with uses."[18]

Pope has expressed his admiration for Hayy Ibn Yaqzan. It is no wonder, therefore, that his didactic poem *Essay on Man* exalts all men regardless of their race or religion. But admiration takes different forms. The literary model can be imitated, then reproduced, or it can be interpreted in a new light, and then irredeemably changed. It is only natural that some European thinkers have borrowed from Ibn Tufayl. But while some follow in his footsteps, others subvert his ideas. The latter tend to divide men into categories—one superior, the other inferior.[19] Color, religion and other considerations are taken into account. Slavery and exploitation of other races become the cornerstone of their philosophy.[20] Commerce assumes a very important role in the state which they have described. Commercial activities are exalted and even linked to personal freedom. On the contrary,

Ibn Tufayl's protagonist sees a potential hazard in commerce. Wealth is not only likely to create conflicts within society, but also masters and slaves. For Hayy, man is born equal to his other fellowmen. Commerce will only disrupt this notion of equality and subsequently destroy human freedom. He himself owns nothing and has no desire to own anything. Nevertheless, he comes to understand the craving of some men for buying and selling when he lives among other human beings. His conclusion is that commerce if not regulated by a just king will lead to greed and moral corruption. Conventional religions in this case can possibly check people's desires.

Many Western writers have been attracted to this *philosophus autodidactus*. They have given Hayy different names and depicted him in different places. But at the same time they have subverted some of his traits and changed his basic message. Hayy, for instance, has appealed to Daniel Defoe mainly because of his ethical values, but on the other hand, he is rejected precisely because of some of these values. As a self-taught man who thinks for himself, solves his daily practical problems and recognizes the existence of the one true being without the help of conventional religions, he is wholly embraced by Defoe in *Robinson Crusoe*. Hayy's notion of religious toleration, in particular, seems to have appealed to Crusoe and many other Western characters. But then the question is asked: How realistic can Hayy be in a human society? For Daniel Defoe, a nation cannot consist only of saints. If commerce is not allowed the nation is easily transformed into masses of beggars. Perhaps for this reason Defoe finds another classical figure in Arabic literature, namely Sinbad the Sailor, in order to balance the equilibrium. A saint and a merchant in this case are more likely to build the empire. Since Crusoe is meant to be allegorical and historical as its author tells us, Defoe is neither a saint nor a merchant, neither a redeemed sinner nor a restless traveler, but a mixture of all these figures. In this sense, the moralist and the economist as an empire builder can exist together even in the same person.

Not only the traits of Hayy have been changed and subverted by many Western writers, but also some of the basic messages of *Hayy Ibn Yaqzan*. Knowledge is divided into two categories in this Arabic book: material and metaphysical. The material knowledge can easily be acquired through observation of all natural things. The methods can vary from simple watching to imitating, from inspecting to chance discovery, from necessity as the mother of all inventions to experimenting, from empirical testing to comparing, from analogy to deduction, from conjecture to the study of behavior of every material body in the universe. This knowledge is acquired and never static. Its purpose is for the well-being and preservation of all humans, plants and animals. Hayy's theory of knowledge is applauded once it is discovered in Europe. But with the colonial project this knowledge becomes perverted. Its main purpose has shifted to exploitation of other races and the rape of their landscape. Yet the colonial powers have masqueraded this purpose and spoke about lofty civilizational missions and the immense benefits for the natives.[21]

One of Said's main concerns in *Orientalism* is the relationship between knowledge and power. In his chapter on "The Scope of Orientalism," Said analyzes one of Balfour's speeches on Egypt in front of the House of Commons in 1910. He argues that two themes dominate Balfour's remarks: "knowledge and power, the Baconian themes. As Balfour justifies the necessity for British occupation of Egypt, supremacy in his mind is associated with 'our' knowledge of Egypt and not principally with military or economic power. Knowledge to Balfour means surveying a civilization from its origins to its prime to its decline. . . . To have such knowledge of such a thing is to dominate it, to have authority over it"[22] But according to Balfour, British knowledge of the Orient reveals only despotism and the inability of Egyptians to govern themselves. Consequently, the next part of the argument moves on to the benefits that Egyptians will have once they are governed by the British. This argument will be repugnant to Hayy Ibn Yaqzan for it falsely assumes that human beings are not equal, and that knowledge can be used to dominate others. No benefit will result from domination. On the contrary, this policy will lead to disaster for both colonizer and colonized. Balfour's perverted happiness of the colonized is doomed to failure.

Hayy's other ideas, such as on religious toleration, have been mimicked by many Western thinkers. Yet at times it seems that toleration is not always meant to be for everyone in his or her work. H. M. Bracken, for example, wonders about Locke's reputation as a tolerant person. He argues that Locke "has acquired a grand reputation as a man of religious tolerance. Yet he apparently had no difficulty in excluding Catholics from the body politic. I find it remarkable that Locke should have been canonized as the father of religious toleration. There were, after all, people around who had expressed genuinely tolerant sentiments. But one should not lose sight of the alteration in thinking about persons introduced by Locke together with his defences of the revolution."[23] Bracken also refers to Locke's justification of slavery in his position as the administrator of slave-owning colonies in America. "While people spoke of the rights of man in ever grander terms from the eighteenth century on wards," he argues, "more and more men were being enslaved."[24] But the reason for human enslavement lies squarely in the new methodology adopted by European thinkers.

According to Bracken "empiricism has provided the methodology within which theories of political control were successfully advanced, and by means of which colour/brain-weight, IQ, etc., correlation studies have been pursued, and in terms of which the liberal ideology has been cast. Hence the role of empiricism has in fact been decisive within the English-speaking community."[25] This shocking link between empiricism and domination in human societies stands in sharp contrast to Ibn Tufayl's philosophy. Human beings may be different in many ways, but they still belong to the same species. All of them, regardless of their differences, are born equal and free.[26] They are endowed with reason. But if some do not use their reason properly at one time or another, no one has the right to enslave them or exploit them. Ibn Tufayl's empiricism highlights man's rational power and ability not only to control nature, but also to live in harmony with nature. Happiness derives from knowledge that is directed toward the benefit of mankind.

Ibn Tufayl's philosophy was appropriated, subverted, or reinvented for many centuries. But the memory of the man who wrote such an influential book was buried in the dust of history. His disciples, many of whom were Europeans, became the pillars of Western Civilization. Did they betray him? Or did they not know him? The answer is not easy. It is likely that some of them read him, or heard about his philosophy, but kept silent and never acknowledged his influence on their work. Others did not read him or hear about him, nevertheless, they used his much discussed ideas and concepts.

The real problem may lie elsewhere. It is, perhaps, our tendency to glorify ourselves, while denigrating others whom we deem to be different from us. In this light, lofty ideas, such as equality, freedom and toleration cannot possibly originate or flourish except in our culture. This xenophobic outlook may explain why many Western theorists have neglected or marginalized Ibn Tufayl's philosophical work. The racist thesis that advocates the division between people and civilizations is very well described by Samuel Huntington. "People," he says, "define themselves in terms of ancestry, religion, language, history, values, customs, and institutions. They identify with cultural groups: tribes, ethnic groups, religious communities, nations, and, at the broadest level, civilizations. People use politics not just to advance their interests but also to define their identity. We know who we are only when we know who we are not and often only when we know whom we are against."[27] Hayy Ibn Yaqzan never identified himself in terms of ancestry, language, religion, or history. He has none of these criteria. He is a human being who is very much concerned about the welfare of humanity.

In conclusion, ideas about God, nature, man, society and history are not the exclusive product of Western societies. Concepts such as modernity, the triumph of reason over superstition, and the scientific revolution should not be loosely attributed to a specific species of human beings. All civilizations influence each other and are dependent on each other. Ibn Tufayl has ancient and contemporary mentors who belong to different races, religions and cultures. In acknowledging his debt to them he acknowledges the fact that all humans are endowed with reason and can influence each other regardless of their race, religion and language.

NOTES

1. Edward Sapir, *Language: An Introduction to the Study of Speech*, 1921 (London, Toronto, New York: Granada Publishing, 1978), 192–94.

2. See for instance Cannon, Garland. *The Arabic Contributions to the English Language: An Historical Dictionary*. Wiesbaden: Harrassowitz, 1994; Habeeb Salloum and James Peters. *Arabic Contributions to the English Vocabulary: English Words of Arabic Origin: Etymology and History*. Beirut: Librairie du Liban, 1996; Juan Goytisolo, *Count Julian*, trans. into English by Helen Lane (London: Serpent's Tail, 1989); Montgomery Watt, *Influence of Islam on Medieval Europe* (Edinburgh: University Press, 1972) and many others.

3. On a lighter note, a few years ago I read an article in the *Sydney Morning Herald* about artichoke as the aristocrat of all vegetables. Trying to find the root of this word, the author concludes that artichoke must be of Italian origin, and that it has spread from Sicily to the rest of Europe. I wrote to the paper explaining that artichoke comes from two Arabic words: *Ardi* which means belonging to the earth and *choke* means thorns, and that the Arabs have cultivated this vegetable in both Sicily and Moorish Spain. In my brief letter I also referred to the Spanish writer Juan Goytisolo who not only scolds his people for not wishing to admit any Arabic influence on the Spanish language, but satirically asks them to stop using many things in their daily life, including the famous Olé when they are watching the bullfight. The newspaper published my response. But after a few days I have received several hate letters. I was really stunned. Where did I go wrong? It is a simple matter. There is nothing serious. I was not writing about Copernicus, or Spinoza, or Locke. It is only artichoke. With the time, however, I forgot these hate letters. But a few months ago here in Cambridge, MA, I was talking to a visiting professor whose specialization was Renaissance music. I asked him about the state of research in this area, and whether there were new articles or books that discuss the interaction between Arabic music in Moslem Spain and Renaissance music. He was not happy about my question. Toward the end of the evening I mentioned the artichoke anecdote. He answered me sharply that in Italian they don't even use the word

artichoke, but something else. He pronounced the word clearly for me. I laughed. It was another Arabic synonym, *al-khurshuf*. My point is that there is this mental block among many Westerners about anything Arabic or Islamic that has influenced the West.

4. See Magdy Gabriel Badir, *Voltaire et l'Islam* (Banbury Oxfordshire, 1974), 94.

5. Angela C. Pao, *The Orient of the Boulevards*, 60.

6. Samuel Huntington, *The Clash of Civilizations and the Remaking of World Order* (New York: Simon & Schuster, 1996), 54–55.

7. Cited in Huntington, *The Clash of Civilizations*, 55. Cf. Arnold Toynbee, *A Study of History*, abridgement of volumes I–VI by D. C. Somervell (New York, Oxford: Oxford University Press, 1974), 37.

8. Huntington, *The Clash of Civilizations*, 55. Cf. Fernand. Braudel, *A History of Civilizations*, trans. Richard Mayne (New York, London: Allen Lane, The Penguin Press, 1994), xxxiii.

9. Huntington, *The Clash of Civilizations*, 311.

10. Edward Said, "Afterword," *Orientalism* 1978 (New York: Vintage Books, A Division of Random House, 1979), 347.

11. Take for instance the notion of "individualism." *Hayy Ibn Yaqzan* is one of the earliest philosophical novels that construct an autonomous individual who does not belong to a group. He has no family, no religion, and no language. He is neither white nor black. Hayy advocates the primary importance of the individual and the virtues of self-reliance and personal independence. He is totally autonomous, free of any external influence. He is independent in mind and judgment and can be considered the supreme ruler of himself. No one has supremacy or authority over him or his actions. His self-realization, the significance of his conscience and self-development are necessary stages toward his ultimate freedom and happiness, provided no harm is done to other beings, be humans, animals, or plants. In his short essay on "individualism" Bryan S. Turner speaks of two broad definitions "In political terms," he says. "it is a political doctrine associated with liberalism that emphasizes the autonomy, importance, and freedom of the individual in relation to society and state. Secondly, it is the culture associated in modern society with private property, consumption, and subjectivity. Individualism is often thought to be an important component of Western culture. . . . The doctrine had its modern roots in seventeenth-century religious dissent . . . and it is interpreted as a fundamental ideology of capitalism. . . . Robinson Crusoe is often taken to be the quintessential representative of individualistic capitalism." See *Encyclopedia of Social Theory*, ed. George Ritzer, vol. 1 (Thousand Oaks, London, New Delhi: Sage Publications, 2005), 399. Turner seems to be unaware of the impact of a dangerous book, such as *Hayy Ibn Yaqzan* on the dissenters, particularly the Quakers, or on Crusoe's author, Daniel Defoe. On the other hand, Alan Macfarlane claims that the word "individualism" is modern. He traces its usage to the English translation of Tocqueville's *Democracy in America* and quotes Tocqueville as saying in a later work "our ancestors had not got the word 'individualism'—a word which we have

coined for our own use, because in fact in their time there was no individual who did not belong to a group, no one who could look on himself as absolutely alone." See *The Social Science Encyclopedia*, 3rd ed., vol. 1, ed. Adam and Jessica Kuper (London and New York: Routledge, 2004), 486. See also Macfarlane's book, *The Making of the Modern World: Visions from the West and East*. New York: Palgrave, 2002. Ibn Tufayl's thesis is that the individual is prior to society and history. Hayy symbolizes the self-sufficient and ethical person who thinks for himself without the help of social, political, or religious institutions and makes his own judgment within a moral framework. His love for self and Other is a cornerstone in his philosophy. Many western theorists have subverted the meaning of individualism. The term became associated with egoism.

12. Pearson, *The Fables of Reason*, 248.

13. Pearson, *The Fables of Reason*, 249. Rushdi's quotation is taken from his "Good Faith," *Independent on Sunday*, 4 Feb., 1990.

14. See Geoffrey Brereton's Introduction to *French Thought in the Eighteenth Century: Rousseau, Voltaire, Diderot*, presented by R. Rolland, A. Maurois and E. Herriot (London: Cassell & Company LTD, 1953), viii.

15. *The Encyclopedia of Religion*, ed. Mircea Eliade, mentions, in particular, toleration as a constant concern for the Quakers or the Religious Society of Friends. "Pen spoke for increasing groups of Englishmen convinced of the need to allow 'dissenting' or 'nonconformist' worship outside the national Anglican Church, which led both to the Toleration Act of 1689 and the tradition of liberal Protestant reformers, he made moral appeals to all consciences, advising nonviolence and 'loyal opposition' to government policies and people in power" (131). Cf. *Crusoe*, 241. ". . . we had but three Subjects, and they were of three different Religions. My Man Friday was a Protestant, his father was a Pagan and a Cannibal, and the Spaniard was a Papist: However, I allow'd Liberty of Conscience throughout my Dominions."

16. Edward W. Said, *Orientalism*, 1978 (New York: Vintage Books, A Division of Random House, 1979), 2–3.

17. Said, *Orientalism*, 13. Bracken's argument is quoted from *Hermathena* 116 (Winter 1973): 81–96.

18. Said, *Orientalism*, 45.

19. Kant who exalted the autonomous rational individual as a moral agent—just as Ibn Tufayl did—did not hesitate to differentiate between races and describe the white race to which he belonged as humanity's greatest perfection in contrast to the inferior "yellow Indians" and the "negroes." Examine, for instance, Kant's notorious comments on the mental capacity of blacks in "Observations on the Feeling of the Beautiful and Sublime, trans. John T. Goldthwait (Berkeley: University of California Press, 1960), 111–13. Cf. Emmanuel Chukwudi Eze, "The Color of Reason: The Idea of 'Race' in Kant's Anthropology" in *Anthropology and the German Enlightenment: Perspectives on Humanity*, ed. Katherine M. Faull. Bucknell Review (London, Toronto, Lewisburg: Bucknell University Press, 1995): 200–41. Examine particularly 218. Kant's "Of the Different Human Races" is one of the

earliest attempts to define the concept of race and to distinguish between species and races. The original article "*Von der verschiedenen Rassen der Menschen*," 1777 was translated into English by Jon Mark Mikkelsen, 1999 and published in *The Idea of Race,* ed. with an introduction by Robert Bernasconi and Tommy L. Lott (Indianapolis, Cambridge: Hackett Publishing Company, Inc., 2000), 8– 22. Cf. Kant's "On the Different Races of Man" 1775 in *This is Race*, selected and edited by Earl W. Count (New York: Henry Schuman, 1950), 16–24. See also Robert B. Louden, Kant's *Impure Ethics: From Rational Beings to Human Beings* (New York, Oxford: Oxford University Press, 2000), 62–106. Note that Kant had appropriated David Hume's racist dogma. In a footnote to his essay "Of National Characters" (1748) Hume argued that the blacks in general were inferior to the whites. See *Essays: Moral, Political, and Literary*, revised edition, Eugene F. Miller (Indianapolis: Liberty Fund, 1987).

20. Compare what Voltaire says in one of his letters "On Commerce" and Lord Cromer's views on the strong relationship between British colonialism and commerce. Voltaire exalts the British merchant as someone who "enriches his country, sends orders from his office to Surat and to Cairo, and contributes to the well-being of the world." But the merchant here is tied to the British Empire. Voltaire argues that "Commerce, which has brought wealth to the citizenry of England, has helped to make them free, and freedom has developed commerce in its turn. By means of it the nation has grown great; it is commerce that little by little has strengthened the naval forces that make the English the masters of the seas. At present they have nearly two hundred warships. Posterity may learn with some surprise that a little island with nothing of its own but a bit of lead, tin, fuller's earth, and coarse wool, became, by means of its commerce, powerful enough by 1723 to send three fleets at one time to three different ends of the earth. . . ." See "Letter Ten On Commerce" in *Voltaire: Philosophical Letters*, trans. Ernest Dilworth (New York: The Bobbs-Merril Company, Inc., 1961), 39–40. On the other hand, Cromer talks about his vision of British imperialism in a specific way and concludes that if his advice is followed, no Egyptian will side with the enemies of England, and that every colonial subject will sing the praises of the mother country. But above all, commerce will flourish. See Said's *Orientalism*, 37. Of course, both Voltaire and Cromer do not consider that commerce is only for the well-being of Britain, but certainly not for its colonies or colonial subjects.

21. Unfortunately, Ibn Tufayl is never discussed with what Western writers call "classical theorists," such as Locke, Kant and Rousseau. No one seems to be aware of his existence or influence on these thinkers. The father of equality, freedom and toleration is forgotten. Scholars continue to produce books either praising the men who wrote about the state of nature and the social contract, or condemning them for their racism and capitalism. See for instance, Sankar Muthu, *Enlightenment Against Empire* (Princeton, Oxford: Princeton University Press, 2003) and Charles W. Mills, *The Racial Contract* (Ithaca, London: Cornell University Press, 1997).

22. Said, *Orientalism*, 32.

23. H. M. Bracken, "Essence, Accident and Race" Hermathena, 116 (Winter 1973): 84. Note that in his introduction to Locke's *Two Treatises of Government and A Letter Concerning Toleration* (New Haven, London: Yale University Press, 2003), Ian Shapiro justifies Locke's exclusion of Catholics and Muslims on political ground, xiii.

24. Bracken, "Essence," 89.

25. Bracken, "Essence," 86.

26. Although women are absent in Ibn Tufayl's allegorical novel, there is no reason to believe that they, as human beings, are not endowed with reason and free will. There is no explicit or implicit statement about women in the text. Also we never think of Hayy or Asal as men, rather as human beings with no specific gender. But at the beginning when Hayy is an infant and a boy, the image of the female deer as a mother is overpowering. She represents all that is good in nature. Furthermore, the position of women in Moslem Spain during Ibn Tufayl's life was quite good. Women were highly educated and played an important role in society.

Contrast what Kant specifically says about women and their rational ability in his essay "An Answer to the Question: What is Enlightenment?" (1784) In *Practical Philosophy*, translated and edited by Mary J. Gregor (Cambridge: Cambridge University Press, 1996), 8:35, 8:36, 17. "I need not think, if only I can pay; others will readily undertake the irksome business for me. That by far the greatest part of humankind (including the entire fair sex) should hold the step toward majority to be not only troublesome but also highly dangerous will soon be seen to by those guardians who have kindly taken it upon themselves to supervise them; after they have made their domesticated animals dumb and carefully prevented these placid creatures from daring to take a single step without the walking cart in which they have confined them, they then show them the danger that threatens them if they try to walk alone. Now this danger is not in fact so great, for by a few falls they would eventually learn to walk; but an example of this kind makes them timid and usually frightens them away from any further attempt."

27. Huntington, *The Clash of Civilizations*, 21. Note that in the March edition of the magazine *Foreign Policy*, 2004, Huntington repeats his old thesis about 'us' and 'them,' but focusing this time on the differences between Mexicans and Anglo-Protestant society in the USA. His book, *Who Are We?* has already appeared in May 2004. See Daniel J. Hemel, "Critics Claim Huntington Is Xenophobic" *The Harvard Crimson*. 16 March 2004: 1 and 3. In reply to Hemel's article, Huntington stresses that his new book is on identity, not immigration. "Mexican immigration," he says, "is dealt with in one chapter out of twelve. The book argues that Americans have historically defined their identity in terms of four major components: race (white) which involved the enslavement, subordination and segregation of blacks, the massacre of Indians and the exclusion of Asians; ethnicity (British and then Northern European) which led to the mutual exclusion after 1924 of southern and eastern Europeans; Anglo-Protestant culture including deep religiosity; and an ideology (the 'American Creed')

articulated in the Declaration of Independence and other central documents. Happily in the past half-century, Americans have pretty much abandoned their racial and ethnic definitions of their national identity. American cultural identity, however, is now under challenge from a variety of sources, only one of which is Hispanic immigration." See Samuel P. Huntington's Letter to the Editors, *The Harvard Crimson*, 19 March 2004: A8.

SELECTED BIBLIOGRAPHY

Primary Sources: Arabic

Ibn Tufayl. *Hayy Ibn Yaqzan*. Ed. & Introd. by Albert Nasri Nadir. 2nd. ed. Beirut: Catholic Press, 1968.

——. *Hayy Ibn Yaqzan*. Ed. and Introd. by Faruq Sa'd. 3rd. ed. Beirut: Dar Al-Afaq, 1980.

——. *Hayy Ibn Yaqzan*. Ed. and introduced by Jamil Saliba & Kamil 'Ayyad. 5th ed. Damascus: Damascus University Press, 1962.

——. *Hayy Ibn Yaqzan*. Ed. and Introduced. 'Abd al-Karim al-Yafi. Damascus: Tlas Press, 1995.

Primary Sources: English

Ebn Tophail. "An Account of the Oriental Philosophy Shewing, The Wisdom of some Renowned Men of the East; and Particularly, The profound Wisdom of Hai Ebn Yokdan. Trans. from Latin into English. George Keith. London, 1674." In Antonio Pastor's *The Idea of Robinson Crusoe*. Vol. I. 305–66. Watford: The Gongora Press, 1930.

Ibn Tufail, Abu Bakr. *The History of Hayy Ibn Yaqzan*. Trans. Simon Ockley. Revised with an introduction by A. S. Fulton. London: Chapman and Hall Limited, 1929.

——. al-Qasi, Abu Bakr Muhammad. *The Improvement of Human Reason Exhibited in the Life of Hai Ebn Yokdhan*. Trans. Simon Ockley. 1708. Hildesheim; Zurich; New York: Georg Olms Verlag, 1983.

——. *The Awakening of the Soul*. Rendered from the Arabic with Introduction. Paul Bronnle. London: John Murray, 1910.

Ibn Tufayl. *Hayy Ibn Yaqzan*: A Philosophical Tale. Trans. with introduction and notes. Lenn Evan Goodman. New York: Twayne Publishers, Inc., 1972.
———. *The Journey of the Soul: The Story of Hai bin Yaqzan as told by Abu Bakr Muhammad bin Tufail*. Trans. Riad Kocache. London: The Octagon Press, 1982.

Primary Sources: French

Ibn Thofail. *Hayy Ben Yaqdhan: Roman Philosophique D'Ibn Thofail*. Trans. into French and introduced. Léon Gauthier. Alger, Imprimerie Orientale, 1900.
———. *Hayy Ben Yaqdhan: Philosophique D'Ibn Thofail*. 2nd ed. Trans. into French and introduced. Léon Gauthier. Beyrouth: Imprimerie Catholique, 1936.
———. *Le Philosophe Sans Maitre*. 1900. Traduction de Léon Gauthier. Présentation de George Labica. Alger: S.N.E.D., 1969.

Primary Sources: Latin

Ibn Thofail. *The Romance of Hayy ibn Yaqzan*. Trans. from Arabic into Latin. Edward Pococke. Oxford, 1671–1700.

Secondary Sources

Abbas, Hasan Mahmud. *Hayy Ibn Yaqzan wa Robinson Crusoe: Dirasa muqarana (Hayy Ibn Yaqzan and Robinson Crusoe: A Comparative Study)*. Beirut: al-Mu'assasa al-'amma lildirasat wa al-nashr, 1983.
Abun-Nasr, Jamil M. *A History of the Maghrib in the Islamic Period*. Cambridge: Cambridge University Press, 1987.
Adorno W., Theodor. *Kant's Critique of Pure Reason* (1959). Ed. Rolf Tiedemann. Trans. Rodney Livingstone. Oxford: Polity in association with Blackwell Publishers Ltd., 2001.
Alf Layla wa-Layla. Cairo: Bulaq, 1252 H.
Alford, C. Fred. *The Self in Social Theory: A Psychoanalytic Account of its Construction in Plato, Hobbes, Locke, Rawls, and Rousseau*. New Haven & London: Yale University Press, 1991.
Anawati, Georges C. "Philosophy, Theology, and Mysticism." In *The Legacy of Islam,* 2nd ed. Ed. Joseph Schacht and C. E. Bosworth, 350–91. Oxford: Oxford University Press, 1979.
Arberry, A. J. *Oriental Essays: Portraits of Seven Scholars*. London: George Allen & Unwin LTD, 1960.
Aristotle. "Politics." Trans. Benjamin Jowett. In *The Basic Works of Aristotle*. Ed. Richard McKeon. 1941, 1111–1316. New York: Random House, 1966.

Atkinson, Geoffroy. *The Extraordinary Voyage in French Literature Before 1700*. New York: AMS Press, Inc., 1966.

Attar, Samar. "'I am Spanish,' Said the Frightened Lebanese Woman: The Aftermath of September 11, 2001 in Australia." *Al-Mustaqbal*. Beirut. (20 January 2002).

Attar, Samar. *The Intruder in Modern Drama*. Frankfurt am Main: Lang, 1981.

————, and Fischer, Gerhard. "Promiscuity, Emancipation, Submission: The 'Civilizing Process and the Establishment of a Female Role Model in the Frame-Story of *1001 Nights*." *Arab Studies Quarterly*. 13, No. 3 and 4 (Summer/Fall 1991): 1–18.

Ayers, Robert W. "Robinson Crusoe: 'Allusive Allegorick History,'" *PMLA*. 82. 5 (Oct. 1967): 399–407.

Bacchelli, F. "Pico della Mirandola: traduttore di Ibn Tufayl." *Giornale Critico della Filosofia Italiana*. 72 i (1993): 1–25.

Backscheider, Paula R. *Daniel Defoe: His Life*. Baltimore, The Johns Hopkins University Press, 1989.

Bacon, Francis, 1561–1626. *The Advancement of Learning*. New York: Modern Library, 2001.

————. *New Organon. Works*. Trans. J. Spedding et al. New York: Hurd & Houghton, 1870–1872.

————. *The New Organon*. Ed. Lisa Jardine, Michael Silverthorne. Cambridge (U.K.); New York: Cambridge University Press, 2000.

Badawi, 'Abdurrahman. "Ibn Tufayl." In *Histoire de la Philosophie en Islam*. Vol. 2. 718–35. Paris: Librairie Philosophique J. Vrin, 1972.

Badawi, Abd Al-Rahman. "Ibn Tufayl." In *Tadrees Al-Falsafa Wa Al-Bahth Al-Falsafi Fi Al-Watan Al-'Arabi*. Beirut: Dar Al-Maghrib Al-Islami, 1987.

Badir, Magdy Gabriel. *Voltaire et l'Islam. Studies on Voltaire and the Eighteenth Century*, vol. 125. Ed. Theodore Besterman. Banbury, Oxfordshire: Voltaire Foundation, 1974.

Baeshen, L. M. S. "Robinson Crusoe and Hayy Ibn Yaqzan: A Comparative Study." Diss. The University of Arizona, 1986.

Bailey, Richard. *New Light On George Fox and Early Quakerism: The Making and Unmaking of a God*. San Francisco: Mellem Research, University Press, 1992.

Baker, Dora. *Giovanni Pico della Mirandola: Sein Leben und sein Werk*. Dornach, Schweiz: Verlag am Goetheanum, 1983.

Barbour, Hugh and Arthur O. Roberts. Ed. *Early Quaker Writings 1650–1700*. Grand Rapids, Michigan: William B. Eerdmanns Publishing Company, 1973.

Barclay, Robert. *An Apology for the True Christian Divinity: As the Fame is Held Forth, and Preached by the People Called, in Scorn, Quakers*. London, 1678.

Bastian, F. *Defoe's Early Life*. London: Macmillan, 1981.

Baumer L. Franklin. *Modern European Thought: Continuity and Change in Ideas, 1600–1950*. New York; London: Macmillan Publishing Co., Inc.; Collier Macmillan Publishers, 1977.

Beckson, Karl and Arthur Ganz. *Literary Terms: A Dictionary*. 2nd ed. New York: Farrar, Staus and Giron, 1975.

Berlin, Isaiah. Ed. *The Age of Enlightenment: The 18th Century Philosophers*. New York: The New American Library, A Mentor Book: 1956.

Bernasconi, Robert and Tommy L. Lott. Eds. *The Idea of Race*. Indianapolis, Cambridge: Hackett Publishing Company, Inc., 2000.

Best, O. F. *Der Ur-Robinson*. München: Mattes & Seitz Verlag, 1987.

Boden, M. A. *Piaget*. Brighton: Harvester, New York: Viking Press, 1979.

(The) Book of the Thousand Nights and A Night. Trans. Richard Burton. London, 1885-1888.

Braudel, Fernand. *A History of Civilizations*. Trans. Richard Mayne. New York; London: Allen Lane, The Penguin Press, 1994.

Brennan, Andrew. *Conditions of Identity: A Study in Identity and Survival*. Oxford: Clarendon Press, 1988.

Bronowski, Jacob and Bruce Mazlish. *The Western Intellectual Tradition From Leonardo to Hegel*. 1960. New York: Books for Libraries A Division of Arno Press, 1979.

Brooks, Richard A. *Voltaire and Leibniz*. Geneve: Librairie Droz, 1964.

Bülbring, Karl D. Ed. *The Complete English Gentleman*. London, 1890.

Bürgel, J. C. "Ibn Tufayl and his Hayy Ibn Yaqzan: A Turning Point in Arabic Philosophical Writing." In *The Legacy of Muslim Spain*. Ed. Salma Khadra Jayyusi, 830–46. Leiden: Brill, 1992.

Al-Bustani, Butrus. *Da'irat al-Ma'arif*. Vol. III, 299–307. Beirut, 1960.

Butterfield, Herbert. *The Origins of Modern Science: 1300–1800*. 1957. Revised edition. New York: The Free Press, 1965.

Cadbury, M. Christabel. *Robert Barclay: His Life and Work*. 1912.

(The) Cambridge Medieval History. Vol. II. New York, 1922.

Cannon, Garland. *The Arabic Contributions to the English Language: An Historical Dictionary*. Wiesbaden: Harrossowitz, 1994.

Caracciolo, Peter L. Ed. *The Arabian Nights in English Literature*. London: Macmillan, 1988

Cassirer, Ernst. *Kant's Life and Thought*. Trans. James Haden. Introduction by Stephan Korner. New Haven and London: Yale University Press, 1981.

———. *The Philosophy of the Enlightenment*. Trans. Fritz C. A. Koelln and James P. Pettegrove. Princeton: Princeton University Press, 1951.

Cave, Terence. "Fictional Identities." In *Identity: Essays Based on Herbert Spencer Lectures Given in the University of Oxford*. Ed. Henry Harris. Oxford: Clarendon Press, 1995.

Chejne, Anwar G. *Muslim Spain: Its History and Culture*. Minneapolis: The University of Minnesota Press, 1974.

Cohen, Bernard. *Revolution in Science*. Cambridge, MA and London: The Belknap Press of Harvard University Press, 1985.

Cohen, H. Floris. *The Scientific Revolution: A Historiographical Inquiry*. Chicago and London: The University of Chicago Press, 1994.

Coleridge, Samuel Taylor. *Miscellanies, Aesthetic and Literary: To Which is Added the Theory of Life*. Collected & arranged T. Ashe. London: George Bell and Sons, 1885.

Collins, J. Churton. *Voltaire, Montesquieu and Rousseau in England*. London: Eveleigh Nash, Fawside House, 1908. Rpt. Folcroft Library Editions, 1980.

Collins, James. *A History of Modern European Philosophy*. Lanham; New York; London: University Press of America, 1986. Originally published: Milwaukee: Bruce Pub. Co., 1954.

Conant, Martha Pike. *The Oriental Tale in England in the Eighteenth Century*. 1908. New York: Octagon Books Inc., 1966.

Conrad, Lawrence I. Ed. *The World of Ibn Tufayl: Interdisciplinary Perspectives on Hayy ibn Yaqzan*. Leiden; New York; Koln: E. J. Brill, 1996.

Corbin, Henry. *History of Islamic Philosophy*. 1964. Trans. Liadain Sherrard. London: Kegan Paul International, 1993.

Count, Earl W. Ed. *This is Race*. New York: Henry Schuman, 1950.

Cross, F. L. *The Oxford Dictionary of the Christian Church*. London: Oxford University Press, 1974.

Crump, Thomas. *A Brief History of Science As Seen Through the Development of Scientific Instruments*. London: Constable & Robinson Ltd, 2001.

Cuddon, J. A. *A Dictionary of Literary Terms and Literary Theory*. 4th ed. Revised by C. E. Preston. Oxford: Blackwell, 1998.

Darwin, Charles. *Autobiographies*. Ed. Michael Neve and Sharon Messenger. London: Penguin, 2002.

———. *On the Origin of Species By Means of Natural Selection*. Ed. Joseph Carroll. Peterborough, Ontario; Orchard Park, NY: Broadview Press, 2003.

Da Vinci, Leonardo, 1452–1519. *The Notebooks of Leonardo Da Vinci*. Selected and Edited. Irma A. Richter. Oxford, New York: Oxford University Press, 1980.

De Boer, T. J. *The History of Philosophy in Islam*. 1903. Trans. Edward R. Jones. Richmond, Surrey: Curzon Press, 1994.

Defoe, Daniel. *Complete English Gentleman*. Ed. Karl D. Bülbring. London, 1890.

———. *The Life and Strange Surprising Adventures of Robinson Crusoe of York, Mariner*. Ed. with an Introduction. Donald Crowley. London: Oxford University Press, 1972, reprinted 1983.

———. *Review*. VII. No. 114 (Saturday, December 16, 1710).

———. *Review*. VIII. 739 (May 27, 1712).

———. "Serious Reflections of Robinson Crusoe," *The Works of Daniel Defoe*. Vol. 3. New York: The Kelmscott Society, 1903.

Dictionary of the Middle Ages. Joseph R. Strayer, editor in chief. New York: Scribner, 1982–1989. "Science, Islamic." Vol. 11, 81–89.

Dictionary of Philosophy. Revised, 2nd ed. Ed. Anthony Flew. 1979; New York: St. Martin's Press, 1984. "Person; Personal identity" 265.

Dictionary of Philosophy and Psychology. Ed. James Mark Baldwin. "Personal identity; Individual." Vol. II. Gloucester, Mass.: Peter Smith, 1957. 283–84.

Dottin, Paul. *The Life and Strange and Surprising Adventures of Daniel Defoe.* Trans. Louise Ragan. New York: The Macanlay Company, 1929.

Earle, Peter. *The World of Defoe.* New York: Atheneum, 1977.

Eddy, William A. *Gulliver's Travels: A Critical Study.* 1923. New York: Russell & Russell, Inc., 1963.

Eliade, Mircea. Editor in Chief. *The Encyclopedia of Religion.* Vol. 12. New York: Macmillan & London: Collier, 1987.

Elias, Norbert. *The Society of Individuals.* Ed. Michael Schroter. Trans. Edmund Jephcott. Oxford, Cambridge, MA: Basil Blackwell, 1991.

Ellis, Frank H. "Introduction." In *Twentieth Century Interpretations of Robinson Crusoe: A Collection of Critical Essays.* Ed. Frank H. Ellis, 1–18. Englewood Cliffs: Prentice-Hall, 1969.

Encyclopedia of the Enlightenment. Ed. Alan Charles Kors. Oxford: Oxford University Press, 2003.

The Encyclopedia of Islam. New Edition. Ed. B. Lewis et al. Leiden & London: E. J. Brill & Luzac Co., 1971.

The Encyclopedia of Islam: A Dictionary of the Geography, Ethnography and Biography of the Muhammadan Peoples. Ed. M. Th. Houtsma et al. Leyden Brill; London: Luzac, 1913–1934.

Encyclopedia of Religion. Ed. Mircea Eliade. Vol. 12. New York: Macmillan, 1987.

Encyclopedia of the Social Sciences. Vol. II. Editor-in-Chief Edwin R. A. Seligman. 1933; New York: The Macmillan Company, 1959.

Erikson, Erik H. *Childhood and Society.* 2nd ed. New York: Norton, London: Hogarth, 1965.

———. "Growth and Crisis of the Healthy Personality," *Psychological Issues* (1959) 1: 50–100.

———. *Identity in Youth and Crisis.* New York: Norton, 1968.

Eze, Emmanuel Chukwudi. "The Color of Reason: The Idea of Race in Kant's Anthropology" in *Anthropology and the German Enlightenment: Perspectives on Humanity,* ed. Katherine M. Faull. Bucknell Review. London, Toronto, Lewisburg: Bucknell University Press, 1995: 200–241.

———. Ed. *Race and the Enlightenment: A Reader.* Oxford: Blackwell Publishers, 1997.

Fakhry, Majid. *A History of Islamic Philosophy.* London: Longman, New York: Columbia University Press, 1983.

Farrukh, 'Umar. *Ibn Tufayl wa qissat hayy ibn yaqzan.* 2nd ed. Beirut, 1959.

Fradkin, Hillel. "The Political Thought of Ibn Tufayl." In *The Political Aspects of Islamic Philosophy: Essays in Honor of Muhsin S. Mahdi.* Ed. Charles E. Butterworth, 234–61. Cambridge: Center for Middle Eastern Studies, 1992.

Franklin, Benjamin. "The Autobiography." In *A Benjamin Franklin Reader.* Edited and Annotated by Walter Isaacson, 395–551. New York: Simon & Schuster, 2003.

Gauthier, Léon. *Ibn Thofail, sa vie, ses ouvres*. Paris: Publications de L'Ecole des Lettres d'Alger, tome XLII, 1909.

Gerber, Jane S. *The Jews of Spain*. New York: The Free Press, 1994.

Gerhardt, Mia I. *The Art of Story Telling*. Leiden: E. J. Brill, 1963.

Germain, Carel Bailey. *Human Behavior in the Social Environment*. New York: Columbia, 1991.

Gilmour, Peter. Ed. *Philosophers of the Enlightenment*. Totowa, New Jersey: Barnes & Noble Books, 1990.

Girdler, Lew. "Defoe's Education at Newington Green Academy." *Studies in Philology*. 50, 1 (1953): 573–91.

Glick, Thomas F. "Ethnic Relations." In *Islamic and Christian Spain in the Early Middle Ages*, 165–93. Princeton: Princeton University Press, 1979.

Goldmann, Lucien *The Philosophy of the Enlightenment: The Christian Burgess and the Enlightenment*. 1968. Trans. Henry Maas. London: Routledge & Kegan Paul, 1973.

Goytisolo, Juan. *Count Julian*. Trans. into English. Helen Lane. London: Serpent's Tail, 1989.

Guichard, Pierre. "The Social History of Muslim Spain: From the Conquest to the End of the Almohad Regime (Early 2nd/8th Early 7th/13th centuries)." In *The Legacy of Muslim Spain*. Ed. Salma Khadra-Jayyusi. 697–723. Leiden: Brill, 1992.

Halewood, William H. "Religion and Invention in Robinson Crusoe." In *Twentieth Century Interpretations of R.C.* Ed. Frank H. Ellis, 79–89. Englewood Cliffs: Prentice-Hall, 1969.

Harris, Henry. Ed. *Identity: Essays Based on Herbert Spencer Lectures Given in the University of Oxford*. Oxford: Clarendon Press, 1995.

Hawi, Sami S. *Islamic Naturalism and Mysticism*. Leiden: E. J. Brill, 1974.

Hitti, Philip K. *History of the Arabs*. 1937. 10th ed. London & New York: Macmillan & St. Martin's Press, 1970.

———. *History of the Arabs*. Revised 10th ed. with New Preface by Walid Khalidi New York: Palgrave Macmillan, 2002.

Hobbes, Thomas. *Leviathan*. Edited Richard Tuck. Revised Student Edition. Cambridge Texts in the History of Political Thought. Cambridge: Cambridge University Press, 1996.

Hodge, Jonathan and Radick, Gregory. Eds. *The Cambridge Companion to Darwin*. Cambridge: Cambridge University Press, 2003.

Hollis, Martin. Ed. & Selected. *The Light of Reason: Rationalist Philosophers of the 17th Century*. London: Fontana, Collins, 1973.

Horton, John and Susan Mendus. *Aspects of Toleration: Philosophical Studies*. London & New York: Methuen, 1985.

Hourani, Albert. *A History of the Arab Peoples*. Cambridge, Mass.: The Belknap Press of Harvard University, 1991.

Hourani, George F. "The Principal Subject of Ibn Tufayl's Hayy Ibn Yaqzan." *Journal of Near Eastern Studies* XVI, (Jan. 1956): 40–46.

Hume, David 1711–1776. *Essays: Moral, Political, and Literary.* Revised edition, Eugene F. Miller. Indianapolis: Liberty Fund, 1987.

———. *A Treatise of Human Nature.* 1739. Edited by David Fate Norton, Mary J. Norton; introduction by David F. Norton. Oxford; New York: Oxford University Press, 2000.

Huntington, Samuel P. *The Clash of Civilizations and the Remaking of World Order.* New York: Simon & Schuster, 1996.

Hunter, J. Paul. *The Reluctant Pilgrim.* Baltimore: The Johns Hopkins Press, 1966.

Ibn Bajja, or Avempace d. 1138. *Kitab Tadbir Al-Mutawahhid,* or *Guide of the Solitary.* Edited and Introduced by Ma'n Ziyada. Beirut: Dar al-Fikr, 1978.

Ibn Rushd, or Averroes, 1126–1198. *Kitab Al- Kulliyat.* Edited and Introduced by Muhammad Bin 'Abd al-Jalil Balqziz. Al-Dar al-Bayda': Al-Najah al-Jadida Press, 2000.

Ilyas, Mohammad. *Islamic Astronomy and Science Development: Glorious Past, Challenging Future.* Selangor Darul Ehsan, Malaysia: Pelanduk Publications, 1996.

'Inan, M. A. *Duwal al-Tawa'if wal-muwahhidin fi al-maghrib wal-Andalus.* 3 vols. Cairo, 1964.

James, Sydney V. *A People Among Peoples: Quaker Benevolence in Eighteenth Century America.* Cambridge: Harvard University Press, 1963.

Johnson, Samuel. *Rasselas and Other Tales.* Ed. Gwin J. Kolb. New Haven and London: Yale University Press, 1990.

Joyce, James. "Daniel Defoe." Trans. from Italian. Joseph Prescott. *Buffalo Studies.* Buffalo, State University of New York at Buffalo, 1964.

Kant, Immanuel, 1724–1804. "Analytic of the Sublime" in *Critique of the Power of Judgment,* ed. Paul Guyer, trans. Paul Guyer and Eric Matthews. Cambridge: Cambridge University Press, 2000.

———. *Anthropology from a Pragmatic Point of View.* Trans. Victor Lyle Dowdell. Revised and edited Hans H. Rudnick, with an introduction by Frederick P. Van De Pitte. Carbondale & Edwardsville, London & Amsterdam: Southern Illinois University Press, Feffer & Simons, Inc., 1978.

———. *Critique of Practical Reason.* Translated by Werner S. Pluhar; introduction by Stephen Engstrom. Indianapolis: Hackett Pub. Co., 2002.

———. *Critique of Pure Reason.* Translated by Norman Kemp Smith; with a new introduction by Howard Caygill. Revised 2nd ed. Houndmills, Basingstoke; New York: Palgrave Macmillan, 2003.

———. *Observations on the Feeling of the Beautiful and Sublime.* Trans. John T. Goldthwait, 2nd pbk ed. Berkeley, California; London: University of California Press, 2003.

———. "On the Different Races of Man."1775. In *This is Race.* Ed. with an introduction Earl W. Count. New York: Henry Schuman, 1950. 16–24.

———. "What is Enlightenment?" In *On History*. Ed. Lewis White Beck. 3–10. Indianapolis: Bobbs-Merrill, 1963.

———. "An Answer to the Question: What is Enlightenment?" (1784). In *Practical Philosophy*. Translated and edited by Mary J. Gregor. Introduction by Allen Wood. Cambridge: Cambridge University Press, 1996. 11–22.

Kaplan, Morton A. *Alenation and Identification*. London & New York: Collier Macmillan; The Free Press, 1976.

King, Preston. *Toleration*. London: George Allen & Unwin, 1976.

Kirby, Ethyn Williams. *George Keith (1638–1716)*. New York: D. Appleton-Century Company, 1942.

Knapp, Bettina L. *Voltaire Revisited*. New York: Twayne Publishers, 2000.

Kopping, Klaus-Peter, Michael Welker and Reiner Wiehl. Eds. *Die Autonome Person-Eine Europaische Erfundung?* München: Wilhelm Fink Verlag, 2002.

Kuhn, Thomas.S. *The Copernican Revolution: Planetary Astronomy in the Development of Western Thought*. 1957. Cambridge: Harvard University Press, 1971.

Laroui, Abdallah. *The History of the Maghrib*, trans. Ralph Manheim. Princeton: Princeton University Press, 1977.

Leibniz, Gottfried Wilhelm, 1646–1716. *Theodicy: Essays on the Goodness of God, the Freedom of Man, and the Origin of Evil*. 1710. Edited with an introduction by Austin Farrer; translated by E. M. Huggard from C. J. Gerhardt's edition of the collected philosophical works, 1875–1890. La Salle: Ill.: Open Court Pub. Co., 1985.

Locke, John, 1632–1704. *An Essay Concerning Human Understanding*. 1690. Ed. Roger Woolhouse, 1997. London; New York: Penguin Books, 1997.

———. *Two Treatises of Government, and; A Letter Concerning Toleration*. Ed. with an introduction by Ian Shapiro; with essays by John Dunn, Ruth W. Grant, Ian Shapiro. New Haven, Conn.; London: Yale University Press, 2003.

Louden, Robert B. *Kant's Impure Ethics: From Rational Beings to Human Beings*. New York, Oxford: Oxford University Press, 2000.

Loukes, Harold. *The Discovery of Quakerism*. London: George G. Harrap, 1960.

Macdonald, Duncan B. *Development of Muslim Theology, Jurisprudence and Constitutional Theory*. New York: Russell & Russell, 1965.

Macfarlane, Alan. "Individualism" in *The Social Science Encyclopedia*, 3rd edition, vol. 1. Ed. Adam and Jessica Kuper. London, New York: Routledge, 2004.

———. *The Making of the Modern World: Visions from the West and East*. New York: Palgrave, 2002.

Machan, Tibor R. *Classical Individualism: The Supreme Importance of Each Human Being*. London, New York: Routledge, 1998.

MacKay, Angus. *Spain in the Middle Ages: From Frontier to Empire, 1000–1500*. London: Macmillan Press, 1977.

Makki, Mahmoud. "The Political History of al-Andalus 92/711–897/1492." In *The Legacy of Muslim Spain*. Ed. Salma Khadra Jayyusi, 3–87. Leiden: Brill, 1992.

Malti-Douglas, Fedwa. *Woman's Body, Woman's Word*. Princeton: Princeton University Press, 1991.

Al-Marrakushi, 'Abd Al-Wahid. b. 1185. *The History of Almohades* [*Kitab Al-Mu'jib*]. Ed. R. Dozy. Leiden, 1881.

———. *Al-Mu'jib Fi Talkhis Akhbar Al-Maghrib*. Cairo, 1949.

Mason, Haydn. *Voltaire*. London: Hutchinson, 1975.

Mills, Charles W. *The Racial Contract*. Ithaca and London: Cornell University Press, 1997.

Moore, John Robert. *Daniel Defoe Citizen of the Modern World*. Chicago: The University of Chicago Press, 1958.

———. "Mandeville and Defoe." *Mandeville Studies: New Explorations in the Art and Thought of Dr. Bernard Mandeville (1670–1733)*. Ed. Irwin Primer, 119–25. The Hague: Martinus Nijhoff, 1975.

Muthu, Sankar. *Enlightenment Against Empire*. Princeton and Oxford: Princeton University Press, 2003.

Nasr, Seyyed Hossein and Oliver Leaman. *History of Islamic Philosophy*. Vol. I. London & New York: Routledge, 1996.

(*The*) *New Encyclopaedia Britannica*. 15th edition. 2002.

Nicholson, Reynold A. *A Literary History of the Arabs*. Cambridge: Cambridge University Press, 1969.

Noonan, Harold. *Personal Identity*. Dartmouth: Dartmouth Publishing Company, 1993.

Novak, Maximillian E. *Defoe and the Nature of Man*. Oxford: Oxford University Press, 1963.

———. *Economics and the Fiction of Daniel Defoe*. 1962. New York: Russell & Russell, 1976.

O'Callaghan, J. F. *A History of Medieval Spain*. Ithaca & London, 1975.

Olofsson, Leif Eeg. *The Conception of the Inner Light in Robert Barclay's Theology: A Study in Quakerism*. Lund: CWK Gleerup, 1954.

The Oxford Companion to Philosophy. Ed. Ted Honderich. Oxford, New York: Oxford University Press, 1995.

The Oxford Dictionary of the Christian Church. Ed. F. L. Cross. London: Oxford University Press, 1974.

Pao, Angela C. *The Orient of the Boulevards: Exoticism, Empire, and Nineteenth-Century French Theater*. Philadelphia: University of Pennsylvania Press, 1998.

Pastor, Antonio. *The Idea of Robinson Crusoe*. Vol. 1. Watford: The Gongora Press, 1930.

Pearson, Roger. *The Fables of Reason: A Study of Voltaire's 'Contes Philosophiques.'* Oxford: Clarendon Press, 1993.

Pellat, ch. "The origin and development of historiography in Muslim Spain." In *Historians of the Middle East*, edited. B. Lewis and P. M. Holt, 118–25. London: Oxford University Press, 1962.

Piaget, Jean. *Judgement and Reasoning in the Child*. 1929; London: Routledge & Kegan Paul, 1962.

———. "Piaget's Theory," in *Handbook of Child Psychology*. 4th ed. Vol. I, ed. W. Kessen. New York: Wiley, 1983.

Pico, Giovanni Della Mirandola, 1463–1494. *Oration on the Dignity of Man.* Trans. Elizabeth L. Forbes. Lexington, Ky: Anvil Press, 1953.

————. *On the Dignity of Man, On Being and the One, Heptaplus,* trans. Charles Glenn Wallis, Paul J. W. Miller, Douglas Carmichael. 1965; Indianapolis: Hackett Publishing Company, Inc., 1998.

Pope, Alexander. *The Correspondence of Alexander Pope. 1719–1728.* Vol. 2. Ed. George Sherburn. Oxford: Clarendon Press, 1956.

Randall, John Herman. *The Making of the Modern Mind.* 15th ed. New York: Columbia University Press, 1976.

Rodinson, Maxime. *Europe and the Mystique of Islam.* Trans. Roger Veinus. Seattle: University of Washington Press, 1991.

Rogers, Pat. *Robinson Crusoe.* London: George Allen & Unwin, 1979.

Rousseau, Jean Jacques. *A Discourse On Inequality.* Trans. With an introduction and notes by Maurice Cranston. New York: Harmondsworth, Middlesex, England, Viking Penguin, 1984.

————. *Émile.* Translated from the French by Barbara Foxley. London: Dent; New York: Dutton, 1974.

————. *Émile, Or Concerning Education. Extracts.* Trans Eleanor Worthington. Boston: D. C. Heath & Co., Publishers, 1883.

————. *The Social Contract.* An Eighteenth-Century Translation Completely Revised, Edited with an Introduction by Charles Frankel. New York: Hafner Publishing Company, 1947.

Rousseau, Voltaire, Diderot. *French Thought in the Eighteenth Century.* Presented by Romain Rolland, André Maurois and Edouard Herriot. Introduction by Geoffrey Brereton. London: Cassell & Company Ltd., 1953.

Rundorff, Dorothy. "European Influence of Hayy Ibn Yaqzan." *Islamic Literature,* 4 (1952): 277–81.

Runciman, Steven. *A History of the Crusades.* Vol. 3. 1954. London: Penguin, 1978.

Russell, G. A. Ed. *The 'Arabick' Interest of the Natural Philosophers in Seventeenth-Century England.* Leiden; New York; Koln: E. J. Brill, 1994.

Sa'id al-Andalusi, Abu al-Qasim, 1029–70. *Tabaqat al-Umam. (Classification of Nations).* Edited by Husayn Mu'nis. Cairo: Dar al-Ma'arif, 1998.

————. *Science in the Medieval World: Book of the Categories of Nations.* Trans. & ed. Sema'an I Salem and Alok Kummar. Austin: University of Texas, 1991.

Said, Edward. *Orientalism.* 1978; rpt. London: Penguin, 1991.

————. *Orientalism.* 1978; rpt. New York: Vintage/Random House, 1979. "Afterwod" c. 1994.

Salih, Madani. *Ibn Tufayl: Qadaya wa-mawaqif.* 2nd ed. Baghdad: Wizarat Al-Thaqafa, 1986.

Salloum, Habib and James Peters. *Arabic Contributions to the English Vocabulary: English Words of Arabic Origin: Etymology and History.* Beirut: Librairie du Liban, 1996.

Sapir, Edward. *Language: An Introduction to the Study of Speech.* 1921. New York: Granada Publishing, 1978.

Sarton, George. *Introduction to the History of Science. Vol. II from Rabbi Ben Ezra to Roger Bacon*. In Two Parts. Baltimore: The William & Wilkins Company, Carnegie Institution of Washington, 1931.

———. *The History of Science and the New Humanism with Recollections and Reflections by Robert K. Merton*. New Brunswick, USA and Oxford, England, 1988.

Sayf, Antoine. "Introductory Remarks. Seminar on Ibn Rushd." *Al-Fikr al-'Arabi* 81. Summer 1995: 5–7.

Schlereth, Thomas J. *The Cosmopolitan Ideal in Enlightenment Thought*. Notre Dame & London: The University of Notre Dame Press, 1977.

Secord, Arthur Wellesley. *Studies in the Narrative Method of Defoe*. New York: Russell & Russell, 1963.

Seigneuret, Jean-Charles. Ed. *Dictionary of Literary Themes and Motifs*. 2 Vols. New York: Greenwood Press, 1988.

Shah, Idries. *The Sufis*. London: Allen & Co., 1977.

Sharif, M. M. Ed. "Ibn Tufayl." *A History of Muslim Philosophy*. Vol. 1 1963, 526–40. Karachi: Royal Book Company, 1983.

Sherburn, G. Ed. *The Correspondence of Alexander Pope 1719–1728*. Vol. II. Oxford: Clarendon Press, 1956.

Shoemaker, Sydney and Richard Swinburne. *Personal Identity*. Oxford: Basil Blackwell, 1984.

Sigler, Julius. A. et al. *Symposium Readings: Classical Selections on Great Issues: Human Nature*. 2nd ed. Lanham, Maryland: University Press of America, 1997.

"Sindbad the Sailor." *Alf Layla wa Layla* (*The Arabian Nights Entertainments*). Vol. 2. Cairo: Bulaq, 1252 H.

———. Trans. Richard Burton. *The Book of the Thousand Nights and a Night*. Vol. 6. London: 1885–1888.

Singer, Peter. *A Darwinian Left: Politics, Evolution and Cooperation*. London: Weidenfeld and Nicolson, 1999.

Smith, Anthony D. "The Formation of National Identity." In *Identity: Essays Based on Herbert Spencer Lectures Given in the University of Oxford*. Ed. Henry Harris, 129–53. Oxford: Clarendon Press, 1995.

Smith, Joseph. *Descriptive Catalogue of Friends' Books*. 2 Vols. London: 1867 & New York: Kraus Reprint, 1970.

The Song of Roland. Trans. Dorothy I. Sayers. 1957; Harmondsworth: Penguin, 1967.

Sorell, Tom. Ed. *The Rise of Modern Philosophy*. Oxford: Clarendon Press, 1993.

Spinoza, Benedictus de, 1632–1677. *Ethics*. Edited and Translated by G. H. R. Parkinson. Oxford; New York: Oxford University Press, 2000.

Starr, G. A. *Defoe and Spiritual Autobiography*. 1965. New York: Gordian Press, 1971.

Sutherland, James. "The Author of Robinson Crusoe." In *Twentieth Century Interpretations of Robinson Crusoe*. Ed. Frank H. Ellis, 25–33. Englewood Cliffs: Prentice-Hall, 1969.

———. *Daniel Defoe: A Critical Study*. Cambridge, Mass.: Harvard University Press, 1971.

Taylor, Charles. *Multiculturalism and "The Politics of Recognition."* An Essay by Charles Taylor with commentary by Amy Gutmann et al. Princeton, Princeton University Press, 1992.

———. *Sources of the Self: The Making of the Modern Identity.* Cambridge: Cambridge University Press, 1989.

Toynbee, Arnold J. *A Study of History.* Abridgement of Volumes I–VI by D. C. Somervell. 1946. Oxford, New York: Oxford University Press, 1987.

———. *A Study of History.* A new edition revised and abridged by the author and Jane Caplan. London: Oxford University Press and Thames and Hudson Ltd., 1972.

Turner, Bryan S. "Individualism" in *Encyclopedia of Social Theory*, vol. 1. Ed. George Ritzer. Thousand Oaks, London, New Delhi: Sage Publications, 2005.

———, Nicholas Abercrombie and Stephen Hill. *Sovereign Individuals of Capitalism.* London: Allen & Unwin, 1986.

Voltaire. *Candide.* 1966. 2nd ed. Translated and Edited by Robert M. Adams. New York: W. W. Norton, 1991.

———. *Candide.* Translated, Edited with an Introduction Daniel Gordon. Bedford, Boston & New York: St Martin's, 1999.

———. *Candide and Other Writings.* 1956. Ed. with an Introduction Haskel M. Block. New York: Modern Library, 1984.

———. *Voltaire's Candide, Zadig and Selected Stories.* Trans. with an Introduction Donald M. Frame. Bloomington: Indiana University Press, 1961.

———. *Letters Concerning the English Nation.* Edited with an Introduction and Notes, Nicholas Cronk. 1994. Oxford, New York: Oxford University Press, 1999.

———. *Mahomet: The Prophet or Fanaticism.* Translated with an Introduction Robert L. Myers. New York: Fredeick Ungar Publishing Co., 1964.

———. *Philosophical Letters.* Trans. with an Introduction Ernest Dilworth. New York: The Bobbs-Merrill Company, 1961.

Wackwitz, Friedrich. *Entstehungsgeschichte von D. Defoes 'Robinson Crusoe.'* Berlin: 1909.

Watt, Ian. "Individualism and the Novel." In *Twentieth Century Interpretations of Robinson Crusoe: A Collection of Critical Essays.* Ed. F. H. Ellis. Englewood Cliffs: Prentice-Hall, 1969.

———. *The Rise of the Novel.* London: Chatto & Windus, 1957.

Watt, M. W. *A History of Islamic Spain.* Edinburgh (Islamic Surveys, 4), 1965.

Watt, Montgomery. *Influence of Islam on Medieval Europe.* Edinburgh: University Press, 1972.

Wild, Stefan. "Samuel P. Huntington wa-Ibn Rushd: Al-Tanweer wa-sira' al-hadarat." ("Huntington and Ibn Rushd: Enlightenment and the Clash of Civilizations"). *Al-Fikr Al-'Arabi.* No. 81. (Summer 1995): 24–33.

Williams, C. J. F. *Being, Identity and Truth.* Oxford: Clarendon Press, 1992.

Wright, Thomas. *The Life of Daniel Defoe.* London: Cassell, 1894.

Zimmerman, Everett. *Defoe and the Novel.* Berkeley: University of California Press, 1975.

INDEX

Abu Ya'qub Usuf, xv, 63; allowed philosophers to indulge in religious speculation, 27, 37, 65; death in a battle against Castile and Portugal, 68, 133; encounter with Averroes, 116–17; protected philosophers from harm and participated in religious speculations, 116

Abu Yusuf Ya'qub al-Mansur, 41; asked by Saladin to assist Muslims against the Crusaders, 68; imprisoned the most important rational philosopher, 65

Addison, reader of the *Thousand and One Nights*, 20

Adorno, Theodor W., on Kant's and Voltaire's enlightenment, 111n32

Albertus Magnus, xii, xv–xvi, 14n22

al-Bitruji, the Latin Alpetragius, 6

al-Farabi, 114

al-Ghazali, skepticism, 8n29; his books banned, or burnt, 67

al-Kindi, Ya'qub, truth must be taken wherever it is to be found even among foreign peoples, 134

allegory, 27; definition, 116

Arab, Muslim, as Other, 2, 12n6, 8, 11; the anecdote of artichoke, 139n3; Defoe and Voltaire on Moslems, 129; interpreting Salman Rushdi's controversial book, *The Satanic Verses*, 132

Aristotle, xv, 2, 15n28, 16; *Politics*: man as a beast, or a god, 63; 88, 116

Ashwell, George, xvii, 20, 37

Atkinson, Geoffroy, *The Extraordinary Voyage in French Literature Before 1700*, 97; claims that *Hayy* has not influenced French literature before the eighteenth century, 97–99

autobiography, 27, 113, 114; autobiographical elements in *Robinson Crusoe*; 118

Averroes. *See* Ibn Rushd

Bacon, Francis, 2; emphasizing the significance of human power, 83; *New Organon*, Bacon's dismissal of Arabs' achievements, 4, 13

Bacon, Roger, 2, 14n17, 53

ABOUT THE AUTHOR

Samar Attar was born in Damascus, Syria. She studied at Damascus University (two Licence es Lettres degrees, English and Arabic Literature), Dalhousie University, Canada (M.A., English Literature), and State University of New York at Binghamton (Ph.D., Comparative Literature: English, French, German). She taught English, Arabic, and Comparative Literature in the United States, Canada, Algeria, West Germany, Australia, and Turkey. During 1990–1991, she was a Rockefeller Fellow at the University of Michigan, Ann Arbor, and in 1994–1995, 1999–2000, and 2003–2006 a visiting research scholar at Harvard.

She has extensive publications in both English and Arabic in the fields of literary criticism, gender studies, migration, philosophy, translation, language teaching, and creative writing. Her books include *The Intruder in Modern Drama* (Frankfurt am Main 1981), *A Journey at Night: Poems by Salah 'Abd Al-Sabur* (Cairo, 1970), *Modern Arabic For Foreign Students*, four volumes plus teacher's manual and seventeen cassettes (Beirut, 1988 and 1991), *The Arab European Encounter: An Advanced Course for Foreign Students* (Beirut, 1998) and *Grammar in Context* (Beirut, 1998). She has two novels: *Lina: A Portrait of A Damascene Girl* (Beirut, 1982 in Arabic and Colorado Springs, 1994 in English), and *The House On Arnus Square* (Sydney, 1988 in Arabic and Pueblo, Colorado, 1998 in English). Her poems have appeared in anthologies in Canada, the United States, and England, including *The Penguin Book of Women Poets* (London, 1978) and *Women of the Fertile Crescent* (Washington, 1981). Her radio play *Australia Day* appeared in *Australian Writing* 1988 (Penguin). Among her many articles are, "Promiscuity, Emancipation, Submission: The Civilizing

Process and the Establishment of A Female Role Model in the Frame-Story of *1001 Nights.*" *ASQ* 13, Nos. 3 and 4 (Summer/Fall 1991); "'Find me this friend and take the Caliphate': Abu Hayyan al-Tawhidi and the Paradox of Friendship," Fusul 14 (Cairo), Fall 1995; "Conflicting Accounts on the Fear of Strangers: Muslims and Arab Perceptions of Europeans in Medieval Geographical Literature," Arab Studies Quarterly. 27.4 (Fall 2005); "The Price of Dissidence: A Meditation on Creativity, Censorship, and Exile," Meridians: feminism, race, transnationalism. Vol. 6., No. 2 (Spring 2006). Her latest article, which appeared in *ASQ*, Spring 2007, deals with the vision of two different Palestinian writers of the city of Haifa. Attar was an invited speaker at various international universities and organizations in Egypt, Syria, United States, Canada, England, Australia, Spain, Germany, and the United Arab Emirates. Her book, *Debunking the Myths of Colonization*, will appear in 2010 by the University Press of America.